Israel's Southern Land

Your Guide to Eilat and the Negev
Aviva Bar-Am & Yisrael Shalem

Front cover: Ein Avdat
Back cover: Fun in the Sun,
   Pink Canyon, Rappelling,
   Rahat Bedouin Heritage Center,
   Sunroses, Sapir Park

Publisher	Yisrael Shalem
Photographs	Shmuel Bar-Am
Typesetting	Phyllis Shalem
Editor	Wendy Elliman
Cover design	Debby Rubin
Production	Yisrael Shalem

© Copyright 1995 by Aviva Bar-Am and Yisrael Shalem.
All rights reserved.
Reproduction in any manner, in whole or in part, of texts or photographs in this publication is prohibited without written permission from the authors.

Yisrael Shalem, Sprinzak 329/27, 13351 Safed, Israel.
ISBN 965–90048–4–2

Printing by Graphica-omanim, Tel Aviv.

Other Books by the Authors

GUIDE TO THE GOLAN HEIGHTS
by Aviva Bar-Am and Yisrael Shalem

SAFED — SIX SELF-GUIDED TOURS IN AND AROUND THE MYSTICAL CITY
by Yisrael and Phyllis Shalem

THE COMPLETE GUIDE TO TIBERIAS AND THE SEA OF GALILEE
by Yisrael and Phyllis Shalem

About the Authors

Aviva Bar-Am was born in a suburb of Minneapolis, Minnesota. Following the Six Day War she immigrated to Israel, married an Israeli, studied at the Hebrew University and graduated with a degree in social work. She lives in Jerusalem with her husband and two teenagers.

In 1983 she began writing articles for the Jerusalem Post on subjects relating to social issues, and eventually initiated an Action Line for dealing with the problems of English-speaking Jerusalemites. Her consumer column ran in the Jerusalem Post local paper, *In Jerusalem*, for five years.

When Aviva began traveling around the country, her family encouraged her to share her discoveries with the general public. Aviva's "Off the Track," "Roadstop," "Scouting About" and "Landscape" columns were in great demand over the years.

Aviva now writes books for tourists and English-speaking Israelis. In a weekly radio segment she suggests travel sites throughout the country; she also participates in monthly panel discussions on issues of the day. Aviva's husband Shmuel is a professional photographer and TV cameraman.

Yisrael Shalem was born in Chicago and immigrated to Israel in 1970. He lives with his wife Phyllis and four children in Safed, where he lectures at Safed Regional College. Yisrael has worked as a tour guide for the past 20 years and is currently studying for a doctorate in Land of Israel Studies at Bar-Ilan University.

This is Aviva and Yisrael's second book together.

Acknowledgments

Dozens of people helped us prepare this comprehensive volume and we are enormously grateful. We owe a special debt of gratitude to: the Negev Tourism Development Administration for the use of their map in this edition.

For guiding us through the Negev, reading large portions of the manuscript and/or proffering other invaluable assistance, we thank: Yehuda Honeybud, Director, Negev Highlands Tourism; Rony Malka, Deputy Director, Nature Reserves Authority (NRA); Raz Ertracht, Director, Society for the Protection of Nature in Israel (SPNI) Sde Boker Field Study Center; Joe Schwartz, Managing Director, Western Negev Tourism Development Society; Dror Levy, Director, northern region Israel Youth Hostels Association; Bunny Alexandroni, Foreign Press Liaison, Jewish National Fund (JNF); Dina Winstein, NRA Spokesperson; Israel Gilad, Director, National Parks Authority (NPA); Adam Sela, Challenging Experience Desert Tours; Tali Erickson-Gini, Israel Antiquities Authority (IAA); Yael Finkelman-Dror, NRA; Eitan Romem, SPNI Sde Boker; and Orit Nevo, SPNI Spokesperson.

We greatly appreciate the help of other Negev experts: Kher Albaz, Director of Social Services for Bedouins, Masos Regional Council; Nabhan Al-Makawi, Tel Sheva; Hanni Alon, Director, Hai Ramon (Bio Ramon); Nurit Bakalash, Kibbutz Gevulot; Prof. David Faiman, Solar Energy Center, Sde Boker; Edna Feinstein, Director, southern region information division of JNF; Shani Granek, SPNI; David Heller, Herbarium Curator, Hebrew University; Rnana Ilan, Yeruham; Gidi Katanov; Shika Katzir, Kibbutz Yad Mordecai; Paula Levine, Dolphin Reef; Rhita Lippitz; Ayal Mardix and Dani Moloch, NRA; David Meninger, Director of Judean Desert, NRA; Nimrod Negev, Northern Negev District Archaeologist, IAA; Alfonso Nussbaumer, Eilat; Yarona and Yossi Politi, Jeepsee Tours; Peter Rabin, NRA; Michal Raz and Aviv Shapira, SPNI; Sas Fialco, Director, Arad Visitors Center (NRA); Niza Yasur, Mitzpe Revivim; and Nisan Zuri, Kibbutz Nir Am.

Many people inspired us to write this, and other books. Aviva is grateful for the encouragement of husband, Shmuel, for his support and the gift of his beautiful photographs. She is especially grateful to her parents, Barbara and Irvin Schermer, for their encouragement, reassurance and technical assistance with the manuscript. Yisrael wants to extend a special thanks to his wife Phyllis for her painstaking work and the many long hours she devoted to the production.

From the Authors

Nowhere in the world is there a country so small, with landscapes so various, as the State of Israel. Nightly weather reports feature a dozen different forecasts within an area no bigger than New Jersey; it takes only a few hours to drive from Israel's southern deserts to snow-capped northern mountains. Even more incredible are the scenic differences found within each tiny geographic region. And Israel's Negev—which stretches from Beer Sheva to Eilat—is the most exciting of them all.

Our love for the Negev is so overpowering that we felt it must be shared with others. We hope that *Israel's Southern Landscapes—Your Guide to Eilat and the Negev*—will be both useful and entertaining. Like our first book, *Guide to the Golan Heights*, it is small enough for your glove compartment yet chock full of traveling tips, information and family jaunts.

While the book's color photographs will entice you to visit the Negev, if you can't get there *Israel's Southern Landscapes* takes you on a vicarious trip. Whether used as resource material, read for pleasure or brought to the Negev as a guide, this is one book you should thoroughly enjoy!

Israel's Negev contains an awesome variety of landscapes

Table of Contents

Introductions

Introducing the Negev...1

How to Use This Book..3

Tips to Traveling in Israel 4

Hiking in the Negev..6

The Western Negev

Introducing the Western Negev...8

Western Negev Route No. 1 10

Yad Mordecai Battle Site..12

Museum From Holocaust to Revival 14

Kibbutz Nir Am 16

Old Be'erot Yitzhak 18

Kibbutz Be'eri Complex 20

Tel Jamma..25

Western Negev Route No. 2 27

The Besor Scenic Route 28

Mitzpe Revivim 35

Western Negev Route No. 3 38

Maon Synagogue 40

Magen...41

Mitzpe Gevulot...43

Golda Meir Park..45

Bir Asluj (Be'er Mashabim) 46

Western Negev Route No. 4 49

Eshkol National Park..51

Additional Sites Not Along Routes

Jeep Trip in the Western Negev 53

Dangur—Old Nirim 59

Steel Monument (*Andartat Haplada*).....................................60

The Northern Negev

Introducing the North Central Negev.....................................61

Route No. 5: Through the Northern Negev 62

Route No. 6: Yatir Forest to the Dead Sea 67

The Modern City of Arad...75

Arad Visitors' Center...75

Tel Arad National Park...77

Introducing Beer Sheva 81

Beit Yad Labanim 88

Air Force Museum...89

The Yiftah Memorial..92

Bedouin Heritage Center, Rahat 93

Negev Brigade Memorial..95

Tel Beer Sheva National Park 96

The Negev Highlands

Introducing the Negev Highlands 99

Route No. 7: Beer Sheva to the Arava 100

Yorkeam Spring (*Ein Yorkeam*) 109

Ein Tzin 112

Introducing Yeruham..114

Dimona..117

Route No. 8: To Mitzpe Ramon via Avdat 118
Ben Gurion's House 123
Ben Gurion's Burial Ground..125
National Solar Energy Center 126
Ein Avdat National Park 127
Sde Boker Field School..133
Avdat National Park...136

Mamshit National Park..143

Route No. 9: Sinai Border Scenic Drive 147
Shivta National Park...157
The Lotz Cisterns (*Borot Lotz*)...161
Arod Observation Point (*Mitzpe Arod*)................................166

Introducting the Negev Craters 167
Big Crater Walk..168
Wadi Yemin and Wadi Hatira 171
Wadi Hava 177

Introducing the Sites in Mitzpe Ramon 183
Mitzpe Ramon Visitors' Center...184
Bio Ramon (*Hai Ramon*) 185
Ramon Crater (*Machtesh Ramon*) 188
Jeep Trip Through Ramon Crater 194
Promenade Along the Crater 198
Desert Sculpture in Mitzpe Ramon 198

The Arava

Introducing the Arava 200
Route No. 10: The Southern Dead Sea to Eilat.......................202
The Dead Sea..208

The Dead Sea Works 209

Wadi Tzafit...210

Shezaf Nature Reserve 215

Spices 219

The Spice Trail by Jeep...221

In and Around Eilat

Introducing Eilat 226

The Underwater Observatory 228

Coral Beach Nature Reserve.................................230

Dolphin Reef...231

International Birds Center 233

Um Rashrash...235

Evrona Spring (*Be'erot Sharsheret*) 236

Amram's Pillars 238

Wadi Shehoret..240

Timna Park...245

Yotvata Hai Bar 251

Mount Yoash..254

Wadi Gishron and Wadi Yoash 256

Droplet Spring (*Ein Netafim*).............................265

Red Canyon..268

Jeep Trip through Uvda Valley..............................270

The Ancient Leopard Temple 272

General Information

History of Man in the Negev 274

The Negev's History: Key Events 278

History of the Nabateans 281

The Bedouin 284

Modern Challenges in the Negev..288

Index of Sites..290

Hike Index 292

Important Phone Numbers 293

Youth Hostels and Field Schools 294

Dictionaries 297

Glossary..301

Introducing the Negev

The Negev's dark granite mountains were formed when molten rocks reached the earth's surface. Oceanic waters covered the rocks and deposited marine life which eventually turned into limestone. Intense tectonic forces "twisted" mountains and forged valleys, while millennia of erosion ground some hills to dust and, in others, built up new peaks.

Combined together, these natural forces created striking hills decorated with colorful sandstone, the largest crater* in the world and the Dead Sea, where you float effortlessly in heavy, murky waters. Prehistoric temples have been discovered at the base of many mountains, and Israel's southern deserts provided inspiration for the three great monotheistic religions.

Abraham lived for many years in Beer Sheva, tending his flock and holding dialogues with God. The Jews received the Torah at Mount Sinai. Elijah fled to the desert and heard the still, small voice of God. Jesus met John the Baptist near the Dead Sea and, centuries later, monks came to meditate in the Negev. Muhammad's first revelation took place in the

Ibex roam the cliffs of Ramon Crater.

Introducing the Negev

desert. And no wonder: in the quiet starry night man stands alone, forever touched by infinity.

Israel's stark and seemingly barren Negev desert supports an amazing variety of plants and wildlife. Despite the desert's incredible evaporation rate and the irregularity of its very low precipitation, there are over 1,200 species of foliage in the Negev. No sight is more breathtaking than the awakening of Israel's desert plains after the winter rains. Riverbeds fill with flowers, covering the landscape like a carpet.

Eilat's coral reefs contain some of the world's most wondrous life forms and you can view them while swimming in the Red Sea or visiting the Underwater Observatory. You can gaze at the heavens as millions of birds fly overhead, migrating back and forth between Asia and Europe.

This is your chance to dance—not with wolves, but with ibex and gazelles! If you don't come across them on your hikes, you can observe them in one of Israel's southern wildlife centers or large reserves. Here, you will learn how creatures, from insect to mammal, survive in the desert.

Contrary to popular belief, the Negev was not always populated by Bedouin riding mangy camels. Large Israelite towns mentioned in the Bible thrived in the Negev well over three thousand years ago. During the Greek and Roman periods, the Nabateans* amassed great fortunes transporting precious spices across the desert, and built large cities equipped with luxurious homes and Roman baths.

On your visit to the Negev you can stop in at Chalcolithic* copper mines, the earliest in history. Gaze at an ancient synagogue with mosaic floors and see spacious Byzantine* churches that were paved with marble.

Scientific research in Israel is at the forefront of the world effort to roll back the desert and open up land for future generations. On your visits to the Negev you can visit solar research installations and experimental farms. Everywhere you see how Israel's unique Jewish National Fund has turned much of the Negev's brown sands into a bright, flourishing green.

"Whoever drinks the water from Abraham's Well in Beer Sheva will return again for more" is an ancient Bedouin saying in which we find special meaning. After "tasting" Israel's south you will feel the pull of the Negev's incomparable attractions. And you will want to return again—and again.

How to Use This Book

Israel's Southern Landscapes is divided into five sections, according to the Negev's five distinct geographical regions: 1) northwest, along the Mediterranean coast; 2) northern Negev, in and around Beer Sheva; 3) Negev highlands, the high and cooler area in the central Negev; 4) the Arava, the narrow strip along the eastern edge of the Negev from the Dead Sea to Eilat; and 5) the Eilat region, which ends along the Red Sea.

In each section you will find detailed articles on the major sites and suggested touring routes. Many places are easy to get to with minimum walking. We offer easy hikes for all the family and off the beaten tracks for experienced hikers; you might want to splurge and take a jeep or camel tour, as well. All hikes and trips are infused with Israel's unique blend of nature and history.

Site descriptions are followed by important reference information: the history of the Negev and a timeline, the people of the Negev and a glossary. A special feature is the book's unique English-Hebrew dictionary of Negev flora and fauna.

At the end of *Israel's Southern Landscapes*, readers will find an alphabetical index of Negev sites and a section containing useful telephone numbers. A listing of tourist services, lodgings and restaurants makes it easy to plan your trip.

Names that appear in SMALL CAPS refer to sites that are explained in detail in their own chapter. Look for them in the alphabetical index of sites. Words marked with an "* "are explained in the glossary.

Don't be surprised to find that you can't make it to all of our suggested routes. The Negev has so much to offer that it would take months to cover all its wonderful sites! Pick and choose which you prefer, depending on your personal inclinations and the season of the year.

Tips to Traveling in Israel

HOW TO SURVIVE IN THE HOLY LAND

You don't have to know Hebrew to manage well in Israel. **Most** Israelis know basic English and love to give instructions. A common answer is "go straight ahead, then ask."

News in English. There is one daily English-language newspaper, "The Jerusalem Post" and a biweekly English-language magazine called the "Jerusalem Report." Weekdays news is broadcast in English on television's channel 1 at 18:15, Fridays at 16:30 and Saturdays at 17:00. There are radio broadcasts in English at 7:00, 13:00 and 17:00. The radio frequency is 1458 or 576 KHz AM depending on your location.

Money. Israeli currency is called shekels, and there are 100 agorot to a shekel. Most tourist enterprises honor major credit cards or travelers' checks but not personal checks.

Telephones. Almost all public phones are operated by inserting magnetic telecards which can be bought at all post offices. Information (144) and the overseas operator (188) do not require a card. Shops and restaurants often have coin-operated phones that take only shekel coins. Use of these phones is generally double the cost of a telecard.

Public bathrooms. Keep a roll of toilet paper in your car at all times.

Money savers. Students, senior citizens and school-aged children are entitled to a discount on buses and children up to the age of five ride free. Very young children are often admitted into tourist sites at no cost, so don't hesitate to ask. If you plan to visit several national parks and/or nature reserves throughout the country, you can buy an inexpensive pass that is good for them all.

Restaurants. Not all restaurants and hotels are kosher. Those that are, display a certificate from the local rabbinate. If you want cold water in a restaurant, ask for ice. Many restaurants include service in their price; this will be written on the menu. If it is not, the amount of the tip is up to you.

Meet the Israeli. Many tourist information centers in the large cities have a list of Israeli families happy to invite you for tea. Unique to Israel: the Jewish Sabbath starts late Friday afternoon and ends after sundown on Saturday night. Most sites and shops close early on Friday and on the day before Jewish holidays. Buses do not run (except for inner city buses in Haifa) on holy days.

Phone numbers. Important public phone numbers are listed in the index at the back of *Israel's Southern Landscapes.*

Tips to Traveling in Israel

TRANSPORTATION

Buses. Israel has excellent and inexpensive public transport. You can purchase a ticket on the bus with no need for exact change.

Shared public taxis (*sherut*). In the major cities, often near the main bus depot, there are intercity taxies which charge fixed rates. They leave when full, and hold about seven people.

Private taxis. They take you anytime, anywhere. Taxi drivers are obliged by law to turn on their meters; do not drive off if they do not turn the meter on.

Driving. Many Israelis learn to drive a tank before they sit in the driver's seat of a car, and horns are used far more often than brakes. Road signs along highways are in English. Refrain from picking up hitchhikers, with the exception of Israeli soldiers. Israel honors foreign driving licenses for up to three months.

You may find driving within cities complicated, for traffic lanes merge and unmerge with no apparent rationale. Speed limits between cities are usually 90 kph. There are occasional changes, so watch the signs.

If you drive outside of city limits the law requires you to turn on your headlights from November 1 to March 31.

Hitchhiking. Though it was once common for civilians to hitchhike, we very strongly suggest you resist the temptation to do so.

SPECIAL NEGEV TIPS

In the Negev, it is common to see the sign "Firing Zone, Both Sides." Don't let this worry you; just don't go wandering around off the road.

When traveling in the Negev, you should bring food and water with you in your car. There are few restaurants and they may be closed on Saturdays and Jewish holidays. Gas stations are also few and far between, so fill up whenever you can.

If you have any suggestions that you would like to share with us after your visit, please write.

Hiking in the Negev

If you want to experience the Negev with your feet, a few basic safety rules can help guide you on your way. Please read this chapter carefully before you hike through Israel's incomparable riverbeds, canyons and mountains.

WHERE TO HIKE

Before starting out, read the trail description from beginning to end to ensure it is suitable for you and your companions. Walk only on marked trails. At times the colored trail-markers (stripes on rocks or poles) are bent at an angle. This is a signal to turn.

Special maps which indicate marked trails (*mapot simun shvilim*) are published by the Society for the Protection of Nature in Israel (SPNI) and are available at SPNI stores all over the country. The colors marking nature trails on the map correspond to the colors of the markers on the paths, so you can follow the map even without knowing Hebrew. The Eilat marked-trails map is available in English.

What if you get lost? Reread the route, and make sure that the map is pointed north! Retrace your steps looking for trail-markers. Tell someone in advance where you plan to hike. Trained people will know where to find you.

WHAT TO BRING

This book; at least three liters of water per person; good walking shoes; a broad-brimmed hat; suntan lotion or sunscreen; and food. It is also a good idea to have a detailed map, compass and camera and a bathing suit where relevant. Bring friends or family. NEVER HIKE ALONE.

Drink water! In the dry heat you perspire more than usual and feel it far less. You need to drink at least every 15 minutes.

Please help keep the Negev beautiful and avoid harming animals! Bring along bags for your garbage; keep them with you, and dispose of them in an appropriate manner after you return home from your excursion. Many sites—and all hikes—are within nature reserves and every flower and rock is protected by law. You may examine the flowers, but do not pick them; if you pick up a fossil or a rock, return it to its place.

Hiking in the Negev

WHEN TO HIKE

The coolest times are early morning and late afternoon. Most tours described here take two to three hours and can easily be completed within the suggested time span. NEVER HIKE AT NIGHT.

We suggest you call the local field school (see IMPORTANT PHONE NUMBERS) before hiking, in order to check on any recent changes in the route and weather conditions. Though the weather may be sunny and clear where you are, run-off from winter storms in the highlands can result in sudden flash floods below.

Swimming: There are many beautiful spots to swim along nature trails, but no life guards. We have tried to indicate the few known sites where the water will be above your head (or those of young children) but winter floods can create dangerously deep water holes. Be careful.

TRANSPORTATION

You need private transportation unless specifically mentioned otherwise. Many hikes can be managed with one car. Having two or more cars, however, is very helpful in a few family outings and especially when hiking off the beaten track.

If you are taking only one vehicle and haven't a car to leave at the end of a riverbed hike, you can either walk back to the beginning of the trail, ask a friend to pick you up at the end or perhaps arrange a time with a taxi.

Hikers with two or more vehicles have two alternatives: If you can all squeeze into one car, leave a vehicle at the end of the hike and return together in a second car to the beginning of the path. Otherwise, drivers leave passengers at the starting point, take two cars to the end of the trail and leave one car there. The drivers then return in the other car to the waiting hikers.

Miscellaneous: Leave nothing of value in your car and nothing at all in plain sight—good advice anywhere in the country!

ENJOY YOUR HIKE!

Introducing the Western Negev

Is there more to Israel's south than the city of Eilat with its glistening Red Sea? The answer, of course, is a resounding "Yes!" For among the vast wastelands of the Negev you encounter enchanting nature reserves bursting with colorful blossoms, picturesque canyons and majestic riverbeds. Negev visitors encounter riveting historical ruins and explore Spartan outposts where pioneers risked their lives to defend the new State of Israel.

Laden with history and lush with forests, springs and vegetation, the untamed western Negev is one of Israel's most delightful holiday spots. Among its attractions are pioneer outposts, reconstructed battle sites, the second largest national park in Israel, ancient synagogues and tels,* a mini-zoo, vast sandy wastelands filled with mazes and rock formations and a famous flower reserve. Almost all of these attractions are easily accessible and require little or no walking.

Although it stands proudly on its own as a superb vacation site, the western Negev can also be incorporated into a drive from northern Israel to Eilat. The four routes described in this section lead you on a fascinating tour of the western Negev. You can stay overnight at the end of each route, or drive a few hours further south to reach Eilat.

Dangur, a monument to pioneer courage (see NIRIM).

Introducing the Western Negev

Western Negev Route No. 1

Western Negev Route No. 1

*Route No. 1 begins at Ashkelon. It leads you through battle sites at
KIBBUTZ YAD MORDECAI and BE'EROT YITZHAK,
the reservoir inside KIBBUTZ NIR AM, an ancient tel*
and the incomparable natural and historical complex at KIBBUTZ BE'ERI.*

The birth and survival of modern Israel is an unsurpassed saga of courage, foresight and dumb luck. On a trip through the western Negev you can explore, at first hand, sites which played a major role in this extraordinary story.

Begin at Ashkelon and drive south on Coastal Highway 4. Your first stop is KIBBUTZ YAD MORDECAI, to visit an unusual battlefield and the museum called "From Holocaust to Revival."

The kibbutz* is to your right immediately past Mordecai Junction, a major intersection featuring a restaurant and gas station complex. Across from the gas station is a small memorial to Israeli tourists who were killed in Egypt by Islamic extremists.

After viewing the attractions at Kibbutz Yad Mordecai return to Mordecai Junction. Turn right (east) on Road 34 in the direction of Gush Katif and the tourist sites.

Next stop is NIR AM, one of the first pre-state Negev settlements. Turn right at the sign (just before Gevim Junction) and follow the directions given in the site description (chapter on Nir Am).

After seeing Nir Am's reservoir and pump house return to the main road and continue to Gevim Junction. Turn right onto Road 232 leading towards Kibbutz Sa'ad. At Sa'ad Junction turn left towards Beer Sheva, then take the first right to Gush Katif and Hevel Habesor. When you see the sign for BE'EROT YITZHAK, turn right and follow instructions to a battle scene from the War of Independence.*

After stopping at the memorial and perhaps having a picnic, return to Road 232, turn right, and drive as far as KIBBUTZ BE'ERI. The kibbutz features a unique variety of historical and natural sites, including a flower reserve, an old sulfur factory, an unusual quarry and a glistening lake!

From the kibbutz, return to Road 232 and turn right. Pass Gerar Nature Reserve (on your right, after you have driven about four kilometers). In February, the ground will be covered with anemone and groundsel, for this

10

Western Negev Route No. 1

is a region blessed with rain. You can picnic in the forest here, or walk on the paths.

Now continue on, past Re'im Junction towards Gush Katif and Hevel Habesor. A few hundred meters from the intersection, look for a tel on your right: this is TEL JAMMA, containing ruins thousands of years old.

After your detour into ancient history return to Road 232 and turn right. Continue on to Maon Junction, from which three routes (ROUTE NO. 2, ROUTE NO. 3 and ROUTE NO. 4) cross the western Negev.

Vital Information
Sites in SMALL CAPS are described in detail in special chapters.

Yad Mordecai Battle Site

Yad Mordecai Battle Site

Like other tales of heroism during Israel's War of Independence,* the story of Yad Mordecai seems the figment of an overactive imagination. Yet when Israel declared independence on May 15, 1948, and Egypt invaded from the south, Yad Mordecai's small community of ill-equipped pioneers had no choice but to fight. Incredibly, they held the Egyptian army at bay for almost a week. And although the battle for Yad Mordecai ended in a Jewish retreat, it probably saved Tel Aviv—and the State of Israel—from ultimate destruction.

This historic event has been immortalized in a most unusual manner, for the kibbutz* has preserved one of the settlement's undermanned defense posts and you can climb the small hill to its top. When you reach the peak you will probably pause in dismay; throngs of enemy soldiers appear to be racing towards the hill, prepared to attack your position.

During the fighting, defenders spaced a few meters apart stood inside iron-reinforced tin bunkers pointing rifles at their assailants. Their weapons remain, trained on the enemy: Victorian rifles, sten guns, French carbines, Canadian rifles and an anti-tank Piat. You can climb inside the bunkers which encircle the hill.

 To reach Kibbutz Yad Mordecai take Coastal Highway 4 going south from Ashkelon. The kibbutz is on your right immediately past Mordecai Junction. Turn in and follow blue signs to the battle site, located within the settlement. After you ascend the low hill where the battle for Yad Mordecai was fought, loudspeakers will begin relating the story of the skirmish. Choose the language you prefer when you pay your entrance fee.

Immediately following Israel's independence, Egyptian troops moved north towards Tel Aviv. Egypt assumed it would take no more than a few days to win a mere 48 kilometers of coast and then move on Israel's main city.

Egypt also expected help from Arab villages located along the coast, up to the very outskirts of Tel Aviv. Scattered among these villages were four young kibbutzim: NIRIM, Kfar Darom, Nitzanim and Yad Mordecai. Of these settlements, only Yad Mordecai lay directly in the army's path.

When the Egyptians failed to overrun Nirim and Kfar Darom, further south, they simply abandoned the fight and continued on to Yad Mordecai.

Yad Mordecai Battle Site

Egyptian forces approached the kibbutz on the morning of May 18. At the time of the assault there were about 150 people defending the settlement. Between them they possessed approximately 50 light weapons, one two-inch mortar and a Browning hand machine gun. In a desperate move to barricade the road, they threw eucalyptus trees across the way.

Opposing the settlers was an infantry brigade of 2,500 troops with cannons, tanks, armored trucks and two airplanes. On the second day of battle the kibbutz came under aerial attack and within hours it was in flames. At night the settlers descended the hill and took weapons from fallen Egyptian soldiers.

The Egyptians finally entered the kibbutz on the fifth day of battle, pushing forward in tanks and armored cars followed by infantry. The tank which remains below the hill was one of those used to capture the post and kill its defenders.

Although the tank was damaged in a counterattack and the post retaken, the cost in human life was horrendous. Almost half the Israelis were either killed or wounded and survivors had run out of ammunition. Those who remained decided to retreat. When night fell, they picked up the wounded and managed to break through the Egyptian lines which surrounded the kibbutz.

Egyptian soldiers attack positions at Yad Mordecai.

Museum From Holocaust to Revival

During the six days of battle, Egypt was prevented from advancing to Tel Aviv. Enemy losses were high and their spirits low. The battle bought Israel enough time to fortify defense lines, collect arms, acquire four airplanes and organize its forces between Yad Mordecai and Tel Aviv.

The Egyptians stayed in Yad Mordecai for five and a half months, completely demolishing the kibbutz. Yad Mordecai was liberated on November 5, 1948. That very same day, the survivors returned and rebuilt their settlement.

Vital Information

Open every day 8:00–17:00. The entrance fee includes the MUSEUM FROM HOLOCAUST TO REVIVAL.
Tel.: 07–720528.
Wheelchairs can ascend a special ramp. There are picnic tables at the entrance, and next to the famous statue of Warsaw Ghetto commander Mordecai Anielewicz.

Museum From Holocaust to Revival

One of several gripping sites within the confines of Kibbutz Yad Mordecai, the Holocaust Museum traces Jewish life from the Eastern European ghettos before World War II through the despair of the Holocaust. It proceeds with the 1940's, the years when refugees immigrated "illegally" to the Jewish homeland, and leads you through pre-state pioneer settlement. Finally, you witness the establishment of Israel against all possible odds.

Kibbutz Yad Mordecai was founded in 1943. Its name immortalizes Mordecai Anielewicz, commander of the Warsaw Ghetto Uprising. Original settlers were from the Polish Hashomer Hatzair movement who escaped from Europe before World War II.

 While you stop at the kibbutz* primarily for its restored BATTLE SITE, the museum is well worth a visit. To get there follow Coastal Highway 4, going south towards Ashkelon. You will leave the highway long before you reach Gaza (often spelled Azza). Kibbutz Yad Mordecai is located just south of Mordecai Junction. Turn right to enter the kibbutz and follow the signs to the museum.

14

Museum From Holocaust to Revival

Once inside, walk down the stairway in a narrow passageway. From this lowest level you begin going up a few steps to the year 1933, when the Nazis came to power in Germany. An entire wall is covered with photos of children in the Eastern European ghettos. These heart-rending pictures are all authentic, and include identity cards and the yellow stars the Jews were forced to sew onto their clothes.

Another display depicts the heads of the Jewish resistance in Europe. One photo shows a child selling cigarettes as a cover for passing information to the unbelieving outside world. Look for the last letter written by Mordecai Anielewicz.

In the middle of your visit you are led outside, to the cemetery where kibbutz defenders are buried. Then, return to the indoor museum, to view exhibits which deal with the revival of the Jewish People.

You may not notice the museum's water motif at first. A blue water conduit represents the sewage tunnels through which children smuggled food in and out of the ghetto. These were used as escape routes when the ghetto was destroyed by the German army. Water also played a crucial role in immigration to this country, as most "illegals" attempted to enter pre-state Israel by ship. Blue also represents the sky, or hope.

Without water there would have been no Negev settlement. A map on the wall clarifies the problem: distances between water sources and settlements were enormous and long pipelines had to be laid to the 11 settlements set up on the night after Yom Kippur, 1946 (see GEVULOT).

An unusual display exhibits a typical picture from each settlement. One includes a tent, another has tin shacks, and in a third photo pioneers dance the hora by wooden huts.

Vital Information

Open every day 8:00–16:00. The entrance fee includes the battle site as well. Tel.: 07–720528; fax: 720594.

15

Kibbutz Nir Am

Kibbutz Nir Am was founded in 1943, shortly before the establishment of the first three Negev outposts. The rich absentee Arab landlord who sold this particular plot of land knew that it contained a badly constructed well which wouldn't last the Jews for very long. And, indeed, the well collapsed soon after the deal went through. Settlers were left literally high and dry, with no choice but to buy water from the Arab village of Beit Hanun and cart it home.

Eventually, they consulted geologist Leo Picard. Professor Picard carefully studied the terrain and decided which site he would suggest to the pioneers as the most promising location for finding water.

When Picard met with settlers at the kibbutz he carried only one tool—a stick. Together they walked into the wilderness. Suddenly the professor stopped, pointed with his rod and said, "Dig here!" The settlers did so and, to their amazement, came up with water! Needless to say, when they wanted to find a second water source the kibbutzniks called upon Picard again who repeated the act in a different site.

To visit Nir Am, drive to Mordecai Junction. Turn left at the intersection onto Road 34 in the direction of Gush Katif and the tourist sites. It's a lovely drive, for the highway is lined with a multitude of flourishing eucalyptus trees.

Turn right at the sign for Nir Am (just before Gevim Junction) and drive to the yellow gate of the kibbutz. Do not go inside the kibbutz; instead, drive left around the fence, on a paved road. Eight hundred meters further on is a blue gate. If you have called in advance it should be open—see Vital Information below.

Drive inside and park next to a lone white building with a red roof.

Walk up the path next to the gate, through an opening in the thicket and onto the top of a water reservoir. From here you can see Nir Am's trees and the Hebron Mountain ridges to the east. Gaza, is off to the west and to the south, about two kilometers away, is a patch which served as the British Mandatory airport until World War II. Behind it is the hill called Mount Ali Montar, the site of many battles over the millennia. It is mentioned in the Bible as the hill Samson climbed after he spent the night with a prostitute in

Kibbutz Nir Am

Gaza and tore down the city gate. "He lifted them [the doorposts] to his shoulders and carried them to the top of the hill that faces Hebron" (Judges 16:1-3).

Water from the Nir Am area played a crucial role in Negev settlement, which grew by leaps and bounds through 1946. The two Negev water carriers established in early 1947 both led out of Nir Am; they were supplied by hundreds of kilometers of six-inch pipes which had put fires out in the London blitz during World War II.

So miraculous was the blooming desert created by Negev settlements that members of a United Nations commission visiting REVIVIM and Nir Am in the summer of 1947 couldn't believe their eyes. Commission Chairman Justice E. Sandstrom, certain the flowers he saw couldn't possibly be rooted in the soil, decided to find out for himself whether he and his committee were being duped and plucked a gladiolus right out of the ground!

Nir Am's 11 wells flowed into the cistern on which you are standing, and pipes from the cistern supplied water to the kibbutzim. Water from the Nir Am area allowed southern settlements to stand firm during the Arab siege of the Negev during the War of Independence* in 1948.

Walk back down to the reservoir's entrance. To get a feel for its size, go inside through a huge pipe like those used in the National Water Carrier in the north.

Now return to the parking area and stroll past the white house to a fortress-like edifice which houses the pumps. Built to withstand enemy attack, this structure has reinforced windows. A special command center was established in Nir Am to guard the water carriers.

During the War of Independence Nir Am operated a field hospital. Israel's president and former air force commander Ezer Weizmann was a pilot in 1948. According to one oft-repeated story, he was flying a gravely injured soldier from Mitzpe Beit Eshel to Nir Am when he was astonished to hear the young man yell "right! right!" Then he saw the lights of Gaza in front of him and realized that had he veered any further to the left he would have flown into enemy territory.

Vital Information
To make certain the gate and pump house are open, call 07–809918.

Old Be'erot Yitzhak

Once a year a memorial ceremony is held on the site of Kibbutz Be'erot Yitzhak. Not the thriving religious community near Ben Gurion Airport, but the original settlement, established in 1943 as the first kibbutz* south of Gaza. The rest of the year the deserted water tower stands alone, all that remains of the courageous settlement that faced a brutal attack by the might of the Egyptian army.

To reach Old Be'erot Yitzhak, begin at Mordecai Junction on the Coastal Highway (Highway 4). Turn left (east) on Road 34 in the direction of Gush Katif and the tourist sites. At Gevim Junction turn right onto Road 232 towards Sa'ad. At Sa'ad Junction go left to Beer Sheva and then, almost immediately, take a right turn leading to Gush Katif and Hevel Habesor. Continue until you see the sign for Be'erot Yitzhak, then turn right and follow the road 2.7 kilometers through the fields of Kibbutz Alumim. At a Hebrew sign pointing to Be'erot Yitzhak turn left in the direction of the water tower you see in the distance.

When it was first established, Be'erot Yitzhak developed by leaps and bounds. The land was fertile and by 1948 the settlement had grown to 200 members—an enormous number for the times. But its location just east of Gaza was its downfall, for Be'erot Yitzhak was a major obstacle to the Egyptians as they advanced towards Tel Aviv during the War of Independence.*

The Egyptians first attempted to conquer Dangur (NIRIM) slightly further south. Failing to capture this settlement, they invaded Be'erot Yitzhak, whose water towers made it a natural target. As you see by the battle scars, the towers were heavily bombed.

Despite the large-scale battles and high casualties here, the kibbutz was never captured. Yet Be'erot Yitzhak, once a symbol of Negev development, was completely demolished in the battle and its settlers moved further north.

From the memorial site you can see Gaza directly to the west. Distinguish Israel from autonomous Palestinian Authority by the trees; planted by the Jewish National Fund, the forests form a "green line" along Israel's pre-1967 border.

Old Be'erot Yitzhak

Several other settlements that were established in the region during the 1940's are doing well. NIR AM, Dorot and Ruhama all benefit from the Mediterranean climate and the 350 millimeters of rain which fall each year. This is well over the drought line of 232 millimeter average rainfall and the settlements grow crops without irrigation. Indeed, this climate is responsible for the incredibly massive quantity and variety of wildflowers at KIBBUTZ BE'ERI, only a few kilometers away.

Be'erot Yitzhak was replaced in 1966 by Kibbutz Alumim, whose settlers are young, observant, energetic Israelis. Many immigrated to Israel from English-speaking countries.

The antenna directly before you in the distance belongs to Kibbutz Nahal Oz, the first *Nahal* settlement in Israel (communities established by soldiers who combine agricultural work with defense of Israel's borders). From the early 1950's until 1967, this area suffered from terrorist attacks originating in Gaza. Since the autonomy of 1994, it has once again become a border community, patrolled by the army and surrounded by electric fences.

Before you are fields of wheat and barley, two of a variety of crops which grow well in this area. Kibbutz Alumim also raises and exports banksia, lovely Australian and South African flowers which are partly cactus.

You will probably see the stunning, spur-winged plover on your visit to Be'erot Yitzhak. This striking creature has a quill on each wing to fend off its enemies and an interesting lifestyle. Once a couple mates, the two birds stay together for as long as they live. When one dies, the other does not mate again.

Plover parents can communicate with their young, and even to embryos still in their shells. After building their nests on hot sand or dirt, they shade their standard four eggs with their bodies. Because they can't care for offspring and cool off the nest at the same time, they send messages to the eggs and all four hatch within hours of one another.

Newborn plovers can leave the nest immediately and hunt for food in the company of one of their parents. If an enemy approaches, the parent signals its arrival and the young plovers immediately lie down on the ground to avoid detection.

Recently developed by the Jewish National Fund, Old Be'erot Yitzhak is a terrific place for a picnic. While you are eating and enjoying the silence, search the ground for a marbled polecat. The tiny creature with a long tail is Israel's smallest predator and this is the furthest south where the marbled polecat can be found.

Kibbutz Be'eri Complex

Shortly after the onset of World War I, leaders of the Turkish Empire declared a *jihad*, or holy war, on Britain and France and joined the German effort. Together Turks and Germans formulated a plan for keeping England busy on a second front: on February 3, 1915, they attacked the British-controlled Suez Canal. Although the Turks were roundly defeated, British commander Archibald Murray determined to prevent further assaults on the canal by capturing all of the Sinai Peninsula. The drive to the Turkish-held Palestine border in 1916 met with minimal Turkish resistance. Encouraged by their success, the British decided to take the Holy Land itself.

Two bloody frontal attacks on Gaza, the traditional port of entry into Israel, failed miserably. Over 10,000 courageous men from the Australia-New Zealand Corps (Anzac) were killed or wounded in battles over the city, despite the fact that in Gaza the British used new secret weapons—tanks and gas shells—for the first time.

A visit to the dramatic Anzac Memorial can be part of an unusual outing at Kibbutz Be'eri, half an hour southeast of Ashkelon. In February and March it includes an incredible flowering in which breathtaking carpets of brilliant red anemone completely cover the landscape. Delicate white and yellow irises (and some exceptional pale blue specimens) peek out from among the bright red blossoms.

Look for luscious lavender orchids. Each flower produces practically a million seeds that the wind can carry for hundreds of kilometers. Orchid flowers take an unusually long time to develop, sometimes as long as 15 years, for the plant depends on nourishment from outside sources for germination.

While a trip to Kibbutz Be'eri is exceptionally colorful in late winter, much of this singular excursion does not depend on seasonal blooms. So if you are too late to enjoy the area's resplendent floral offering, you can still take advantage of other novel attractions: a concrete bridge, deserted sulfur mine, gleaming lake and unusual memorial.

 Begin at the entrance to Kibbutz Be'eri. To get there, drive along Highway 4 south of Ashkelon to Mordecai Junction. At the intersection, turn left (east) on Road 34 to Gevim Junction. There turn right in the direction of Kibbutz Sa'ad (Road 232) and at Sa'ad Junction swerve with Road 232 to

Kibbutz Be'eri Complex

the left and to the right. Continue on 232 until you reach the sign for the Be'eri tourist sites. An orange sign directs you to an excellent dirt road some 20 meters before the entrance to the kibbutz.* Turn right and follow it around the kibbutz's outer fence towards the Anzac Memorial.

PIf you come fairly early in the morning, chances are you will be able to glimpse only a few of the thousands of flowers along the road. Don't worry: you'll get the full, heady view as the sun shines down upon them when you return.

On your way to the memorial stop at Nahbir, two bullet-ridden structures which are all that remain of Be'eri's original kibbutz. Be'eri was one of 11 Negev settlements set up overnight in 1946 in an effort to influence the U.N. map makers who were drawing up boundaries for future Jewish and Palestinian states. Jewish leaders hoped that a Jewish presence in the Negev would stop the U.N. from including the Negev in a Palestinian state.

From the hill across the road you have an excellent view of the Mediterranean Sea, the city of Gaza and the western pre-'67 border ending in forests planted by the Jewish National Fund. If it's not muddy you can

Bullet-ridden structure and fortifications are all that is left of Be'eri's original settlement, Nahbir.

Kibbutz Be'eri Complex

walk through the trenches across the road and if you have very strong arms you can very carefully climb the ladder to the top of the water tower.

By autumn 1996, 50 years after the founding of Be'eri, old Nahbir is expected to house an extensive museum relating the history of the Negev settlements. Its two floors will contain a model of the original Nahbir; the roof will house an observation deck.

Back on the road, turn right at the first fork. You will find yourself on a very special byway, called Concrete Road. When first built in 1933 it was only a dirt road stretching from Be'eri to the port at Gaza. At the time it was used by a company mining sulfur in these parts, to transport its product to the Gaza port.

During World War II, when Rommel began his advance east from Africa, the British established an air force base and ammunition complex near the sulfur factory (over 170 structures altogether). The road was then topped with concrete slabs and serviced the Royal Air Force by connecting the base with the airport in Gaza.

Stop at Concrete Bridge over Wadi Sahaf, specially designed to accommodate the Negev's overflowing rivers. You will see how huge empty pipes permit excess water to flow under the bridge during floods. At the same time you can examine the fascinating riverbed, unusually attractive in winter, when the water's harsh flow creates imaginative shapes in the sand.

Continue on Concrete Road past the next mini-junction to some sloping hills to the left. Park at the side of the road just past the hills and follow a path left into the fields. It takes you straight towards a delightful picture-book lake.

Negev soil is composed largely of loess,* which seals off the ground below when the top level gets wet. During rainfall, the drops soak through less than 10 millimeters of ground: excess water flows to the lowest possible spot. While the western Negev is blessed with several seasonal ponds, this picturesque lake is the largest of them all and brims with water well into June.

Australian tourists are inevitably reminded of home by the western Negev's multitude of eucalyptus trees, rolling hills and pretty valleys. Here the eucalyptus shade the roads, surround the lake and populate the forest surrounding your next stop, the Anzac Memorial. To reach the memorial, continue on the road several hundred meters, and you will see an orange sign pointing left to "Yad Anzac."

British forces first invaded Gaza on March 25, 1917. Since they had the superior navy, they planned to bombard the enemy from the water as they

Kibbutz Be'eri Complex

advanced towards the city. They chose a road parallel to the ocean, the same route followed by conquering armies from the early Egyptians to Alexander the Great and Napoleon. All had taken advantage of a Negev coast bursting with cisterns, which provided water for men and beasts.

In spite of severe fog and apparently some serious blunders by their commanders, British troops circling around the city managed to wrest control of a strategic hill above Gaza. Unfortunately, before they completed their conquest of the city they were ordered to retreat. On April 17 Allied forces moved straight into Gaza, across Wadi Habesor. Analysts say that due to a fatal complacency and a whole string of foul-ups the army was soundly defeated.

The tide turned five months later on October 31, 1917. General Allenby, the new commander, carried out a sophisticated deception and faked a Gaza attack as he captured Beer Sheva. Within the year, the 400-year-old Turkish empire in the Holy Land fell and the Turks left Israel, never to return.

The Anzac Memorial was established in 1967, 50 years after the Gaza battles took place. Climb to the top for an excellent view of Gaza—west, past the clearing. From here you can easily see the water tower of old BE'EROT YITZHAK, a settlement heavily bombarded by the Egyptians in 1948.

 Retrace your car's tracks but this time, when you reach the fork leading to Nahbir, remain on Concrete Road. Stop next to an open pit on your left—you are about to explore a sulfur mine.

Millions of years ago, there was a gigantic canyon between Kibbutz Be'eri and Kibbutz Sa'ad to the north. Sulfur strata are common in shallow, fresh water where the climate is warm, and they were probably deposited here by flood waters flowing in and out of this huge, deep gulf. Oxidation of exposed sulfur caused the rocks to turn yellow.

A British officer and geologist discovered the western Negev's sulfur during World War I (some say what he smelled wasn't sulfur, but money). In 1933 an English-Arab concern began producing and exporting the mineral, eventually reaching 1,200–1,800 tons of purified sulfur each year. See if you can find the sulfur yourselves, by walking right into the pits and "nosing" around. Then follow Concrete Road a further 100 meters and turn right to see the factory.

The skeletal building before you was once a vigorous, going concern which processed natural sulfur (15 to 20 percent pure) and ended up with an unnatural 98 proof. Unfortunately for the company, parts were

23

Kibbutz Be'eri Complex

unavailable during World War II, markets were closed off and the price of labor rose to new heights. It shut down in the early 1940's.

Watch out for pits as you walk near the factory. Around the side you will see a well about 50 meters deep, apparently dug from the top down as needed. Water was crucial for the crushing and preliminary purification carried out in the factory.

An open building to the left of the factory contained laboratories, and the overgrown field nearby was where sports enthusiasts probably played tennis during World War II. If you walk to the road you will notice the letters RAF inscribed in the concrete and see the concrete post which held the gate. During the War of Independence* the buildings were taken over by the Egyptian Moslem Brotherhood.* They were defeated by Israeli forces in October 1948.

 Now leave the factory and head for the fields. At the main road turn left, and at the intersection go right, again to pass Nahbir on your return to the kibbutz entrance. If it is anywhere near noon, the sun will be sparkling on a profusion of wildflowers.

Dominating them all are resplendent anemones, but you will also spot a flower commonly called Aaron's rod, which blooms all through the winter. The relatively tall stalk is topped by a long, green-striped white flower which curves at the end. Look for pink butterfly orchids, whose flowering reaches a peak in late spring. Note the strange bee-orchid as well. It masquerades as a female bee to attract the male of the species.

Vital Information

Suitable for all ages.

Tel Jamma

So wild and untamed that cows graze on the weeds and wildflowers cover the slopes, Tel Jamma was once a thriving city on the frontier of civilization. Its eastern edge features remains of a small Chalcolithic* settlement; in the southern field archaeologists discovered evidence of a large Byzantine* city.

Early civilizations built towns, cities and fortresses atop the hills of the western Negev to control the region's large riverbeds with their abundant winter flow. Tel Jamma was one such site and experts believe the tel* to have been populated from the Chalcolithic period to the second century B.C.E. During the War of Independence* the Egyptian army used it as a base from which to attack Israel.

To reach Tel Jamma, drive along Highway 4 south of Ashkelon to Mordecai Junction. At the intersection turn left (east) on Road 34 to Gevim Junction. Then head right in the direction of Kibbutz Sa'ad (Road 232) and at Sa'ad Junction swerve with Road 232 to the left and to the right. Continue to Re'im Junction. Tel Jamma is about one kilometer further south.

A few hundred meters from the intersection begin looking for a hill on your right, Tel Jamma. Immediately past the metal railings which indicate you are on a bridge, turn right on the road leading to the tel. There may be no sign and if there is, it will read "Tel Gama." Follow this paved road to the foot of the tel, approximately 500 meters, then park and follow the path to the top.

In ancient times farmers at Tel Jamma grew excellent crops. But it was impossible to cultivate the land that lay to its south. So, in the 18th century B.C.E., the Egyptians developed the site as a major storage area for agricultural produce supplying food for the city of Gaza. Consequently, most of the tel's remains are storerooms for wheat and barley. Look for an ancient mud brick Assyrian building, still partially intact because the bricks were underground. Nearby is a large granary, one of ten that were found on the tel. In the Byzantine period, Tel Jamma also served as a way station along the trade route between the Greek islands and Arabia.

Tel Jamma was originally identified by modern archaeologists as the biblical Gerar. It was at Gerar that Isaac "had so many flocks and herds and

Tel Jamma

servants that the Philistines envied him" and filled Isaac's wells with earth. To avoid strife, Isaac moved away and dug more wells, also rich with water. Seeing how successful he was, the king of the Philistines decided to make peace with Isaac, and did so at Gerar (Genesis 26:12–29).

Some archaeologists suggest that Tel Jamma is not Gerar, but the city of Yurza. An important Canaanite city, Yurza is mentioned in early Egyptian documents.

From your vantage point on top of the hill you can appreciate the strategic importance of Tel Jamma. This position enabled successive rulers of Israel to control the water supplied by Wadi Habesor, a key to power in the parched, dry Negev. Notice how foliage in the riverbed below lies on its side, pushed down during annual winter floods. Floods have also eaten away at the tel itself, and decreased its size.

26

Western Negev Route No. 2

*Route No. 2 includes a scenic drive through
a unique collection of natural and prehistoric sites and
a cave where early pioneers set up the Negev's southernmost outpost.*

In 1938, the British Woodhead Commission proposed dividing Palestine into three parts: a tiny portion in the north and center of the country would be Jewish; Jerusalem would become an international city; and everything else, including the entire Negev, would fall into Arab hands.

Alarmed, the country's Jewish leaders devised a plan to place the Negev inside a future Jewish state. Their scheme involved finding a way around the British restriction on Jewish settlement in the south. They did so by sending three little groups into the Negev in 1943, ostensibly to conduct agricultural research but actually to gain a foothold on the land. One of them was MITZPE REVIVIM, a restored outpost which is located along an unusually exciting route through the western Negev.

Begin at Maon Junction, where Roads 232 and 241 intersect. Turn left (east) onto Road 241 and continue several kilometers to the sign BESOR SCENIC ROUTE. Take the two-to-three hour scenic drive, stopping for enchanting little walks and at historical sites, then proceed to Tze'elim Junction. Here turn right onto Road 222 and continue to Mashabim Junction.

During the next part of your ride, you will explore MITZPE REVIVIM and will drive past two attractions described in ROUTE NO. 3: BIR ASLUJ and GOLDA MEIR PARK.

After your visit to Revivim, return to the main road. About two kilometers southeast of Revivim, as you continue on Road 222, you reach Golda Meir Park. Just across from the park is Be'er Mashabim, known as Bir Asluj to local residents. Mitzpe Revivim's first settlers drew their water from the well of Bir Asluj and carted it home.

Continue further along Road 222 to reach Mashabim Junction. From here you can turn right to MITZPE RAMON and EILAT or left to BEER SHEVA.

Vital Information

Sites in SMALL CAPS are described in detail in special chapters.

The Besor Scenic Route

Developed by the Jewish National Fund (JNF) in 1994, the Besor scenic route is our favorite type of tourist attraction. Not only are its historical sites and little ponds easily accessible but the delightful outing is FREE. Do take this leisurely, unforgettably lovely trip, which leads you through 18 kilometers of natural landscape.

The scenic drive runs along a small part of Wadi Habesor, one of Israel's longest intermittent streams. Although the Besor flows only during winter floods, erosion on its banks has created exciting desert badlands. Little springs surrounded by river foliage contain water all year long; ancient tels* and other remains from antiquity are common near the river.

 To reach the Besor scenic route from Maon Junction, follow Road 241 east, turning right at the signs between Urim Junction and Maon Junction.

At the beginning of the route a large billboard offers historical and geographical explanations in English; 14 more (green) signs appear along the route. Explanatory pages in English should be available under the map at the entrance. If a site interests you, park your car—usually there is a small clearing nearby—and look for the excavations, railroad tracks, well or pool it describes. To get to a few of the suggested attractions you are directed onto an extension road, then returned to the main route.

Former jeep roads have been closed off to vehicles and are meant exclusively for visitors on foot. As a result, even strollers should be able to maneuver the desert sands. Blue trail-markers along the road follow the scenic drive, while black markers point to nature paths for hikers.

As you begin the excursion, note young trees surrounded by plastic sleeves. Sleeves have a greenhouse effect which enable the saplings to grow faster and with less water than under natural conditions. They also help the shoots grow straight and tall and protect them from hungry hedgehogs, porcupines and gazelles. When the trees are strong enough, the sleeves are removed and the shoots released.

In late winter and early spring the ground is covered with bright yellow chrysanthemum and groundsel. In Hebrew groundsel is called *savion*, probably from the word for grandfather, *sav*. When it dries the groundsel's petals become white and wispy; blow on them and they drift away in the wind. Around February, red anemones are at their peak—later on, bright

Tall white asphodels dominate a field of blood-red blossoms.

The Besor Scenic Route

The Besor Scenic Route

red tulips take their place. Other flowers you will see include milk vetch, scarlet pimpernel, Negev colchicum and desert stork's bill.

Your first stop is an historical site located near sign number one. When you park you will see a dirt embankment next to the riverbed. Look to your left (or walk in that direction) to observe the concrete bases which once held a wooden bridge.

During World War I the British were based south of Gaza. In mid-1917, before they seized Beer Sheva from the Turks, the British desperately needed water from the Besor riverbed. With construction of railroad tracks and a railway bridge they were able to operate a train running from Gaza to the Besor springs and as far as Beer Sheva.

Climb atop the embankment. In winter and spring it bursts with anemones and colorful chrysanthemums, as well as marigolds and tall asphodels. The Greeks considered tall asphodel a symbol of nature's awakening and of resurrection. When someone died, it was customary to say he had "gone to the dwelling place of the asphodel." Even today, Greeks sometimes plant this graceful flower in cemeteries, for their white color symbolizes the purity of those who have passed away.

From here you can gaze down at what remains of the bridge. Across from the riverbed are trees and picnic tables, part of ESHKOL NATIONAL PARK.

If you like, leave the car and ascend the scenic road a few meters. Across from a black trail-marker a path leads down to the wadi, where there are pools of water in winter, spring and summer. It is a short, easy descent: you can stroll in the direction of the river as far as you want and back again.

You are now driving along Wadi Habesor, which is lined with green foliage and twists and turns like a serpent. Even in summer the ravine is wet in parts, forming a refreshing contrast to the desert sands.

Wadi Habesor is mentioned in the Bible in connection with David's battle against Amalek. "David and the six hundred men with him came to the Besor Ravine...some stayed behind, for two hundred men were too exhausted to cross the ravine" (I Samuel 30: 9–10). Although this is the ravine officially identified as Besor, some experts argue that biblical Besor is, instead, the nearby Wadi Gerar.

Site number two is Chalcolithic,* and includes an ancient quarry. Follow the path to the left, across from the sign. Look for remains from numerous dwellings dug into the ground by ancient residents around 6,000 years ago, as this was the perfect spot for grazing their animals and watering their flocks.

Then take a short stroll down to the wadi, especially delightful in late winter and early spring when the ground is covered with a vast array of

30

The Besor Scenic Route

dazzling wildflowers. At the bottom you will see two hollows which contain water all year long. Next to the left recess are remains of the ancient quarry. You can sit on the edges of the rock and gaze at the ground—where you just might discover a porcupine's den. Jackals and wild boars are also known to roam this part of the riverbed.

Back on the road note the contrasting scenery. On one side is a plateau, filled with waving wheat, green in winter and spring, yellow in summer. On the other are flowers, hills and strange, swirling badlands. Here in the Besor riverbed the badlands constantly change their shape, for the thick layer of loess* soil is eroded by infrequent strong rains.

In the distance to your left you will eventually see Tel Sharuhen, the region's only natural hill. Fortified by the Egyptians, Canaanites and later by the Israelites, Tel Sharuhen was subsequently populated during the Roman period as well.

Park near sign number four (not at the first clearing across from the tel), then follow the path up the hill. You will pass a dry moat, in winter and spring full of flowers. This tel was naturally defended on all but the western side, which was unprotected and required a moat. Atop the hill is a lookout which blends beautifully into the landscape and offers an excellent view of the town Ofakim, of Kibbutz Be'eri and of Wadi Habesor below. On a good day you can also see Ashkelon and occasionally all the way into Sinai. Soon after the British occupied Palestine in 1917, they decided to map out the land of Israel. They began here because the western Negev is almost a total plateau and from Tel Sharuhen they could see great distances in every direction.

Look for a trail leading along the rim of the tel to an adobe (sun dried brick) wall, and examine the gate which has remained. Thousands of years after the Canaanites built with mud, pioneers at MITZPE GEVULOT utilized the same kind of materials to construct their outpost. Now return to your car.

Scenic Detour and Swimming Hole

From the 4,000-year-old adobe wall you can take a fantastic hike. Walk through the "gate," and start your gradual descent. Make sure you go down, not up, when the path splits near the end. Pass through a tamarisk jungle and come out into the dry riverbed.

Now stroll atop the pebbles in the wadi, staying close to the shrubs on your right. Eventually you reach a large body of water—Sharuhen Pool—which contains masses of bulrushes stretching further than you can see. If you are hot, have a dip in the water.

31

The Besor Scenic Route

To get back to your car, walk up the dirt path next to the lone tamarisk tree and turn right. You should be on a trail slightly above the riverbed (which is on the right). Take the gradual rise, straight ahead.

When you see a very narrow gully to your right, try to identify hairy leatherwood. Perfectly suited to the desert, this plant has tiny leaves which provide minimal exposure and lessen condensation. Hairy leatherwood may be the rope used by the Jews of Judah to bind Samson before they delivered him to the Philistines. After Samson was turned over to the Philistine enemy, "the spirit of the Lord came upon him in power. The ropes on his arms became like charred flax and the bindings dropped from his hands" (Judges 15:14).

Hairy leatherwood is excellent for making ropes. If you pull off a branch a long, tough string comes with it. Braid a few together and you have your rope. Then walk up the hill to the tel and down from there to your car.

Resume the Scenic Route at Sign Number Six

Continue on the scenic route to sign number six and you will reach Sharuhen Pool. Containing water year round and full of reeds, in ancient times this pool was the main water source for the adjacent city. As you continue the drive, you will see reeds pushed over on their sides by winter floods. Because there are so many rodents near this riverbed you will also see a large number of birds of prey. Hyenas have also been spotted around here!

Twice during this jaunt a dirt road going straight ahead may confuse you. Swerve with the asphalt, watching for blue trail-markers which will help you find your way.

Stop next to sign number seven, called "site B." During the Chalcolithic period there were many settlements in the western Negev, to a large extent built around the area's natural flora and fauna in the area. A great deal of flint and other remnants of settlement were found on this spot.

But the best thing about site B is the view. You can stand on a little hill to your left, right above the riverbed, and gaze at the rich foliage surrounding the wadi. Be careful not to get too close to the edge of the cliff!

Wild boar can often be seen wandering through the wadi. Note how the riverbed twists and turns: there is a lot of hard rock in this region and the water simply takes the easiest path. Look for ducks and frogs in the water. In April, storks—dozens of them—appear on the ground near the wadi and above you in the sky.

Revuva Well at sign number nine is worth a little detour by car. It is one of 12 wells found within the boundaries of the former Bedouin village of Ruweiba, built at the beginning of the century by the Turks for the Tharabin

The Besor Scenic Route

tribe. Over 40 meters deep, Revuva Well was initially a pit carved out by the Turks. It was renovated during the British Mandate period, when the British needed water for their animals. The groves were planted under the Turks to keep Bedouin from claiming ownership of the land.

Potable water from the well was sold to the settlers of MITZPE GEVULOT. Established on May 12, 1943, Gevulot was the first Jewish outpost in the Negev. Kibbutzniks* would harness a horse, bring it to the well, and pay one pound sterling for a big tank of water.

Proceed along the route. To your right are gigantic tamarisks, 80 to 90 years old, where you can picnic. In spring tulips bloom along the road.

You will see trees growing away from the road in long, horizontal rows. Sandstorms pose a major problem in the desert, and the JNF has planted hundreds of kilometers of hedges like these as windbreaks. They keep sand off access roads, fields and agricultural produce.

There is a "drain cliff" at sign number 10, where pipes and natural stone filters raise underground water to the surface. Then, at sign number 11, the JNF is building two huge reservoirs to collect run-off water for agriculture. One will hold about a million cubic meters of water from winter floods; a pump will empty it into an upper reservoir which has more than double the capacity of its companion.

The tractor at Mitzpe Revivim should really be a museum piece (next chapter).

The Besor Scenic Route

At this point several roads intersect: go straight ahead, driving above and along the reservoirs and riverbed. Near the end of the drive you will reach a long swinging bridge over Gev Cliff, fantastic fun for children. On the other side of the bridge is a memorial to two youths from Kibbutz Mashabei Sadeh, killed when they rode their ATV's (all-terrain vehicles, or *tractoronim*) over the cliff.

After an exciting walk back and forth on the bridge continue along the route, which passes two hidden stone picnic tables next to site number 13, the Cliff Pool. This particular part of the wadi is an unusual geological cross-section and a sign explains loess, clay, chalky limestone rock, conglomerate, pebbles, and other stone found in the area. Water seeps under the pebbles on top, and is stopped at the chalk level where a pipe 25 meters deep sucks out the water and diverts it to agricultural fields.

The road loops, then meanders along the riverbed another kilometer and a half. Finally it ascends to the main (Tze'elim-Gevulot) highway. To your left is Tze'elim Observation Tower and if you climb up you can see, below, lots of foliage and an impenetrable layer of white chalky rock. Next to the tower are picnic tables, a garbage bin and some inviting hills where children can run safely up and down while you put out your picnic.

 After descending the tower return to the Tze'elim-Gevulot Highway (222). Take a left and drive a few hundred meters to Tze'elim Junction. To reach Beer Sheva, take a left to Urim Gilat and Beer Sheva. Follow a tree-lined road (234) and continue as far as Road 241, and turn right. This eventually intersects with Highway 25, and leads to Beer Sheva.

If you wish to reach Eilat drive to Tze'elim Junction, where you continue on Road 222. When you reach Mashabim Junction you will be well on your way south.

Vital Information
There is no drinking water on the route. In summer it is usually very hot.

Mitzpe Revivim

If it hadn't been for a handful of brave and hardy pioneers who settled at Mitzpe Revivim, the Negev might not be part of modern Israel. Established in 1943, Revivim was the southernmost of the first three Jewish *mitzpim* ("outposts") in the Negev. Its presence helped influence the United Nations' 1947 decision to include the Negev within the boundaries of the soon-to-be-created Jewish State. Mitzpe Revivim was built like a tiny castle: a two-story security edifice within a courtyard, surrounded by a stone wall. The roof was used as a watchtower. Settlers moved to an adjacent area and built the permanent housing of Kibbutz Revivim in 1950.

Revivim lost several members of its small group in skirmishes with the Arabs before and during the War of Independence.* The pioneers' participation in the battle for BIR ASLUJ, which temporary halted an Egyptian advance, was crucial to the war effort.

Restoration of the original site began in 1983 when Kibbutz Revivim celebrated its 40th birthday. The indoor-outdoor museum is designed to educate visitors about early Negev settlement and agricultural experiments. It also gives you a feel for the community's daily life over 50 years ago.

To visit this fascinating site begin at Mashabim Junction, between Beer Sheva and Sde Boker, on Highway 40. Turn northwest on Road 222 towards Kibbutz Revivim and drive about two kilometers to GOLDA MEIR PARK. It is no accident that the park is named for Golda Meir: the former prime minister's daughter was a founding member of Revivim.

A few kilometers further and you will approach the site of contemporary Revivim. Circle around the kibbutz, following orange signs to the* mitzpe. *The road is marked with a sign in English on the road between Revivim and Retamim. It reaches a palm grove and then turns into a dirt road. Drive along the road for a few minutes until you see a lone old house on the hill. Before you go into the outpost you are going to visit the Revivim Dam, located below the house.*

Like the other two 1943 outposts—GEVULOT and Beit Eshel—Revivim started out with a handful of young men, some of whom left wives and children at home in the north. Life in the Negev was incredibly difficult. Not

35

Mitzpe Revivim

only were they completely isolated and horribly lonely but they were camped on a desert wilderness.

Without water life would have been impossible. Here, at Revivim, a single-minded engineer named Dov Kublanov tried to harness the Mashabim River. Note the fantastic water system he created (and look at the little hut on the hill where he often spent his days and nights). It includes canals, dams and, to the northwest, a cistern lined with tar.

Unfortunately for the settlers, however, Mother Nature had her own plan. Time and again the walls and river channel were destroyed by flooding waters or cracks in the storage area floor, and eventually the system was abandoned.

Desert plants prove, if proof were needed, that Revivim was established on wasteland. Look for saltwort, which in summer absorbs the brackish water that remains deep underground. Foxthorn, a prickly plant common to the Negev, begins to sprout green leaves in October.

White broom, which flowers at Revivim, is a protected plant which blossoms in the winter. It saves surface area by sporting green needles instead of leaves. If you examine a needle you will see slits which cover the stomata within.

The pink and white flowers which characterize the saxaul bloom in summer. Like a few other desert plants, the saxaul is constructed out from joints (thus the Hebrew name, *prakrak*, from the word for joint). During a drought it kills off its outermost joints to economize on water.

Now drive to the outpost entrance to begin your tour of Mitzpe Revivim with the slow-moving but worthwhile audio-visual presentation. It is available in English, Russian, Spanish and Hebrew. Then move on to the outpost, past some rusty barrels once used by the settlers as barriers against enemy vehicles. As you can see, any intruder would have had to swerve back and forth to get inside the outpost.

On top of their geopolitical purpose, the three Negev *mitzpim* performed a major agricultural service. Their diverse geographical settings allowed experimentation with all kinds of soil, weather conditions and seed. Samples are on display along the sidewalk, as you walk over to the outpost fortress.

All the *mitzpim* included a two-story security edifice within a courtyard surrounded by a wall. Here the wall was made of stone and the security building's roof was used as a watchtower.

You can begin your visit to this indoor-outdoor museum with Kublanov's simple cabin. Nearby is the original communications center. Illegal to operate under the British, it is hidden behind a wall with a row of pegs for hanging coats. Settlers pretended that the radio antenna was used for

36

Mitzpe Revivim

testing climatic conditions and were so convincing that the British bought the story. The actual radio was concealed in a first-aid kit. If you press the button on the wall you can hear what the transmissions sounded like.

The culture hall has an old-fashioned gramophone and 78 rpm records, as well as the original backgammon, chess boards and books from the settlement's first library. Take a look at the old favorites in their songbooks—they are still sung today. The radio was a gift from David Ben Gurion, who donated it when he learned the settlers received newspapers only every two weeks. Turn it on to hear the original sound.

From the top of the tower, you will see bunkers and fortifications used through 1948. Note how the dining hall and other communal rooms were part of the wall around the fortress. Below you are agricultural equipment and two exciting caves, your next destination. The tractor should really be a museum piece. It is a little Caterpillar D2, used by the first three settlers when they dug a makeshift border and later for plowing.

Both caves were originally storerooms built by the Nabateans, one of them was used as a cistern. The larger housed the pioneers during their first year in Revivim and later became a field hospital. Pipes, which have become the symbol of the museum, were hastily erected as support when settlers needed to build a back wall to the cave. The medical supplies on display belonged to a British field infirmary during World War II and were brought here after settlers found them in a bomb shelter. Note the chamber pot and the tubing for infusions—one end was inserted directly into the donor's arm and the other into the patient.

The smaller cave was discovered only in 1948 when members were digging a bomb shelter. It became a command post during the War of Independence and still contains vintage weapons and an escape hatch.

Look also for two fighter planes, sitting on the remains of a camouflaged runway. They were among the few planes which were the settlement's only physical connection with the rest of the country when the Negev was under siege in 1948.

Finally, have a picnic in the date grove near the entrance to the outpost. It is part of a lovely rest area built by the Jewish National Fund. Excellent bathroom facilities are located next to the office.

Vital Information
Sun. to Thurs. 9:00–15:00; Fri. & holiday eves 9:00–13:00; Sat. & holidays 9:00–16:00. Entrance fee.
Tel.: 07-562570; fax: 562607.

Western Negev Route No. 3

Western Negev Route No. 3

*Route No. 3 pilots you through a delightful little zoo,
an ancient synagogue and a desert oasis.*

Those in the know plan their Negev trips for late winter and early spring, when the region's spectacular flowers are in brilliant bloom. This particular outing, however, is fun any time of year: it includes historical sites, a Negev oasis (GOLDA MEIR PARK) and desert dunes.

Begin at Maon Junction, where Roads 232 and 241 intersect. Look for a sign leading right (west) to MAON SYNAGOGUE and follow it onto Road 242 in the direction of Kissufim and Nir Oz. After about two kilometers, a wooden sign points to the synagogue. Maon has been developed as a recreation area by the Jewish National Fund and contains water, trees, flowers and picnic tables.

After visiting the ancient site (and modern picnic spot) return to Maon Junction. Now continue right (south) on Road 232 towards KIBBUTZ MAGEN. You will see jojoba fields on your left, about a kilometer past Maon Junction and just after the entrance to the town hall and schoolhouse. Jojoba is a plant which is endemic to Mexico and was first commercialized in the United States. Oil produced from the jojoba plant is an excellent alternative to whale oil, used in delicate motors to prevent friction. Because jojoba plants need little water, they have adapted well to the Negev desert. Today Israelis manufacture soap, body lotion and other cosmetics from jojoba seeds.

Enter Kibbutz Magen to explore part of the original settlement, established in 1949 by a group of young Romanians. Don't forget to visit the lovely kibbutz* zoo.

When you leave Magen, turn right so that you are again traveling south on Road 232. At Gevulot Junction take the left fork onto Road 222. Continue to KIBBUTZ GEVULOT.

Cut across the kibbutz to visit MITZPE GEVULOT, one of the first Negev communities, which was settled by highly motivated pioneers (see also MITZPE REVIVIM). Afterwards return to Road 222, turn right and continue in the direction of Mashabim Junction. About two kilometers past Mitzpe Revivim stop at shady Golda Meir Park, where you can take a short wilderness walk to an observation point with a wonderful view. Bring a fishing rod to cast into the glistening lake, stocked with fish.

38

Western Negev Route No. 3

Just across from Golda Meir Park are the sands of BIR ASLUJ. Here a Bedouin ex-army tracker operates a fleet of camels at Sfinat Hamidbar, or "Ship of the Desert." After your stop for Bedouin hospitality, you continue the last few kilometers to Mashabim Junction. From there, you can turn left, to Beer Sheva, or turn right to Mitzpe Ramon.

Vital Information

Sites in SMALL CAPS are described in detail in special chapters.

Maon Synagogue

It is common knowledge that Jewish communities thrived in the Galilee during the Byzantine* era, the fourth to sixth centuries C.E. What many people do not realize, however, is that there were also prosperous Jewish towns and villages in the Negev throughout the same period. One such community was Maon, whose synagogue was discovered by chance in 1957 as workers paved a new road. The ancient house of study and prayer had a splendid mosaic floor which was chock full of Jewish symbols and animals. An unusual balcony lets you view the floor from above.

 Maon has been developed as a recreation area by the Jewish National Fund and alongside the archaeological remains are water, foliage and picnic tables. To get there from Beer Sheva follow Road 241 to Maon Junction. At the intersection turn onto Road 242 towards Kissufim and Nir Oz. A wooden sign points to the synagogue.

Look for an apse in the wall facing Jerusalem. Perhaps the small platform in front of the apse held the Holy Ark.

Most of the elements that went into typical Byzantine mosaics can be found on this floor, together with distinctive Jewish symbols such as the *menorah* (candelabrum). The mosaic tesserae are of colored glass, marble and clay, forming peacocks, lions, grapevines and a fruit bowl. Mistakes in lettering and language indicate that the Gaza artisans didn't understand Aramaic and were probably not Jewish. In order to create symmetrical designs they apparently added little signs of their own, strange squiggles that you may notice on the tiles.

Interestingly, this synagogue strongly resembles a church located in ESHKOL NATIONAL PARK. Perhaps the same artist decorated both houses of worship.

Magen

Like most kibbutzim* in the western Negev, Magen is a thriving modern settlement and it is hard to comprehend how difficult life was for the early pioneers. Situated in a wasteland, surrounded by hostile neighbors and living from hand to mouth in crowded and primitive quarters, they nevertheless managed not only to survive but also to create a contemporary paradise.

So completely have they succeeded that even their offspring sometimes have trouble understanding the life they led during those first, difficult decades. So kibbutz members created "In the Beginning," a section of the settlement containing one of the original huts, the first outhouse, early communal showers and the original bell.

To visit old Kibbutz Magen follow Road 232 to Sa'ad Junction in the northwestern Negev. Continue on 232 past Maon Junction until you reach the kibbutz.

In the early days, because the British had confiscated their watches at displaced persons camps in Europe, the settlers used a bell for wake-up calls which would send them to work and bring them home. You can see this bell at the entrance to the hut—a large metal ring with a metal hammer.

Local Arabs stole anything not tied down in those days, and sometimes planted explosives. As a result guards from the group climbed the watchtower at night and combed the area with projectors.

Magen's settlers wanted desperately to leave the Diaspora behind them and to become true Israelis. They talked only in (broken) Hebrew and one day burned all their clothes and everything else linking them to their native Romania. Afterwards, they Hebraized all their names.

Photographs in the dining hall illustrate the absolute wilderness they inherited. One shows a stage the settlers set up whenever VIP's appeared, in the futile hope of gaining assistance. Unfortunately, the very important person would make a speech applauding their heroism and leave the kibbutz as he found it—still without water, electricity or other basics.

A British army jacket hangs on the wall. Clothing and other possessions were communal and since this jacket was one of the few decent items they had between them, it was shared among those who wanted to go into town. With luck, the person ahead of you on the sign-up list would return

Magen

the jacket before it was your turn to leave the kibbutz. If he didn't, you went to town in your work clothes.

The second room is a model of the pioneers' bedrooms. As there were never enough rooms, two families shared or one family was joined by a single settler. In the hut's third room you find old tools (the original sickle and an ancient saw, for example) and a model of the kibbutz at its inception. Outside are the old outhouse and the communal shower, divided for men and women. This was where you came to hear the latest news of the day. Look for little holes between the walls and for the wooden clogs they wore in the shower.

During your visit to Magen, plan to stop at an unusually large and interesting kibbutz zoo. It was established so that kibbutz youngsters would learn about animals and the farm is almost exclusively their responsibility. Here you can pet Shetland ponies and watch the antics of several snobbish-looking emus.

Look for deer, ibex, and a snake hut. This latter houses black and red milk snakes, iguanas, king snakes and a baby giant turtle.

Among hundreds of other animals and fowl are porcupines, dwarf deer, and angora goats. A female ibex reared from babyhood by humans still loves to be petted. Cute little capuchin monkeys swing through the monkey house and guinea pigs live next door to parakeets, lovebirds and several lop-rabbits with droopy ears. Dozens of peacocks roam around the animal farm.

Gorgeous black swans from Australia swim in the little ponds with white swans and Canadian geese. Watch them from atop bridges over the water as they mingle with a delightful collection of multicolored ducks.

Vital Information

For details on hours and the entrance fee to the zoo call 07–983080.
The entrance fee includes a visit to "In the Beginning;" for a tour of "In the Beginning" call kibbutznik Arie Barzilai at 07–983275.

Mitzpe Gevulot

A group of children visiting Mitzpe Gevulot walked around the original mud-brick huts, gazed across vast expanses of wasteland and inspected the water system used by the early pioneers. Impressed, one of the youngsters turned to veteran kibbutz* member Shimon Alony and asked, in all seriousness, how the settlers managed without television!

How difficult it must be for today's children (as well as some adults) to comprehend the reality of life in Israel's desert wilderness during the British Mandate. Even a single visit to an early settlement can help them understand the hardships faced by these hardy idealists.

To reach Gevulot from Maon Junction drive south on Road 232. At Gevulot Junction take the left fork onto Road 222 and continue to the kibbutz.

Enter the kibbutz and cut across it to the opposite side. Immediately beyond the border fence turn right and drive around the orchard. When the paved road ends, continue on a dirt road until you get to the signs in front of an abandoned building.

In 1943 Jewish leaders in Palestine organized the establishment of three tiny outposts in the Negev, supposedly for agricultural research. In fact, they were a means of gaining a foothold in the Negev, an area where Jewish settlement was virtually forbidden.

Three years later, just before a United Nations commission visited Palestine to examine the issue of Jewish statehood, hundreds of young people left their homes in central and northern Palestine and moved quietly into existing Negev communities. The night after Yom Kippur, the time when Jews normally break their 24-hour fast, 11 pioneer convoys secretly set out towards new territory. The trucks contained not only the settlers, but also fences, poles, material for walls and everything else necessary to set up new outposts. So clandestine was the mission and so difficult the passage through the desert sands, that at times pioneers had to get out and walk, and even carry the equipment on their backs!

During the night and the following day these stalwart souls built their new homes and by the time the British realized what had happened, each settlement already had a watchtower, perimeter walls and a few huts. Even the most pro-Arab of British rulers was reluctant to wipe eleven established

Mitzpe Gevulot

communities off the map. The settlements stayed—and the Negev eventually became part of the State of Israel.

Mitzpe Gevulot, where you are now standing, was one of half a dozen communities from which the 1946 Yom Kippur convoys started out. It was set up on May 12, 1943, and was the first Jewish outpost in the Negev. (The two that followed were Beit Eshel and REVIVIM.)

Fewer than ten people lived here in 1943. They slept in the cement watchtower and used the mud-brick buildings as kitchen, dining hall and infirmary. Inside the fortress was a regional bakery: during the War of Independence,* when the Negev was under siege, Gevulot settlers provided soldiers and area settlers with all their baked goods. The ruined house outside of the fortress was where Bedouin guests were received. Walk up the hill to see the surrounding sandy wastelands and the outpost below. Nothing you see has been restored or touched in any way: there are adobe buildings, the shower (where settlers poured pails of water over themselves), the bakery and the walled cement security building. Outside the perimeter walls is a complicated water system with asphalt-coated reservoirs.

Pioneers at Gevulot experimented with a mixture of sand and the local loess* in a successful attempt to raise a variety of fruit and vegetables. In an effort to store water they tried collecting dew, which is especially heavy here because of the sharp contrast between day-time and night-time temperatures. They also tried asphalt-coated plates, slanted to carry water into the reservoirs to your left.

Today Gevulot is a prosperous kibbutz with 120 members who work primarily in agriculture. The "old-timers" can reflect on their life's work with a true feeling of accomplishment.

Vital Information

Tel.: 07–983136.

Golda Meir Park

Intended one day to become a major recreational site, the Negev park named for former prime minister Golda Meir offers tourists a shady spot for picnics, a short wilderness walk and an observation point with a wonderful view. Most delightful, however, is a glistening lake which contrasts sharply with the desert sands.

Before the park was established, the lake filled with floodwater during the rainy season and evaporated every summer. Now the water level is stable, for the park's Jewish National Fund developers calculate the rates of vaporization and loss into the ground, and restore the missing volume with brackish water drilled a few hundred meters from the park. The lake is stocked with St. Peter's fish and three species of carp. So far only a small portion of the park's slated 1,000 dunams have been developed, but the lake already hosts hopeful fishermen—mostly, it seems, Russian and American immigrants.

Water for irrigation of the colorful foliage comes from the Mashabim Well right inside the park. Better known by its Arabic name, BIR ASLUJ, it was the only source of water for MITZPE REVIVIM, a frontier outpost established in 1943. It was also the site of a fierce battle during the War of Independence.* A memorial to the soldiers who died there is located on the other side of the road, across from the entrance to the park.

The observation point is named for Tali Rasinsky, who was marketing director of the Negev Tourism Development Association when it was established in 1989.

 To reach Golda Meir Park take Road 222 off the Beer Sheva-Sde Boker Highway (Highway 40). You will see a sign leading to the park on your right, minutes after the turn.

Vital Information
The Tali Rasinsky Observation Point is located on the western side of the lake, accessible by dirt road.

Bir Asluj (Be'er Mashabim)

Bir Asluj (Be'er Mashabim)
"THE WELL OF MASHABIM"

Although a stop at Bir Asluj is a journey into the recent past, this site of famous battles fought during the War of Independence* was developed by the Jewish National Fund and is a wonderful place for a picnic.

Pause here for a tranquil respite next to beautiful sand dunes and a shady grove. For more excitement you can visit the adjacent Sfinat Hamidbar ("Ship of the Desert"), established a few years ago by an enterprising Bedouin.

If you are coming directly to Bir Asluj follow Road 222 northwest of Beer Sheva and very near Mashabim Junction. Bir Asluj is five kilometers east of another attraction—MITZPE REVIVIM—and immediately across from GOLDA MEIR PARK. A large monument to Palmach* soldiers who fought in the War of Independence dominates the intersection where you turn into Bir Asluj.

Bir Asluj is an Arabic name which means "to nurse" or be nourished, as the ground nourishes trees. According to a Bedouin legend, when Abraham banished Hagar she came to Bir Asluj and threw Ishmael down. Wherever he stepped he found nourishment in the ground.

The village of Bir Asluj was founded by the Turks as an administrative center for the Ajame Bedouin tribe. Three stone wells were later built by the British, who set up a regional police station on the site. Bir Asluj was the only source of water for the stalwart pioneers at Mitzpe Revivim, an outpost founded in 1943 and at the time the southernmost Jewish settlement in the Negev.

During World War I Bir Asluj served as a logistic center for the 1915 German-Turkish assault on the Suez Canal. That attack failed and two years later the British conquered BEER SHEVA and based troops at Bir Asluj. All that remains of the British presence at this site are military latrines.

In December 1947, Arab terrorists killed three members of Revivim. The pioneers had been seeking medical aid for friends, wounded when their vehicles were ambushed on the road between today's Mashabim Junction and Revivim.

During the War of Independence,* Egyptian troops and Arab gangs occupied the land around the straw huts of Bir Asluj for six months. Their

Bir Asluj (Be'er Mashabim)

control of the roads to Beer Sheva kept supplies from reaching Negev settlements.

Palmach soldiers and local settlers attacked Egyptian troops and Arab terrorists at Bir Asluj on June 10, 1948. The assault was a last-ditch effort to win this strategic junction shortly before the start of a cease-fire. As a result of the attack, Egypt's advance towards Tel Aviv—and ultimately Jerusalem—was temporarily halted. Five Israelis died in this surprise offensive: 10 more were killed when, disregarding intelligence reports, they moved into the evacuated British police station looking for weapons. A remote-controlled mine exploded and the building collapsed.

Following their defeat the Egyptians built a road circumventing Bir Asluj. Taking up alternative positions in the area, they attacked the site again on July 18. Israel finally liberated Bir Asluj in December of 1948.

Development of the area in the early 1990's required installation of underground pipes, and workers doing so inadvertently disturbed Bedouin graves. Local Bedouin responded by lying atop the graves to prevent installation of the pipes, today visible above ground. According to the Bedouin, when the tractors approached a certain sheikh's grave their motors suddenly died. The revered sheikh—a miracle-worker during his lifetime—continued performing miracles even after his death!

Sfinat Hamidbar provides visitors with a special kind of Bedouin experience. Soft-spoken and rather retiring ex-IDF tracker Farhan Shlibi offers the usual Bedouin hospitality—music on the single-string *rababa*, tea and coffee, and tales of Bedouin lore—as well as freshly baked pita. A camel ride to the dunes is an experience which may never be forgotten.

Our families once spent the night on the sands of Bir Asluj, looking for desert creatures. A large greenish-brown desert turtle held our attention for the better part of an hour. The shell on its back had curled up edges which eased its passage through the sand, and the turtle sported two characteristic black spots on its tummy. Female turtles have flat stomachs, whereas the male has a curved front which enables him to mate. Our youngsters used a magnifying glass to count the rings on "their" turtle's shell. It was already 19 years old.

It was exciting to discover the unusual lizard-like Revivim gecko, found almost exclusively in Israel's Negev. The sand-colored gecko had shutter-like eyes which open and close from the sides, and was only a few centimeters long.

Spider webs covered with dew and clinging to the plants in the morning sun were sensational sights the next day. Dew is very important in the desert, where rain hardly falls: there is even a snake which drinks from the dew on its back!

47

Bir Asluj (Be'er Mashabim)

Vital Information
There is a fee for hospitality and rides at Sfinat Hamidbar. Tel.: 07–557315.

Bedouin hospitality in the Negev.

Western Negev Route No. 4

Route No. 4 steers you towards the springs and pools at Eshkol National Park. Continue on "Hunger Road," then stop to picnic at charming Ofakim Park.

Unless you live in the Negev, Eshkol National Park is Israel's biggest secret. Amazingly beautiful against a brown, barren, desert landscape, ESHKOL NATIONAL PARK is an all-year-round delight. Yet even natives of nearby Tel Aviv seem unaware of its historical attractions and tranquil waters.

To reach Eshkol National Park begin at Maon Junction, the intersection of Roads 232 and 241, then turn onto Road 241. Follow the road east and pass the entrance to the BESOR SCENIC ROUTE. Winter and early spring are cool and inviting months to visit; later in the season you have the added option of swimming in the park's exceptional outdoor pool, splendidly landscaped and the biggest in Israel.

When you finish relaxing at the park, continue on Road 241 all the way to Gilat Junction. The route from Maon Junction to Gilat is often called "Hunger Road," a name dating back to a period in the mid-1940's when the Negev suffered from a severe drought. Local Bedouin couldn't water their flocks and their animals died along with their crops. The people were destitute.

In an attempt to alleviate the situation the British decided to build a road with Bedouin labor, a route that at the time went from noplace to nowhere. Wages paid by the British kept the Bedouin from starvation and hence the name of the road.

At one point you will be driving through a flat plain made of layer after layer of loess* soil—dust particles swept here from the major southern deserts. Every once in a while the plains suddenly break and you descend into a channel carved by flowing, flooding waters over millions of years.

Pass the road leading to Kibbutz Urim, established as one of 11 outposts created on the same single day in 1946. Most of the moshavim* along the route were originally set up to house Jewish refugees from Arab lands who arrived in the late 1940's and early 1950's. The Negev experiment marked the first time Israel's young government settled immigrants in moshavim, instead of within deserted homes and tent cities.

Sad-looking tamarisk trees just outside of Moshav Maslul are planted in rows, and look rather out of date. These were hurriedly cultivated by the

Western Negev Route No. 4

Jewish National Fund (JNF) in the 1950's to keep the sands from shifting and to establish ownership of the land. Today the JNF utilizes run-off water from higher ground to irrigate new forests as well as other modern methods for extracting maximum water from minimal rainfall.

Turn right at Ofakim, a development town established in 1955. Most of the population, like the residents of local moshavim, are immigrants from the early 1950's.

Follow the signs left off Ofakim's main street to Ofakim Park. Developed by the JNF in 1971, the park was donated by Hadassah, the Women's Zionist Organization of America. The lovely landscape is irrigated both with fresh water and purified sewage from Tel Aviv. Here you can rest, picnic, or sit on the grass while your children have fun in the playground.

Now return to Road 241 and turn right. Just before you reach Gilat Junction look left to see some strange plants. Manufacturers imported these agave from South America as raw material for a rope industry. Unfortunately, however, the production of agave ropes requires vast amounts of water and the idea was abandoned. But since the stalks grow out of cacti they continue to flourish, and now these exotic plants cover whole fields.

At the intersection turn right onto Highway 25. Drive straight to Hanasi Junction and continue on 25 in the direction of Beer Sheva. About three kilometers south of the intersection you should spot the bridge which runs over the green riverbed of Wadi Patish. Beside the riverbed is a well, built by the British during the Mandate* for Bedouin use. Even today, you will see Bedouin lowering pails inside and bringing up water for their flocks.

Be sure to stop in BEER SHEVA to enjoy a variety of attractions (see the following section on Beer Sheva and its environs). Then, if you wish, take Highway 25 all the way to the Dead Sea and continue on the Arava Highway (90) to Eilat (see ROUTE NO. 10).

Eshkol National Park

Bursting with natural springs and dazzling against a desert backdrop, Eshkol National Park encompasses 3,000 dunams of water, grass, trees, sand and archaeological sites. In summer, park visitors can swim in Israel's largest pool, where they are surrounded by superbly landscaped lawns.

You can reach the park by taking Highway 40 north of Beer Sheva. Turn right at Kama Junction and head south on Road 264 in the direction of Mishmar Hanegev. At Hanasi Junction (known locally as Mishmar Hanegev Junction) turn right onto Highway 25 towards Ofakim. At Gilat Junction head left (Road 241). Turn at the entrance to the park.

Now drive in the direction of the springs, following the signs (in Hebrew, *ma'ayanot*). You will pass 2,000 luxurious palm trees, half of them greenhouse palms from the JNF Gilat nursery, located just east of the intersection where you turned into the park. The rest were transplanted from Yamit, the Sinai settlement which Israel was forced to evacuate after the 1979 peace accords with Egypt.

Watch for the beautiful spur-winged plover flying among the trees. This splendid tricolored creature has a black cap and a black stripe from its chin to its breast. White cheeks and beige-grey back and wings give it a particularly stunning look. Should you hear it make an incredible amount of noise, you will know that another bird has invaded its territory.

Park your car under the picnic benches and walk up to the observation platform. From this vantage there is a great view of the part of Wadi Habesor which is called "puddle valley" in Arabic and contains a number of springs. To the south note a long line of vegetation. The park's planted foliage is a much darker green than the natural river flora.

The observation platform on which you are standing was once a hill housing a fourth-to-sixth-century Byzantine* church. At the time the western Negev below was populated with Jewish and Byzantine farms and villages. Next to the platform is a reservoir. Since the brackish water in the nearby springs was unsuitable for humans, the reservoir was supplied with fresh water transported by aqueduct. Construction of the aqueduct required precise engineering, for it had to travel four kilometers while descending a mere four meters in height.

51

Eshkol National Park

Walk back down, then turn left in the direction of the springs. Turn right at the first sign and you will reach a large pool, whose brackish water is used to irrigate the park. Originating in underground springs close to the surface, they contain water year round. The tree next to the water is called tipuana tipu and has seeds which look like helicopter rotors when you throw them up and watch them float down. Cross the pool to the other side to reach a jungle of reeds and bowers.

Swimming in the shimmering pools is forbidden but you can try your luck at fishing. On the other side of the water are jungles of reeds and bowers of foliage to explore.

Behind the springs is an archaeological site. It dates from the early Canaanite period (early Bronze Age) and contains remains of Canaanite and Hellenistic settlement.

Vital Information
*Open every day 8:00–17:00. Entrance fee.
Tel.: 07–985110.*

Eshkol Park is one of Israel's best-kept secrets.

Jeep Trip in the Western Negev

lizard in Israel. Its whiplike, rounded tail is very flexible and is a powerful defensive weapon.

Eventually you reach the Keren Mountain range. Because it is endowed with deep valleys, ancient inhabitants collected rainwater streaming down the slopes. A multitude of cisterns, fed by canals at the foot of the slopes, testify to their former presence.

The Nabatean and later Byzantine* city of Rehovot was built on Mount Keren. Now called Rehovot-in-the-Negev, to distinguish it from the town near Tel Aviv, it should not be confused with a similar-sounding city in the Scriptures.

Not only is the climate here cool, dry and pleasant, but from the heights inhabitants could control trade routes below. On a clear day you can see the Mediterranean Sea, REVIVIM, and the sands of Tze'elim.

On your approach to Rehovot you perceive a crumbling Turkish khan or caravan stop. Next to it is the biggest well in the area, 80 meters deep. But the aquifer here was not sufficient for a city the size of Rehovot-in-the-Negev. Here and there the Nabateans built cisterns, huge empty caverns underneath the ground. And because water was such a priceless commodity, owners of the cisterns covered them up with special lids, on view nearby.

In the mid-1970's Israeli archaeologists uncovered a splendid Byzantine church just outside the city. It contains the characteristic three apses and a large atrium, or hall. Saints and priests were buried here and you can see one extremely well preserved Byzantine inscription.

Most interesting of all is the underground crypt, easily reached by descending some stairs. Marble slats once covered the walls, held up with copper pins, and a few of these remain. So does some 1,500-year-old red and white wax from dripping candles.

What makes this church particularly exciting is its lack of signs and reconstruction. When you visit you feel as if you are the first to have discovered this archaeological find!

The wide riverbed called Wadi Lavan ("White Riverbed") begins in AVDAT and descends all the way to Wadi El Arish. Because its aquifer is very close to the surface, the gully is filled with green plants, trees and desert flowers. Wadi Lavan gets its name from its white chalky walls.

After riding through the foliage you reach the riverbed's "big dune," full of clean brown sand. Sinking into sand up to your shins as you walk up the dune is a strange experience. And it's terrific fun to run along the surface as best you can all the way down the hill.

Jeep Trip in the Western Negev

Vital Information
To book jeep tours, call the Negev Highlands Tourism Reservations Center, at 177-022-2646 or 07-588319.

Negev enthusiasts riding camels.

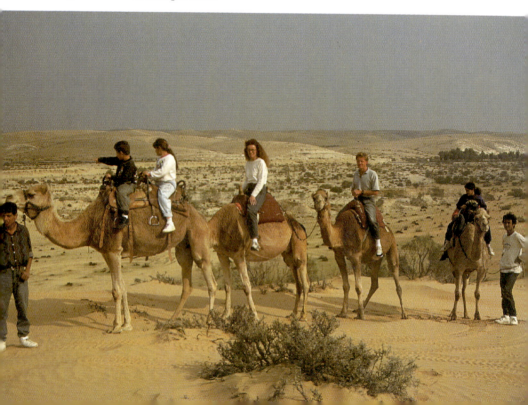

Dangur—Old Nirim

On May 15, 1948, the day after the Jewish State was declared, Arab armies moved into Israel and attacked the tiny settlement of Nirim. Armed with only two pistols, two mortars, seven Italian rifles and a few other weapons, the Israelis managed to force an Arab retreat.

For the next five months the enemy repeatedly attacked Nirim and its settlers were compelled to spend their time inside protective bunkers. One of the pioneers invented a revolving mirror with which to catch the sunlight, so they would not be in complete darkness within the bunkers.

To reach the site where the battles took place, take Road 232 south. At Gevulot Junction follow 232 to the right (southwest) in the direction of Kerem Shalom. Turn right at Sufa-Holit Junction, pass the entrance to Sufa and then make an immediate right turn. Drive another 200 meters or so and you will reach old Nirim, one of 11 Negev settlements set up overnight in 1946 to influence map makers drawing up boundaries on a future Jewish state. See GEVULOT) Contemporary Nirim lies further north.

Bunkers lead to the original settlement's watchtower and to an unusual monument. First look at the model of Nirim, then climb to the tower and gaze around. Not too far away in the distance you will see the Gaza Strip.

From here you can also see the pretty houses of Sufa's settlers. Kibbutz Sufa was originally established in the Yamit region, in nearby Sinai. As part of the 1979 peace treaty, Israel withdrew from the Sinai Peninsula and the kibbutz relocated. Farmers at Sufa grow mango, which thrives in hot weather and sandy ground. In February and March the famous Negev iris—a stunning flower—grows wild in its fields.

Vital Information
On some maps, Old Nirim is called by its original name of Dangur.

Steel Monument (*Andartat Haplada*)

First erected in Yamit, an Israeli town within the Sinai Peninsula, the tremendously impressive Steel Monument honored Armored Corps Battalion 84. Following Israel's evacuation of Yamit in 1982, the memorial was reproduced in the Shalom Region (*Hevel Shalom*).

The monument consists of dozens of tall, silent columns symbolizing the biblical pillars which guided the Israelites to safety when they came out of Egypt (Exodus 13:21). Many of the columns are topped with pieces from armored vehicles and weapons used in battles for the Gaza Strip during the Six Day War.* In the middle is a tower 25 meters high.

 To reach the memorial, take Highway 232 west from Gevulot Junction (south of Kibbutz Magen).

As you drive, look for a strange kind of sprinkler watering the fields. The *kav noa* (which translates as "moving line") seems to be walking! Operated by computer, the sprinkler automatically shuts off when there is too much wind or water pressure. The sprinkler runs along the width of a field, in a circle.

Between the turnoff for Pit'hat Shalom and Kerem Shalom there should be an orange sign indicating the monument. If it is not there, look for a prominent structure on your left.

Visitors can climb 116 steps to the observation point at the top of the tower. The green and flourishing land you see below was barren sand until the evacuation of Yamit. Future plans call for a park here, to be called Park Hashalom ("Peace Park").

Introducing the North Central Negev

Most people assume that the desert is dry, barren, and devoid of vegetation, so get ready for a surprise as you approach the northern Negev from Jerusalem or the coastal plain. Riding down Highway 40 heading south you will find that the familiar sun-scorched sands north of Beer Sheva are covered by rows of seedlings and prospering shoots.

Until the Moslem conquest in the seventh century, all the land here was fertile and green. But over the next 1,500 years the soil was destroyed: the vegetation holding down the rich topsoil was over-grazed and the topsoil was washed away. Farmers could no longer cultivate such mineral-depleted land.

For some time the Jewish National Fund (JNF) has been trying to reverse this long process of desertification. By using contour lines to collect run-off rainwater from the slopes, the JNF has been able to give young trees as much as triple the moisture they receive under natural conditions—similar to the quantity of rainfall in the Jerusalem Hills!

The section entitled "Israel's Northern Negev" includes a number of attractions in and around Beer Sheva, Arad and Sde Boker. Explore biblical and Nabatean* sites while enjoying the flowers and geological formations along the road.

We also suggest four thoroughly delightful routes from which you can eventually reach Eilat. Attractions along these routes can be seen from the car, at roadside stops in relatively unexplored historical sites such as Hurvat Krayot, on stupendous overlooks or at stunning nature reserves* described in the text. Sites which entail walking or take more than a few minutes to scout out are described in detail following each route.

Route No. 5: Through the Northern Negev

Route No. 5
Through the Northern Negev

*Route No. 5 guides you to desert forests, a Bedouin museum,
into remains of a Jewish town from the Bar Kochba revolt and
through a spectacular wildflower reserve.*

Of all Israel's brilliant wildflowers, perhaps the most captiva-

ting is the sternbergia. Named for an early 19th century botanist, sternbergia are often called golden starflowers because they are so exceptionally dazzling.

But the flower's Hebrew name—*helmonit gedola* ("large yolk")—really describes it better. Consisting of a bloom as large as eight centimeters across, it is the bright orange-yellow color of a healthy egg yolk. Sternbergia are especially prized because their short-blooming blossoms splash isolated spots of color within a mass of dry weeds or brown desert sand. Indeed, sternbergia begin blooming even before the soil has been touched by rain!

You can see the glorious sternbergia along Route No. 5, if you visit the northern Negev in late autumn and early winter (and other attractions at other seasons of the year). The route begins within a lush, shady forest planted and developed by the Jewish National Fund (JNF). Keep in mind that while we noted here only a few forest highlights, other attractions are accessible during a forest walk or a leisurely drive.

Begin your excursion south of Kiryat Gat on Highway 40. Six kilometers north of Kama Junction, at kilometer marker 215, you will see a sign reading "Pura N.R." (Pura Nature Reserve). Park your car and walk up the hill.

In winter and early spring the reserve's flowers are exquisite: blue alkanet, tall white asphodel, pink sunroses, a variety of yellow blooms, red anemones, and the small, pointy blue petals of the herbaceous periwinkle.

Once quite common in Israel, the periwinkle is now a rarity and Pura Reserve is one of the few places in the country where it grows wild. The periwinkle's Latin name, *vinca*, means wreath, and is based on the ancient custom of using the periwinkle's leaves for garlands and wreaths.

62

Route No. 5: Through the Northern Negev

When you finish frolicking through the flowers at Pura, return to Highway 40 and continue your ride south. Pass the arches at Kama Junction with their big Hebrew sign reading *"Derech Hahofesh"* (Freedom Road). Continue only a few kilometers more to Devira Junction.

At the intersection turn left onto Road 325 and follow it east to Lahav Forest. Several kilometers past Kibbutz Devir large signs on the right point you into Lahav Forest, a startling green contrast to the dry shrubs and brush which have accompanied you till now. A recreation site offers an innovation increasingly found in JNF forests: picnic sites with cement floors and protruding table tops especially constructed for the wheelchair-bound.

When the JNF plants a forest today it includes palm, acacia, terebinth and fruit trees wherever possible, and puts pine only in stony ground where nothing else will grow. But in the 1950's, when the JNF first began reclaiming the Negev's eroded and overgrazed soil, workers planted huge forests with the easily nurtured pine. Planting trees provided work for thousands of new immigrants—just as it was to do later for Russian newcomers in the early 1990's. Older sections of Lahav Forest and its neighbor Yatir contain millions of flourishing pine trees.

These conifers originated in northern countries, where their strong, thin needles kept them from being crushed under heavy snow. Pine needles contain a special acidic material which repulses most other trees and plants, helping pines vie successfully for soil and water. With no competitors, they can keep all the light they need for themselves; the Hebrew word for pine, *oren*, is derived from the word for light.

An exception is the *ornia*, or pine mushroom, which appears under pine trees after it rains. The pine and the *ornia* complement each other, providing for one another's natural needs. Pine trees supply the *ornia* with nutrients that have formed in their green leaves; the mushroom gives the pine materials from the ground which are difficult for the tree to absorb.

Soon you come to the Joe Alon Center of Bedouin Culture, whose wonderful museum contains three-dimensional exhibits depicting Bedouin life as it used to be. A slide show (available in English) brings the old traditions to life. Included in the admission price is a visit to the Bedouin tent adjacent to the museum, where you share coffee and hear stories about Bedouin life.

On your way to the museum's observation balcony are several delightful walk-through exhibits of nearby archaeological sites. Explore cave replicas, including a columbarium (niches in which to bury the ashes of the dead or perhaps for use as a dovecote) from the Hellenistic period, a Chalcolithic* cave, and a Bar Kochba hideaway (from the Jewish revolt in the second century C.E.).

63

Route No. 5: Through the Northern Negev

Old-fashioned placards line the stairway as you ascend to the second display, aptly named "The Awakening Desert." The posters, some over 50 years old, were used in the past to solicit contributions to the JNF. One is from the 1947 Australian Campaign and it states: "The plough breaks through;" another, from 1946, warns of "The Land at the Hour of Crisis."

What makes the exhibit unusual are photographs illustrating a variety of JNF projects not generally associated with the organization—among them settlement and improvement in Israel's quality of life. Exceptionally interesting is a blowup of a black and white photograph from 1935, in which JNF official Josef Weitz is seen walking through the desert with a cane. At one point on that tour Weitz stuck his rod in the ground and said "Here there will be a forest." Today that forest is Yatir (see ROUTE NO. 6), the largest manmade woodland in Israel. From the roof of the display you have an excellent view of the settlements and Lahav Forest itself.

Drive through the parking lot, continuing one kilometer further into the forest. A sign will point you left, onto a dirt road that leads to Hurvat Rimon. Drive 500 meters to a fork. Do not take the sharp left turn, which heads down into the valley. Instead, you curve mildly to the left, pass a little monument, continue another 700 meters (and up and down a few hills) to the end of the road. Park.

If you gaze across the bare hills to the north you will see ruins from Rimon, a Jewish settlement built during the Second Temple period which was probably inhabited through the Bar Kochba Revolt (135 C.E.). Its synagogue was built in the third century and remained in use until sometime after the Moslems conquered Israel in the seventh. *"Rimon"* is Hebrew for pomegranate and the word was preserved in the local community's Arabic name: *Khirbet Um er-Ramamin.*

The synagogue's inner walls were plastered, painted red, and richly decorated with floral motifs. The niche which faces Jerusalem probably served as the ark.

Caves where the Jews of Rimon buried their dead line the slope below the road. Climb part way down the hill and look for the most promising entrance to a burial cave. Inside there is plenty of light. Just to the left is an open pit, perhaps used as a *geniza* (for storing worn-out holy books), so be careful as you go in. Note the triple tombs and ossuaries.

Now walk along the ridge to the city itself. Hollows on the hills fill with rainwater each winter and every year, without fail, an uncommon species of crab appears in the pools. Beware of ancient wells and cisterns which may be obscured by brush. The ridge contains all kinds of ruins, including ancient walls and underground storerooms.

64

Route No. 5: Through the Northern Negev

Once you enter the city gate look for the synagogue floor with its carved *menorah* (candelabrum) and rosette designs. To the west of the ark area, on a lower level, archaeologists found a hoard of ancient coins.

Return to your car, backtrack to the asphalt road, and continue your ride. Just below the watchtower, at a fork in the road, turn left onto a paved road. Drive about three kilometers to reach Highway 31. You are about to visit the sternbergia.

Go right on Highway 31, then drive northwest for about four kilometers. Pass kilometer marker 7 and before you reach marker 6 you will see a big blue-and-white Hebrew sign on the left that reads *"Brichat Lehavim."* Turn in and immediately take the dirt road to your left. Drive a few hundred meters more and park in front of the wire gate.

A few textbooks describe the sternbergia as endemic to Israel, but the flower has been seen in Lebanon, parts of Asia, northern Iran and Syria as well. What makes the sternbergia unusually interesting is the fact that they are located in only a dozen or so isolated spots that are scattered unevenly throughout Israel. Each site is only a few dunams in size, but the flowers grow so densely together and at such a specific time period that during the season the ground resembles a colorful carpet. Blossoms open in the morning, and close their eyes at night.

Negev sternbergia, like many other desert plants, can generally be found in wadis* and on northern slopes facing away from the sun. Because they store water and nutrients in underground bulbs and are dormant through the summer, they can blossom before the rains come and there is only light competition for pollinators. They would probably have little trouble attracting insects anyway, for they emit a strong scent which pulls in flies and larger pollinators like a magnet. Look for them from late October until early December: their leaves will appear only after the flower has withered away.

To reach BEER SHEVA, or to head north, return to Highway 31 and continue driving northwest—the direction you were going—towards Lehavim Junction. There, you turn left onto Highway 40 towards Beer Sheva or right to return to Kama Junction.

However, if you are continuing on to Eilat, instead, turn right on Highway 31 when you finish viewing the sternbergia, and drive southeast in the direction of the Dead Sea. Here you can connect with ROUTE No. 10 (The Arava route) by turning right at Zohar Junction onto the Arava Highway.

Alternatively, hook up with ROUTE No. 6 (YATIR) at Shoket Junction, on Highway 31.

Route No. 5: Through the Northern Negev

Vital Information

To enjoy the sternbergia take this trip in late autumn or early winter. (Flowers at Pura Nature Reserve bloom from mid-winter to early spring). Pura Nature Reserve is accessible only to drivers traveling from north to south on Highway 40.

Forest roads are almost always passable, although in a few spots you may feel uncomfortable in a low-bottomed vehicle.

The Joe Alon Center is open Sun. to Thurs. & Sat. 9:00–16:00; Fri. 9:00–14:00. Tel.: 07–918597.

There is some climbing involved at Hurvat Rimon.

Sternbergia are often called golden starflowers because of their dazzling beauty.

Route No. 6
Yatir Forest to the Dead Sea

Route No. 6 takes you through a nature reserve with rare flowers,
to ancient synagogues
and for a walk amidst the ruins of a Byzantine church.
Special attraction: a variety of forest recreation sites.

Israel's pre-1967 borders are often called the Green Line, for green is the color of the cease-fire line drawn on maps following the War of Independence.* Negev residents contend that the phrase refers to the trees planted by the Jewish National Fund (JNF) in 1964 along the Jordan-Israel border. Located on the southern slopes of the Hebron Mountains, the forests formed a visible division between the two countries and bestowed a bright green belt of color on dreary brown sands.

Today, the green line of trees is no longer the border. But the four million trees in Yatir, the JNF's largest planted forest, still offer a refreshing change from an otherwise desert landscape. Early spring is the best time for a drive through Yatir Forest, for rare flowers like the Arabian fritillary bloom from late February to April and cherry trees blossom gloriously in March. Clusters of pink sunroses add color to the scene, as well.

Begin at Shoket Junction, northeast of Beer Sheva, where Roads 31 and 60 intersect. A right turn leads to Arad; you head left (northwest) on 60, in the direction of Hebron. Pass the community of Meitar, then drive to the army checkpoint at the end of the former "green line."

You are in the northern Negev, 400 meters above sea level, where the weather is cool and pleasant all year round. The semi-arid region through which you drive is the edge of the desert, a passageway between desert and Mediterranean Sea. It receives more rain than the desert but less than the coastal regions: an average of 200 millimeters a year.

Turn right towards Shim'a and Utniel just before the checkpoint, onto part of the patrol road used before 1967. Fields of wheat and barley on your left are cultivated by Arab farmers who live in the Hebron Mountains. To the right are saplings which suit the region's landscape—pistachio, carob, olive and acacia trees as well as the traditional JNF pine.

Jews lived in the Hebron Mountains in biblical times, in the Second Temple period and throughout the Byzantine* era. The landscape then was

Route No. 6: Yatir Forest to the Dead Sea

similar to the scene you see today. Living, as they did, on the edge of Jerusalem, the Jews could supply the Holy City with wheat and other grains.

Chukars (partridges) flourish in this hilly area, where the forest is out of bounds to hunters. They feel secure enough to walk on the road itself, soaring skyward when disturbed by vehicles.

Just over three kilometers further, a sign to your right points to Yatir Forest. Turn onto the excellent dirt road, to begin part of a 12-kilometer scenic route. These days the forest is prettier than ever, for the JNF scattered their newer trees instead of planting pines close together. In April the ground is covered with red poppies.

As you ride look for modern, recently built stone steps (*terrasot*), intended to keep rain from eroding the soil and to retain water. Together with embankments and canals, these steps make irrigation unnecessary and have been used to "harvest" water in Israel for thousands of years.

The mountain range to your right, which includes an as-yet-unexplored archaeological site, is soon to be declared the Mount Hiran Nature Reserve. Because the Hiran hills are located in a semi-arid zone, this is a meeting point for two distinct kinds of foliage. In fact, within a single dunam, researchers have found 120 separate species of plant life—some Mediterranean and some desert. This mixture is vital to the ecological system, for the encounters result in natural variations of existing species.

Along the sides of the road you may see the little owl. It stands stock still on the rocks, its speckled brown-and-white coat making it almost indistinguishable from the region's light brown stone. Little owls are small and round night birds which are often spotted during the day. They weigh only 160 grams and eat small rodents, birds, lizards, snails and insects. Huge eyes permit the little owl to detect its prey in very dim light for, like other owls, it is a night raptor. Because its eyes are located in front of its head, like those of a human, it has the reputation of being a wise old bird.

To the right of the road is a channel of the Eshtamoa River and just above it towers one of the Mount Hiran hills. Within the little stream are spectacular limestone formations, whose hollows hold rain water in winter and spring.

Pull over to the side and walk down to the stream; if it is warm enough take a dip. On the banks stand tall, white asphodel amid fields of red anemone, buttercups and tulips and yellow dwarf pheasant's eye. You can also cross the stream at a dry point and climb the hill to Mount Hiran; in spring flowers cover the slope.

Back in your car continue your drive. Yatir Forest, which provides Beer Sheva area residents with a bit of green and ungrazed hills full of wildflowers, is also a recreation site. Indeed, nature reserve rangers report

Route No. 6: Yatir Forest to the Dead Sea

seeing immigrants from East European countries visiting it in droves, picking mushrooms after the rain and, in warmer weather, barbecuing breakfast steaks.

Ruins from the ancient Jewish settlement of Yatir are visible from the main road. Swerve with the road to the right and park next to a minute orange-and-brown sign signifying that you are on part of the Israel Trail.* Local Arabs call this hill *Khirbet Atir*, thereby preserving the settlement's biblical name of Yatir. Located in the portion of Israel allotted to the tribe of Judah (Joshua 15:48), Yatir was one of the cities picked to house the descendants of Aaron (I Chronicles 6:57 and Joshua 21:14).

When David defeated the Amalekites, he sent plunder to the elders of Judah, who had helped him when he fled from King Saul. Yatir was among the Judean cities which received the spoils (I Samuel 30:27). Yatir has not yet been excavated and surface remains are from the Byzantine period. The large cistern next to the road where you left your car supplied most of the village's water.

To explore the site walk up the hill, avoiding small cisterns on the slope. You will see caves in the hills opposite, on the other side of the "green line": from biblical times to the present these were home to many villagers. Near the top to the right look for an immense stone, the basin from an ancient oilpress.

The slopes are wild and deserted, the perfect spot from which to spy harriers hovering over the hills. They are searching for cold-blooded agamas and lizards warming themselves in the sun. All kinds of insects roam the hill. In late winter and spring look for strange small piles of dead twigs: incredibly, they house insects called bagworms. When bagworm larvae emerge from their eggs, they make nests of twigs and dead leaves which they tie together with sticky threads from their mouths. Male larvae turn into moths and fly away in summer, while females spend their entire lives as caterpillars inside the nest, and die after they lay their eggs.

Three distinctive Washingtonian palms mark a crossroads into the older part of the forest, thick with trees. Drive uphill until you reach a paved road, turn left and continue until you find a pink sign leading to Soussia. Turn left, and at the next pink sign for Soussia and Shani turn right. Staying on the road straight ahead, instead, takes you to Hebron.

Soon you come to the settlement of Livna, called Shani on some maps. Just past its apple orchards lie the ruins of Anim, another part of the land allotted to the tribe of Judah (Joshua 15:50). You can park at the site.

Most of the visible ruins are from Anim's prosperous Talmudic period, but archaeologists also found ruins from an Israelite fortress 20 meters by 20 meters, its walls five meters thick, on the top of the hill. Because of the

Route No. 6: Yatir Forest to the Dead Sea

location of the citadel, residents in Talmudic times were unable to build their synagogue at the city's highest point, undoubtedly the spot they would have preferred, it is situated further down the slope. Nonetheless, the entrance faces east in accordance with Jewish law.

Mosaic tiles and decorative lintels grace the synagogue's outer entrance. The synagogue altar area faces Jerusalem and takes up a full fourth of a central hall lined with stone benches. Like other local synagogues and churches, the roof was probably a gabled wooden frame. Fragments of roof tiles have been found as well as clay and glass pots which were filled with oil to light the building at night. The synagogue was used for prayer and congregation from the fourth to seventh centuries.

Enjoy exploring the intricate water system above the ground. Caves dug out of the rock were probably used as hideaways in times of danger, and you can climb into several of them. An unusually large number of oilpresses and a winepress in the forest nearby indicate a thriving industry.

Return to the road and continue your ride. At the first major intersection turn right, then right again at a big white sign leading to "Har Hamasa." Drive to Kibbutz Har ("Mount") Amasa, park outside the gate, then walk between two large green nature reserve signs. A stony path leads to the peak: you will know you are there when you reach a double swing,

Decorative lintels graced the Anim synagogue entrance.

Route No. 6: Yatir Forest to the Dead Sea

romantically overlooking the Judean Desert.

Mount Amasa was probably named for Amasa ben Jeter (Amasa son of Jeter). Absalom appointed Amasa commander of his army when he was trying to wrest the throne from King David, his father. After Absalom's army lost to David's troops and Absalom was killed by David's ruthless commander Yoav, David replaced Yoav with Amasa. Soon afterwards Yoav stabbed the unsuspecting Amasa in the belly and in a particularly gruesome episode left his rival to wallow in his blood while he reassumed command of the army (II Samuel 20:8–12). Locals have preserved the name over the years, calling the hill *Jabel Amsha*.

To your left you will see a hill topped by antennas. They belong to a police station which was manned by the Jordanian Legion, guarding the border prior to 1967. Israeli soldiers patrolling the area nicknamed them the "Mickey Mouse police station." From a distance the courtyard with stables and two towers on either side resembled Mickey's ears.

Below the antennas is a concrete reservoir, located along the pre-1967 Israeli-Jordanian border. Today the settlement of Beit Yatir, named for the ancient village, is situated on top of the hill. Due to a conflict with Israel's Official Names Committee, you may see Beit Yatir called Metzadot Yehuda on some maps.

Mount Amasa is a very special nature reserve. Not only is it the easternmost semi-arid nature reserve in Israel, but it also contains a wondrous mix of desert and Mediterranean plants and wildlife. On Mount Amasa the mountain-loving chukar meets the desert-abiding sand partridge; European vipers roam the slopes together with the black desert cobra.

Even more significant is a rare flower called the Arabian fritillary, found in abundance on the other side of the mountain. When the blossom was discovered here one spring in the mid-1960's, Nature Reserve Authority staff believed it to be the only place in Israel where the fritillary grew. Although it has since been spotted elsewhere, the flower is quite rare and is part of the reason that Mount Amasa was declared a nature reserve.

You began your ride from Shoket Junction at 400 meters above sea level and have ascended almost 500 meters to Mount Amasa (857). The trip parallels the journey made by warm air from the Mediterranean Sea as it moves east. During its climb up the mountain it becomes colder, losing one degree centigrade per 100 meters. When the cool air contracts, rain begins to fall, running down both sides of Mount Amasa. The air then moves further east and descends the other side of the mountain. This time it expands, and the rainfall ceases. That is why the Judean Desert below is called a rain shadow desert—it stands, literally, in the shadow of the rain.

Route No. 6: Yatir Forest to the Dead Sea

From the top of the mountain you have a breathtaking view of the Judean Desert. Unlike most of the world's deserts, which are located in a chain around the equator, this one is a local phenomenon and one of the most extreme in the world. The difference between precipitation on the mountain and the rain received by the desert is an incredible 400 versus 30 millimeters!

Across from you is Zealots' Mountain, or Mount (*Har*) Kanaim, resembling a large, flat table. It probably gets its name from Wadi Kanaim below, for the riverbed reaches to Massada and the name may refer to Massada's zealots. Beyond Mount Kanaim are Jordan's Moav Mountains. Across to the right is the Arad Valley.

Because you are on top of the mountain you can clearly see large birds of prey utilizing currents of rising warm air. Look for falcons and harriers, beating their wings to stay aloft.

Now take your car and backtrack to the T-intersection where you turned towards Har Amasa (Road 80). Turn right, in the direction of Arad, and begin a long descent. At the bottom look to your left: you have reached an archaeological site only recently excavated by the Israel Antiquities Authority. Although there are no signs to mark the spot, this is Hurvat Krayot, the ruins of a Byzantine church built over Israelite sites from the First and Second Temple periods.

In its day the church was large and ornate. Pillars remain as they were discovered, in rows within a large courtyard. A well-preserved mosaic has been covered to prevent damage, but you will see decorated capitals and, at a lower level, a grave. Architectural elements from the church are scattered in the area and are used, today, in fences, cisterns and dwelling caves.

West of the church, archaeologists have found portions of strong walls that were apparently part of an Israelite fortress. Pottery shards from the Second Temple period were discovered on its floor.

Return to your car and drive a few dozen meters further, then stop and walk to the left side of the road. From late February to early April the rare Arabian fritillary should be in bloom: if there are no signs indicating the area look for other parked cars to help you find the site. The fritillary's unusual stalk holds upside down purplish-caramel-colored bell-shaped flowers.

Continue on the road, driving through the Arad Valley. One side of the road is deeply green while the other is brown and barren. Normally this difference is related to how the slopes face the sun. Unlike hills in much of North America, the southern slope in Israel is often drier and thus supports less vegetation than the northern slope. Here, however, the phenomenon

Route No. 6: Yatir Forest to the Dead Sea

has little to do with the sun. Rather, the cause is the Bedouin, who live on the green side and let their animals graze in the other.

Turn in at TEL ARAD NATIONAL PARK. From December to early March, the ground around the entrance is covered with stunningly beautiful androcymbium blossoms growing very near the ground. A glorious white or lilac flower with purple stripes, the androcymbium is a desert flower which reached Mediterranean zones from South Africa. The autumn crocus, which it closely resembles, developed from the androcymbium. After visiting Tel Arad National Park drive to Arad, where you will stop in at the Nature Reserves Authority's delightful VISITORS' CENTER.

It's been a long day, hasn't it? If evening has drawn nigh, stay overnight in ARAD, visit the city, and perhaps even explore Tel Arad the next day. Then you can continue to the Dead Sea, and connect up with ROUTE NO. 10 to Eilat if you're going that far south.

If you have time, however, or if you are on your second day, return to the intersection where you entered Arad and pass through the industrial center. Follow signs to *Minhat Metosim Arad*, the "Arad Landing Field." An orange sign leads you to "Mitzpe Zohar, H. Uza." Turn right past some factories to see a second orange sign. Shacks along the road date back to Israel's first oil drilling camp. During the 1950's, entrepreneurs hoping to find oil here did come up with something—natural gas!

Your destination is Zohar Observation Point at a mountain overlooking the Judean Desert. Called *Ras Zohara* by local Arabs, it is known, in Hebrew, as *Rosh Zohar* and controls the road below. Before the War of Independence, British policemen were stationed here in an attempt to prevent smuggling. A second station was built at MAMSHIT, following rumors of oil in the area.

As you drive to the overlook you have an unusually lovely view of Arad. With luck you should see another sign pointing to Mitzpe Zohar; if you don't, look for a right turn taking you to the top of the mountain, 550 meters above sea level. Park next to the pile of stones called Rogem Zohar, part of a fortress that controlled the road from the Edom Mountains and the Dead Sea to Jerusalem and perhaps ancient Beer Sheva as well.

Zohar Observation Point offers two overlooks with entirely different views. Below the first is a strange phenomenon called *hatrurim*, whose wrinkles may remind you of pictures from the moon. Smoke is from the nearby phosphate factory. The *hatrurim*, (sometimes called the "mottled zone") were created when limestone rocks were baked by bitumen lying deep beneath the surface. In Arad the stone is used for making a special kind of marble.

73

Route No. 6: Yatir Forest to the Dead Sea

Long ago, bitumen sank to the ground and was well buried for many thousands of years. When the Syrian-African rift* began to form, the resulting east-west cracks were very large. As a result, a large quantity of oxygen penetrated into the earth's surface, reaching even the deeply buried bitumen. Since bitumen burns when touched by oxygen, it began to smolder at a very high temperature, burning the limestone above and causing it to contract. The limestone wrinkled and hardened into the strange hills you see below.

From this point you can walk to another observation point, for a fantastic view of the 100-meter-deep canyon in Wadi Abuv. The stupendous sight is of the riverbed's sharply angular bend, and from way above the gully you can follow its course in two directions.

Return to the turnoff from which you headed into the overlook and head right to get back to the main road (Road 31). This trip ends at Zohar Junction, facing the Dead Sea. Turning right leads you to Highway 90 (the Arava Highway), south towards Eilat. For an exciting journey along the highway, see ROUTE NO. 10.

The northern Negev bursts with wildflowers in winter and early spring.

The Modern City of Arad

In 1921, veterans who served together in the British Army's Jewish Brigade decided to create an agricultural settlement near ancient Arad. For seven months they lived in very primitive conditions, digging wells which they hoped would supply them with water for drinking and irrigation. When the precious liquid was nowhere to be found the community was disbanded.

Modern Arad was founded in 1962, on 70,000 dunams of land east of the original Israelite city (see TEL ARAD). Best known as a haven for asthmatics, Arad is located some 600 meters above sea level and blessed with an excellent climate. Arad was designed to provide the eastern Negev with a major town, and its residents with easy access to chemical plants along the DEAD SEA.

While it was originally settled by veteran Israelis, its original current population of 23,000 residents includes 6,000 new immigrants from the Soviet Union.

Arad Visitors' Center

Papyrus was expensive and rare during the period when the Israelites lived in Arad, so people wrote letters and made notes on pottery shards instead! Hundreds of such shards, many relating details of daily life at the Israelite fortress, have been discovered at Tel Arad. Some are incised and others are written in ink. One inscribed bowl links the name Arad with the tel; it has the word Arad written on it seven different times, in mirror script.

You can examine these shards and other exciting artifacts at a fascinating museum in the center of the modern city. The museum is located in Arad's Visitors' Center, and contains exhibits which help demonstrate methods used by humans over the millennia, to survive in the desert.

Rooms in the museum are arranged in chronological order, and the first displays findings from the Canaanite city of Arad during its early Bronze Age. Among the exhibits is a fragment from an Egyptian jar. Found within the Canaanite city on the tel, the shard was incised with the name of the

Arad Visitors' Center

founder of the earliest Egyptian dynasty. Not only does this find help archaeologists substantiate the date of that Egyptian dynasty, but it proves there were commercial ties between Arad and Egypt at least 5,000 years ago.

An excellent exhibit illustrates early burial customs, and includes some modern-looking jewelry approximately 5,000 years old. Among the ancient tableware on display are cups, platters and bowls. Checkers discovered on the tel clearly indicate that early residents found time to play board games!

A miniature clay house found at the site may have been used as a model by the architect who designed this and other Canaanite cities, for it closely resembles the houses uncovered during excavation. Seeing the model you can visualize Canaanite houses, complete with doors and roofs.

The Canaanites worshipped forces of nature such as the sea, water and foliage, and three sanctuaries dedicated to these nature gods were discovered in the heart of the town. Archaeologists digging on Tel Arad found the largest and most intricate early Bronze Age sacred precinct ever excavated in Israel. Artifacts from this unusual site are also on view at the museum.

A room containing finds from Arad's Israelite period has a model of King Solomon's fortress. It demonstrates how water was transported from the large water cistern down below.

Part of your visit includes an audio-visual production with special effects. Running about 20 minutes, the show begins by describing the Negev's climate and geology. Views of the region's splendid natural sites will entice you to prolong your visit to the Negev, or to return after the winter floods have created gorgeous waterfalls and rushing riverbeds.

Vital Information

Sun. to Thurs. 9:00–17:00; Fri. 9:00–14:00. Entrance fee.
Tel.: 07–954409.
Call in advance to see when the audio-visual program is shown in English.

Tel Arad National Park

After four hundred years of bondage, the Children of Israel were rescued by Moses and followed him home to the Promised Land. When they reached the borders of Canaan, however, their way was barred by the king of Arad.

For the next forty years the Israelites sojourned in the desert. Then they tried to enter Canaan again—and suffered another decisive defeat at the hands of Arad's ruler. During a later battle the Children of Israel were finally victorious, and the Canaanite city of Arad was destroyed (Numbers 21:1–3).

If you visit the site of ancient Arad, you can explore what remains of its exciting history. Tel Arad is comprised of five layers of Canaanite city as well as ruins from a series of later Israelite fortresses.

Excavations began at the tel* in 1962, the same year that modern Arad was constructed on a ridge only a few kilometers away. Part of the reason for the dig was to provide jobs for the city's new residents.

The oldest findings on the tel are about 6,000 years old, from a time when people generally lived in the caves visible outside of the city walls. But most of the remains are left from a large Canaanite city dating back to around 3000 B.C.E.

Canaanite Arad, whose several thousand inhabitants made it one of the largest cities in Canaan, was surrounded by a wall 2.4 meters thick and over a kilometer long. It served as the regional center for the surrounding villages and based its economy on agriculture, livestock and trade.

Since there are no natural water sources near Arad, the city's entire water supply was based on accumulated rainfall. When it rained, water dripped off the roofs and into the streets, eventually draining into a 20-meter-deep central pit.

Located at the entrance to the ancient city, this cistern has been reconstructed. A blue line divides the original water hole and the modern reconstruction, but in the interest of authenticity workers used only rocks found within the pit during excavations.

Indeed, water was probably one of the main factors that gave rise to this city. The hill, 40 meters higher than the surrounding area, is shaped like a bowl and rain naturally drains into its center. Numerous cisterns were dug in the chalk rock, which is easily worked and retains water well. While today's annual rainfall is only 170 millimeters, there is much evidence that in earlier years rain was more abundant.

Tel Arad National Park

One of ancient Arad's houses has also been restored, giving a feeling for what it was like to live here five millennia ago. Another has been lifted up on short columns, demonstrating the difference between historical periods.

Archaeologists believe that two of the rooms uncovered may have been pagan temples, partly because they discovered a ritual monument nearby. They also found a slab that might be an altar, and a hole which could be a cult basin. The statue is of a standing figure which is reaching its hands towards the sky, above another lying down. You may well shudder when you reach this part of the site, as you imagine animals—or maybe even humans—sacrificed here, their blood running into the basin!

One of the most important finds was made in the cemetery. Research indicates that a skull uncovered there underwent an operation with a surgical instrument some 5,000 years ago, one of the earliest indications of trephining surgery ever discovered.

Arad was destroyed around 2800 B.C.E. and later deserted. The large amount of ash found in the ruins provides clear evidence that it was attacked by a military force—but who the soldiers were and why they assaulted Arad is not known. Since the city was not rebuilt, it remains one of the best preserved Canaanite sites in Israel.

Look for the rare Arabian fritillary (right) near Tel Arad.
The reconstructed cistern in Tel Arad (below).

Tel Arad National Park

Tel Arad National Park

The Biblical exodus from Egypt occurred hundreds of years after Arad was destroyed and so this is probably not the exact place where the king of Arad fought the Hebrews. Or, perhaps researchers should rethink their geography and biblical chronology! Some experts suggest, in fact, that Arad in the Bible refers to an area, not a specific city. Others contend that the biblical Arad is at a different site, Tel Malhata, located 12 kilometers southwest of Tel Arad.

Seventeen hundred years after the demise of Canaanite Arad, King Solomon ordered construction of a fortress on the crest of a hill nearby. This fortress was one of six built near the former city, one atop the other. Inside the remains is one of the most significant archaeological finds in this country: an Israelite temple used by Israelites during the First Temple period, whose layout corresponds in structure and its east-west axis to that of Solomon's Temple in Jerusalem. No other Israelite temple of this kind has ever been discovered.

What you see at the site today are the remains of three separate rooms just like those described in the Bible (II Chronicles, chapters three and four). They are the Holy of Holies, the altar and the temple. The altar is five cubits square, the exact dimensions of the Tabernacle (Exodus 27:1). Interestingly, 107 Hebrew inscriptions were found here, and some of the priests' names mentioned at the site appear in the Bible as well. In addition, the name of the city, Arad, is repeated several times.

This sanctuary was probably destroyed either by King Josiah or by King Hezekiah, both of whom carried out religious reforms and purifications condemning idol worship and emphasizing the centrality of the Jerusalem Temple. Nevertheless, the altar, a column and other parts of the temple are still partially intact.

Tel Arad was fortified continuously through the Roman period. In the seventh century the Moslems built an inn here, destroyed a century later.

The sign-posting is very clear and with the help of a pamphlet available in English at no cost—and this book, of course—you will thoroughly enjoy your visit. Tel Arad is seven kilometers west of contemporary Arad and there are directions on the roads.

Vital Information

Sun. to Thurs. & Sat. 8:00–17:00; Fri. & holiday eves 8:00–14:00. From Oct. to March the site closes one hour earlier. Entrance fee.
Many of the remnants discovered at Tel Arad are on display at the delightful ARAD VISITORS' CENTER *in the modern city.*

Introducing Beer Sheva

Only a few short decades ago the Bedouin market in Beer Sheva was the city's single tourist attraction. But Beer Sheva of the 1990's bears little resemblance to that sleepy little town of the recent past. Today the city is a furiously booming metropolis, with lovely suburbs, well-preserved historical and natural sites and a few impressive shopping malls.

While settlement in the Beer Sheva region dates back at least six millennia, the site of contemporary Beer Sheva was inhabited by Israelites, Romans and Byzantines.* In the seventh century, Arab conquerors completely destroyed Beer Sheva and the city was abandoned.

It wasn't until 1900 that Beer Sheva rose from the dust. The city's resurrection was due to political considerations, for the Turks wanted to keep Bedouin nomads in line. For hundreds of years Bedouin had ruled the Negev sands, fighting fiercely amongst themselves, extracting "protection" money from the villagers and charging merchant caravans a toll. But by the late 19th century, with the opening of the Suez Canal and increased British influence in Egypt, the Negev and Sinai deserts became strategically and politically important. And the Turks, who controlled Palestine at the time, worried that Bedouin Lords of the Desert were threatening the stability of the region.

The Turkish solution was both original and bold: they decided to establish a town so attractive and responsive to the needs of the Bedouin that the eternal wanderers would settle down. Then, hoped the Turks, these former nomads would become farmers and landowners, loyal to the Turkish government and under its control.

Designed by German and Swiss architects together with two local Arabs, Beer Sheva was a wondrous combination of east and west. As in its European counterparts, Beer Sheva's streets were laid out according to a grid and graced with beautiful public gardens. But the buildings were oriental and possessed of a soothing symmetry, with arches, balconies and splendid stone.

A walk around this early 20th century city—today Beer Sheva's Old Town—takes you through reconstructed areas and some of the original buildings. The trail consists of two concentric circles. Park your car or walk to the point at which they meet: Ha'atzmaut Street, between Asaf Simhoni and Herzl. You will first do the northern ring, pass the general area of your vehicle, and then head for the southern circle. The whole walk should take

Introducing Beer Sheva

about three hours. During the week you may need parking tickets (available at many kiosks).

Beer Sheva is the only city that the Turks built from scratch during their 400-year sojourn in Palestine. The site was picked for its easy access to water, the large number of Bedouin tribes in the area, and because it was a crossroads for three major trade routes leading to Gaza, Hebron and the Negev desert.

If you sit on a bench across from Allenby Park on Ha'atzmaut Street, you will see an impressive edifice completed in 1901. Called the *saraya*, which means "palace" in Arabic, it was the first building constructed on the Negev wastelands that became the city of Beer Sheva. Many of its beautifully chiseled stones were stolen from old Byzantine sites and reworked before being placed in the building. The front porch was lined with arches, and the roofs were topped with red shingles visible throughout the little town (the shingles blew off in the early 1930's).

Location was of vast significance to the architects of Beer Sheva and it wasn't coincidence that the *saraya*, a symbol of law and order, was built on a hill and could be seen from afar. There was also a practical reason for choosing this site: the building faced one of the city's two main thoroughfares and a wall of windows was directly across from the second. This gave the Turkish police control over the entrance to the city from Ha'atzmaut Street all the way down Keren Kayemet Street to Abraham's Well and Wadi Beer Sheva.

The *saraya*'s walls encompassed the Turkish courts, special Bedouin courts, the police department and the temporary governor's quarters. A square police fortress in the front of the *saraya* was added by the British, after Arabs burned down the wooden roof in the riots of 1938.

During the War of Independence,* the *saraya* was the scene of bitter fighting between Israeli and Egyptian forces. Following the Egyptian surrender, Beer Sheva became part of Israel.

On the other side of Ha'atzmaut Street is the governor's mansion, a lovely building surrounded by trees. It was constructed in 1906 when Governor Achaf Bey decided that a police station, no matter how elegant, was no place to raise a family. When first built there was a narrow balcony on the second floor—the door which led to the little terrace is still there. Best of all, the mansion had a bathtub, the only one in Beer Sheva! Note the integration of east and west in the building's oriental arches and square European lines. Today the mansion houses archaeological exhibits under the auspices of the Negev Museum.

Beer Sheva was meant to be more than a Bedouin city; its Turkish rulers intended it as an administrative and commercial center for the entire

Introducing Beer Sheva

Negev. Thus in 1906 they put up a magnificent mosque, with a towering minaret which could be spotted long before entering the town. It served not only residents of the city but also local Moslems.

Situated on the far side of the governor's garden, the mosque was built on the diagonal so that the mosque could face south to Mecca. Over the door is a *tughra*, the sultan's monogram. Note the beautiful windows, grouped in three pairs on one side of the entrance and three single ones on the other. You can see the *mikhrab* (prayer niche facing Mecca) through any of the single windows.

Cross the street to Allenby Garden. In 1915 the Turks placed a large stone base in the middle of the park. On top was a marble pillar inscribed with the symbol of the Ottoman Empire. A few years later, Britain's General Allenby took Beer Sheva from the Turks and an artist was hired to sculpt the general's head and shoulders. The new statue was unveiled in 1923. During anti-British riots in 1938, Arabs beheaded the monument and later the statue simply disappeared. The Turkish pillar is in storage; the modern monument is from 1947 and simply says "Allenby, 1917–1918" in English and Arabic.

Leave Allenby Garden and turn left on Ha'atzmaut Street (walking northwest). Past the mosque are remains of an elegant gate which opened onto the second of Beer Sheva's three public gardens. To your left at the next intersection (Asaf Simhoni Street), is a Turkish building that served as an agricultural school for Bedouin children. This was also the site of the third public garden. Reminiscent of other Turkish buildings from this period, the lovely edifice has a slanted roof, arched doorways and windows and an outer entrance.

Government School was part of the Turkish effort to encourage the Bedouin to settle down, and to transform Beer Sheva into a district center. To their disappointment, however, only the children of rich Bedouin sheikhs enrolled. As you continue down Ha'atzmaut, note the building next door to Government School. Constructed by the British, this second school has harsh, squat lines lacking the grace and beauty which make the earlier one so attractive.

Further northwest on the same street is the Beer Sheva cemetery for soldiers of the Commonwealth who fell during World War I. Perfectly tended and splendidly landscaped, the cemetery was built by Jewish labor, completed in 1922, and inaugurated a year later.

During World War I the British made several attempts to conquer the Holy Land. Twice they tried to enter through Gaza, which they thought would be easy to cross with their heavy equipment. Both times they failed

Introducing Beer Sheva

miserably, and two huge cemeteries in Gaza testify to the bitter price they paid (see BE'ERI).

Eventually General Allenby was brought in to replace the previous commander. Information from a Jewish spy ring in Palestine decided him on a different tack: he would gain control by way of Beer Sheva which, since 1915, had been the Turks' most important military center in the country.

Allenby's plan was based on cunning. The Turks were to be tricked into thinking the British would attempt a third Gaza attack, while in reality Gaza would serve only as a diversion while they entered Beer Sheva. A mounted intelligence officer was sent across Turkish lines in hopes that the Turks would shoot; he was to pretend to be wounded and to "drop" his intelligence notebook on the ground. Written in the notebook were false plans for a massive attack on Gaza. Incredibly enough, the first two times the book was "dropped" no one picked it up and the charade had to be repeated!

On the morning of October 31, 1917, the British reached the outskirts of Beer Sheva, attacking Gaza at the same time to confuse the Turks. A brutal battle took place at Tel Beer Sheva, where the Turks had set up substantial fortifications. It lasted eight hours and most of the graves in the cemetery belong to soldiers who fell in that engagement. Part of the attack involved one of the more famous cavalry charges of World War I, during which British troops rode over eight kilometers while exposed to Turkish fire.

The British succeeded in taking the tel* and, despite their fatigue, the British commander decided to move his forces into the city itself before the Turks could destroy the wells. Had he waited even one more day the Commonwealth army might have lost everything, for two German back-up divisions had already set out for Beer Sheva.

The cemetery contains the graves of close to 1,300 soldiers, 80 percent of them British, most of the others from New Zealand and Australia. At the base of almost every monument is a personalized phrase, written by the cemetery's Jewish employees or by the soldiers' families. A Jewish soldier, Captain Seymour Van den Bergh, is buried in the last row. His parents penned the inscription on his tombstone: "So far from home, yet so near to those who love him."

Set off to one side is a monument to eight English flyers who were shot down before the battle of Beer Sheva. As a gesture of respect, the Turks established a memorial to one of the flyers; after the conquest of Beer Sheva, the British expanded the memorial to include all eight.

Immediately past the cemetery, turn right and cross over an open field. Look for a few eucalyptus trees and a house with a red roof. This is the

84

Introducing Beer Sheva

Turkish railroad terminal, and your next destination. Near the gabled roof on the side of the terminal is a sign in Arabic that reads *Bir el-Saba* (Beer Sheva). Climb the three steps next to the blue information sign and you will be on the platform. Railroad tracks ran between the platform and the benches spread out in a semicircle before you.

During World War I, the Turks laid railroad tracks from Beer Sheva to the southern border, hoping the railroad would help them conquer Egypt. Beer Sheva hosted one of the country's five major railroad stations. A very dim plaque on the terminal's wall, located across from a hidden garden, reveals the fate of a group of Jewish artisans waiting to board a train out of Beer Sheva on January 5, 1917. The station was bombed by the British and 16 of the workers were killed. Circumstances dictated burial of all 16—some of them from Jaffa and others from Jerusalem—in one mass grave in Beer Sheva. After the war ended, the Jerusalem victims were taken to the Holy City for re-burial. Jaffa's rabbi would not let the graves of the other victims be disturbed, and the Jaffa-born artisans remain interred in Beer Sheva.

Walk southeast past the platform to see some tall, fairly modern apartment buildings facing Rambam Street. Squatting between them and almost hidden from view is the railway's water tower, which dates from 1915. It had two gigantic round tankers on the roof, which were kept full for the steam-driven locomotives.

On the other side of Rambam Street is the Be'eri School, built by the British in the 1940's. Little holes over the windows are for air circulation. Sometimes water would be placed there, a kind of primitive air conditioning seen in many Turkish homes of the period. Construction of this, a second school, indicates how much the city had grown.

Turn right at Asaf Simhoni Street and follow it back to Ha'atzmaut Street to start the second circle (or pick up your car if you want to conclude here). Your first stop on this leg is at Beit Aref el-Aref, which you reach by passing Allenby Park and crossing Herzl Street. The main entrance to Beit Aref el-Aref, today a grocery store, faces Ha'atzmaut.

Well-to-do Arabs living in Beer Sheva during the British Mandate owned some fabulous homes and this one, belonging to district officer Aref el-Aref and built in 1937–38, was probably the most beautiful of all. Aref el-Aref was an Arab leader who incited Arabs to rebel against the British in 1920, after which he fled to Jordan. Later the British pardoned him and tried to moderate his political views by giving him a role in the British administration.

In the late 1930's the Arabs rioted against the British and Aref el-Aref was faced with a problem of dual loyalty. Although responsible for law and order in his district, in his heart he identified with the Arabs. He permitted

85

Introducing Beer Sheva

Arab gangs to operate freely near Beer Sheva, but to prove his "loyalty" to the British, he arranged for explosions near his home so it would seem he was being attacked as a British agent. Note the Jerusalem stone on every part of the house that faces the street, in sharp contrast with the other buildings.

Continue on Ha'atzmaut for one block, then look across to your right to see the home of Sheikh Farik Abu Medin on the pedestrian mall. Abu Medin lived here when he was mayor of Beer Sheva in the 1920's. Later it became headquarters for Israel's labor union. The second story has been restored; to get a better view, walk across the plaza in the direction of two delightful fountains.

Just past the fountains you reach another pedestrian mall, part of Keren Kayemet Street. Look both right and left. At the top see the *saraya*; way down at the bottom is Abraham's Well.

While each of the perfectly planned streets in Old Town was 15 meters wide, the main thoroughfare, Keren Kayemet, was five meters wider and was called the Street of Twenty Meters. Since it was first built, Keren Kayemet has served as Beer Sheva's main commercial center.

Turn left. As you walk towards the well you pass #94. This was one of the

Government School was part of the Turkish effort to encourage the Bedouin to settle down.

Introducing Beer Sheva

only two-story buildings in Turkish Beer Sheva, for the owners lived above the store instead of in the yard, as was common. While a huge billboard covers the original balcony, the second floor has been preserved and the first story reconstructed.

Continue to #56, the site of Beer Sheva's first flour mill and, at the time, the only one in the Negev owned and operated by Jews. Look down the alley to see two of the original buildings. Jews from the city's tiny Jewish community would congregate here in the courtyard. The owners sold out after the Arab pogroms of 1929 and, together with the rest of the Jewish community, left the city.

The next site, on the corner of Hebron and Keren Kayemet, is known as Abraham's Well. The Bible tells that Abraham dug a well in Beer Sheva (Genesis 21:30) and for centuries this was thought to be the well described in the Scriptures. Archaeologists contend that Crusaders built "Abraham's Well," or believe that it may be a restored Roman or Byzantine well.

Abraham's Well was not only the scene of controversy between Abraham and the Philistines (see TEL BEER SHEVA), but in recent years the fight to control it was re-enacted. As the Turkish moved to establish their presence in the area at the beginning of the century one local leader took over the original well and dug a second, hoping to demonstrate that the Bedouin owned Beer Sheva's water. The Turkish leaders reacted by throwing the sheikh in jail.

Actually there are two wells here, Abraham's under a shelter and Isaac's in the courtyard. Both are next to a wooden cogwheel system built by the Turks. The site is open weekdays, and municipal workers will be happy to tell you all about Abraham's Well and his tamarisk tree. The bridge at the end of the street crosses Wadi Beer Sheva, and is meant for pedestrian use during floods.

Walk back up Keren Kayemet Street to Beit Eshel Street and turn left. Beit Eshel turns into Hapalmach, which you follow as far as Trumpeldor Street. A turn onto Ha'avot Street takes you past a lovely, restored Christian mission with a bell-tower behind it. The building was constructed by a Turkish officer in 1903 and taken over by the mission in 1911. Now stroll up Ha'avot Street to Hehalutz Street and turn left. At the corner of Anielewicz Street is an art center for youth; the central courtyard surrounded by buildings is typical of one style of Arab edifices constructed during the period of the British Mandate and was Beer Sheva's first high school.

Continue right on Anielewicz Street to the corner of Histadrut Street for an example of more westernized Arab architecture during the Mandate—called Beit Hanegbi. Then turn right and cross Hanasi Park. At Herzl Street go right to return to your starting point on Ha'atzmaut Street.

87

Beit Yad Labanim

Vital Information

From the central bus station it is only a short walk to the beginning of the circular route.

Abraham's Well. *Sun. to Thurs. 8:30–16:00; Fri. 8:30–13:00. Tel.: 07–234613.*

Zoological Gardens. *Sun. to Thurs. 9:00–18:00; Fri. 9:00–13:00; Sat. 10:00–16:00. Entrance fee. Tel.: 07–414777.*

Bedouin Market* (Shuk)***. *Open every Thursday.*

Indian Center, Moshav Nevatim. *Not American Indians, but Jewish Indians who moved to Israel in the 1950's from Cochin, India. Here is a replica of a synagogue from India and a small museum on the history of this community. Entrance fee. Tel.: 07–277277 (you must call in advance).*

Beit Yad Labanim

Beit Yad Labanim is a perpetual memorial dedicated to Negev soldiers who died serving their country. Located inside of Beer Sheva along Highway 40, the building is too arresting to miss: it is three stories high and its pillars narrow into gabled windows at the top.

When built close to 40 years ago, the edifice was meant as a non-denominational synagogue. But it was difficult to persuade Jews of varying religious shades to pray together and the structure stood idle for decades. After new residential areas developed, the building became too far away for Sabbath worshipers to reach on foot.

Transformed into a memorial in the early 1980's, Beit Yad Labanim features a central commemorative hall, symbolically designed stained glass windows and an album in which each soldier's biography is written in parchment. Along the wall is an excellent and succinct exhibit of Negev history from Chalcolithic* times to the present. Yad Labanim's third floor houses a rotating art exhibit whose exciting works were created by new and well-known artists.

Vital Information
Sun. to Thurs. 8:30–12:30; 16:30–18:30. Tel.: 07–237744.

Air Force Museum

Shortly after Israel declared independence, a column of Egyptian forces invaded Israel from the south and advanced towards Tel Aviv. Israel's meager ground forces were unable to stop the flow of the Egyptian army and it seemed that Tel Aviv would quickly be overrun.

During those early days of the fight for independence, Israel didn't possess even a single warplane. Israeli agents in Czechoslovakia quickly purchased four small World War II Messerschmidts, took them apart, loaded them into larger aircraft and rushed them to Israel for reassembly.

Israel's newly-acquired planes met and attacked the Egyptians near a bridge a mere 20-minute ride from Tel Aviv. Today the bridge is called Gesher Ad Halom, or "Up to Here Bridge." Although two of the four planes —half of the Israeli Air Force—were damaged, the Arab advance was halted. In part, this amazing success was due to the psychological effect on the Egyptians, who were astonished to find that the fledgling country had any air force at all. One of the planes has been reconstructed, and is on display at the Israel Air Force Museum in Hatzerim, right outside of Beer Sheva.

Exhibits like the famous Messerschmidt with its exciting story are common at Hatzerim. But this museum is not just a collection of planes: it is a living testimony to the State of Israel. Planes flying overhead every few minutes make the Hatzerim museum seem even more alive than it already is!

Hatzerim is located west of Beer Sheva and there are clear, large orange signs on the city's main streets which direct you there. You can also reach the museum by public transport: take bus #31 from the central bus station in Beer Sheva.

The Israel Air Force Museum opened to the public in 1991. Its originator, driving force and director is former pilot and ex-police chief Ya'acov Turner, who began collecting castoff planes in 1977.

Most of the 100 fighter planes and other displays are outside on the beautifully designed and impressive tarmac; a few are under shelter. Look, especially, for a MiG 21, flown into Israel by Iraqi pilot Munir Radfa in 1966. At the time, Israel was determined to get a close look at a MiG 21 and searched high and low for an Arab pilot who would agree to defect.

Radfa, a Christian whose family had been persecuted for its faith, agreed only after ascertaining that Israel would help his family escape by land. He then flew bravely from Iraq to Israel, where pilots dubbed Radfa "007"—incredibly enough, the number of his plane.

The MiG 21 was at that time the predominant fighter plane used by Arab air forces. But when Israeli test pilots examined it carefully in flight they discovered a blind spot, similar to that found in cars. The MiG's is over the cockpit on the left hand side, and can keep a pilot from seeing he's being attacked. Knowledge of the MiG 21's Achilles' heel gave Israeli pilots an edge that was to be significant during the Six Day War* the following year.

Each of the aircraft displayed in the museum has its own story. Look for a plane known as Ezer Weizmann's Spitfire: President Weizmann flew Spitfires in the British Air Force and later in the IAF. When Israel sold its Spitfires to Burma, Weizmann asked that one be left behind for exhibition flights.

Under the shelter is the hang glider used by a terrorist to infiltrate into Israel. He landed in an army base and killed six soldiers.

Two Syrian pilots were on their way to a base in south Lebanon in 1968 when they miscalculated and landed, by mistake, near Nahariya. Both pilots were returned to Syria in exchange for Israeli prisoners of war; one of the planes is on display.

Training planes called Tzukits have two seats—one for the instructor and

This MiG 21 was flown into Israel by an Iraqi defector.

Air Force Museum

one for the cadet. In 1967 the IAF's Tzukits were drafted into the war, carrying bombs under their wings. Many pilots flying in Tzukits were killed during the fighting because the trainer-planes lacked ejector seats.

On your tour you will hear about the Mirage with 13 sticker-medals on its side, and the story of the Superfrelon helicopter and its famous passengers. Find out why long metal rods stick out of the nose of some aircraft on display. See scorched remains from a Scud missile that landed in the center of Israel during the Gulf War, and gaze inside an old blue simulator.

The tour, which lasts approximately an hour and a half, includes a stop at Heritage Hall to view a tiny drone and some fascinating photos. At its conclusion you will sit back in a Boeing 707, the prototype for all Boeing jets, whose special day of glory is a tale in itself. Enjoy the movie (English, Hebrew) about the IAF and its secret weapon: *hutzpa*, or "daring."

Vital Information

Sun. to Thurs. 8:00–17:00; Fri. & holiday eves 8:00–13:00. Entrance fee.
Tel.: 07–906853, 906855; fax: 906314.
Guided tours, in English, Hebrew, and many other languages, are offered every hour on the hour.
As exciting for children as it is for adults.

The Yiftah Memorial

The Palmach's Yiftah Brigade is best known for its role in the liberation of Israel's northern and central cities during the War of Independence.* But it also played a crucial part in battles for the Negev. A memorial to Brigade soldiers who fell in Negev battles is situated within a lovely picnic ground.

To reach the site travel north from Beer Sheva on Highway 40. At Kama Junction, turn left (west) and you will see a restaurant and gas station with picnic tables and play apparatus. The bathroom is accessible to wheelchairs.

Pass the complex and turn left towards Mishmar Hanegev and Shoval. This is Road 264, which leads to a charming recreation area and impressive monument. Yiftah Brigade Memorial and Park, developed by the Jewish National Fund, is situated on the right-hand side of the road soon after you turn onto Road 264.

Shaped like a shield with a sharp point on top, the monument symbolizes both protection and the breaching of barriers. You can walk up to the memorial along an asphalt path, then picnic in the forest or relax on the lawns. Water is available, and there are climbing structures for children.

Yiftah troops first moved south to replace bone-weary Palmach* soldiers from the Negev Brigade who had been cut off from the rest of Israel for months during the Egyptian siege. To get through the Egyptian lines which surrounded the kibbutzim,* soldiers were ordered to infiltrate one by one, and meet near today's memorial site once they made it through.

Equipment was flown into a makeshift airport at Kibbutz Ruhama in a campaign called *Avak* (the Hebrew word for dust). Later the brigade played a crucial role in the famous Yoav Campaign, which liberated part of the Negev.

Bedouin Heritage Center, Rahat

Only a few short years ago, the Bedouin Heritage Center in Rahat, slightly north of Beer Sheva, consisted mainly of craft and hospitality tents. While you can still enjoy tea, coffee, Bedouin music and tales at the center, today visitors also enjoy historical displays and exhibits of contemporary Bedouin art. Youngsters may prefer the huge yard outside, where they can walk among goats, camels, donkeys and turkeys.

To reach Rahat, take Highway 40 directly north of Beer Sheva. At Kama Junction turn right (west). You will immediately see a delightful restaurant-gas-station complex with a shady picnic spot and a little playground. Clean bathrooms include facilities for people in wheelchairs.

Just past the complex turn left, in the direction of Mishmar Hanegev and Shoval (Road 264). Pass the lovely monument and picnic site at the YIFTAH BRIGADE MEMORIAL, *then continue a few kilometers further to see the sign for Rahat, the largest Bedouin city in Israel.*

Rahat has a population of almost 30,000 Bedouin. The houses are unusually interesting, for they are often built like tents with the entrance on the northern side, guest rooms and a women's kitchen.

Inside Rahat, follow signs to the museum of Salem Abu Siam, a Bedouin entrepreneur and the most genial of hosts. Here you can watch Bedouin craftspeople at work, and drink tea or coffee with Salem in the main tent. A Bedouin-style light lunch is often available.

A guided tour in English begins with the herb gardens. Children uninterested in herbs can play with Bedouin toys in the amphitheater. Next stop is a gallery with photographs of Bedouin dancers and riders, while another room has exhibits of striking local paintings. An interesting three-dimensional display depicts the Negev Bedouin's sharp transition from tent to tin shack and finally into permanent housing. Toys change along with the modification in dwellings: plastic soft-drink bottle bottoms are incorporated into the trucks built by today's Bedouin children.

A room full of tools includes a thresher, a wooden plow tall enough for a camel to pull, and a yoke designed for two animals at once. Look for a four-pronged pitchfork and a five-fingered flat winnowing fork, the latter used for scattering and separating grain. Sieves are made of wood and long-lasting

Bedouin Heritage Center, Rahat

goat intestines. You can try working the millstone to see how flour is produced.

On sale are herbs and handicrafts, such as beautiful earrings, embroidered purses, vests, mirrors and skullcaps. There is even a studio where you can have your picture taken in Bedouin garb. Leave plenty of time for the animals, especially if you want a spin on a camel or donkey.

Vital Information

The center and restaurant are open Sat. to Thurs. 8:00–17:00. Closed Fridays. The entrance fee includes the guided tour, drinks and stories. Camel and donkey rides cost extra. For a small fee you can bring a sleeping bag and stay overnight.
Tel: 07-918263.
Evening visits (reserve in advance) include a Bedouin feast (eaten with your hands), tales of traditional life and a performance of local folk dancing.

Camel kissing at Rahat.

Negev Brigade Memorial
ANDARTAT HATIVAT HANEGEV

Immediately after the State of Israel was declared on May 15, 1948, the Egyptian army established its southern command post in BEER SHEVA. For the next five months, all Negev settlements south of Beer Sheva were under Arab siege.

In October of that year, the United Nations put heavy pressure on Israel to agree to a cease-fire. The country's leadership worried that Israel might lose its settlements—and with them the Negev—forever. Prime Minister David Ben Gurion knew that Israel must capture Beer Sheva, the capital of the Negev, before he acceded to the U.N.'s demands.

Ben Gurion waited 24 hours before agreeing to a cease-fire. His delay gained the Israeli army time to win Negev battles, in which Beer Sheva fell into Israeli hands.

Built on a high hill just north of Beer Sheva, the Memorial to the Negev Brigade is a dramatic and powerful monument to fallen soldiers. It covers an area of 100 square meters and consists of 18 symbolic elements. A north-to-south axis represents the Negev water pipeline, and ends in high walls and a path so narrow that visitors must walk single-file. This, too, has meaning, for it leads to a memorial dome for the fallen. Rays of the sun light up their names.

Other symbolic portions of the memorial are an army tent made of cement, a labyrinth with communications trenches, and an underground bunker. The monument is dominated by a water tower and pockmarked with "bullet holes," a reminder of the Negev under siege.

Poems about the Negev, Palmach* songs and passages from the Brigade's campaign diaries are engraved into the stone in Hebrew only. Yet the monument has a powerful impact even on those who don't understand the language. The Hebrew sign at the memorial's entrance reads: "Dear visitor: you are entering a sanctuary which expresses our love for the Negev."

To reach the monument, called "Hanegev Palmach Brigade Memorial" on signs within Beer Sheva, take Highway 60 east out of the city in the direction of Omer. Watch for a green sign on the left hand side of the road.

Tel Beer Sheva National Park

Tel Beer Sheva National Park

When we were children we hated our respective afternoon Hebrew schools with a passion—especially those studies related to the Bible. But after we immigrated (separately) to Israel, our interests in the Scriptures were ignited and, in fact, both of us greatly enjoy treading biblical sites. One of our favorites is ancient Beer Sheva, the scene of powerful political and social events for thousands of years.

Beer Sheva is the only planned Israelite city uncovered in its entirety. Its ruins are encompassed, today, within Tel Beer Sheva National Park. The site has been partially reconstructed with biblical-style mud bricks, which make the ancient city come to life!

Tel Beer Sheva National Park is located east of its contemporary namesake, along Highway 60 (also called Derech Hebron*). To get there, turn towards the Bedouin town of Tel Sheva and drive until you reach the park.*

Once in the park, you ascend a path which lies to the left of the city. This entrance was designed for defensive purposes: since a warrior attacking in ancient times carried his shield with his left hand, his naked right shoulder was exposed to guards manning the walls.

Next to a shaded rest area is a tamarisk tree (see BEER SHEVA). It is meant to remind visitors that, long ago, Abraham planted the same kind of tree in Beer Sheva (Genesis 21:33). Abraham also dug a well in the town, but local shepherds wanted the water for themselves. Eventually Abraham met with the Philistine ruler of the region and the two agreed to make peace. Beer Sheva means that next to the well (*be'er*) they took an oath (*shvu'a*) of peace (Genesis 21:31).

Beer Sheva is the best place in the entire Negev to find water, for its water table lies very close to the surface. The biblical tel* is bordered by two riverbeds that provide ample water during winter floods. The water seeps underground and enriches the aquifer.* As a result, the soil here is very fertile.

According to Jewish commentaries, Abraham strove to spread belief in one God. He gave each of his wells a divine name, and when people came to draw water the name introduced them to his religious idea. Despite the wells' importance to the Negev, the Philistines filled them in after Abraham's death, apparently because they opposed the religious ideology

Tel Beer Sheva National Park

with which the wells were associated. Isaac redug his father's wells and restored their original names (Genesis 26:18).

Archaeologists discovered an ancient well next to the tamarisk tree and the National Parks Authority named it for Father Abraham. The 80-meter-deep well has been beautifully reconstructed so that visitors can imagine a donkey walking back and forth pulling a pail of water. Long ago, a person would stand beside the well, grab the bucket from the donkey with a hook and empty the water into the adjacent trough. Press a button and the inside of the well lights up.

While there are a number of Chalcolithic* sites in the area of Tel Beer Sheva, it was the Jews who first built the city. It was begun as a small settlement about 3,100 years ago, and greatly enhanced some decades later by either King David or his son Solomon.

Beer Sheva was on Israel's southern boundary and the expression "from Dan (in the north) to Beer Sheva" was used to describe the borders of ancient Israel (Judges 20:1). Pharaoh Shishak destroyed Beer Sheva in 924 B.C.E., but the city was rebuilt by the later kings of Judah.

Although Beer Sheva was completely surrounded by protective walls, these fortifications were no match for the Assyrians. They conquered Beer Sheva in 710 B.C.E. and the city never returned to its former prominence. The Romans built a town in the vicinity of modern Beer Sheva and all that remained on the tel was a small fortress. Following the Moslem conquest in the seventh century, the site fell into ruins. Much of the original Israelite entrance remains. Just inside the gate, judges met with the people (you will find plaster still sticking to their benches.) The sons of the prophet Samuel were judges in Beer Sheva (I Samuel 8:1–3), but they were so corrupt that the people rejected them as rulers and demanded that Samuel choose a king to rule over them, instead.

A bit further on you will see huge rooms used for storage. These were royal storehouses, over 600 square meters in size, which housed agricultural produce collected as taxes for the king and tithes for the Temple in Jerusalem.

There were many Jewish temples outside of Jerusalem where pagan gods were worshipped. The prophet Amos harshly criticized the temple at Beer Sheva (Amos 5:5, 8:4). In the year 715 B.C.E., King Hezekiah assembled the country's Jews in Jerusalem and proclaimed an end to all idolatrous shrines. The Jews went home and broke all of their idols (II Chronicles 31:1). It is very likely that this altar and the temple that housed it were destroyed by the Jews during their period of religious fervor. A copy of the altar is on display at the foot of the tel. Stones from an Israelite altar were

Tel Beer Sheva National Park

used to build the storehouses and may provide archaeological confirmation of that biblical religious revolution.

Next you come to the governor's residence, which contained a kitchen, living room, reception hall and a staircase to the second floor. Most houses in this part of the city were two stories high and some even contained cellars.

Walk around a roped off area to view a lower level of pavement. These are remains from ancient Beer Sheva's earliest paved street—the one on which you have been walking is from a second period about 200 years later.

Many dwelling units here were built inside a casement wall. On your left are portions of the wall, incorporated into the homes of residents who were responsible for their maintenance. Short rows of columns divided the rooms and held up the roof.

Recently, an incredibly large and complex water system was uncovered. Complete with huge, high-ceilinged rooms, tunnels and drainage pools, the system is currently being prepared for viewing. During recent excavations of a new storehouse area, Beer Sheva's original building blocks were uncovered. Reconstructed storerooms on the tel are uncannily similar to the genuine article!

Vital Information

Sun. to Thurs. & Sat: 8:00–17:00, Friday & holiday eves 8:00–14:00. The site closes one hour earlier from October to March. Entrance fee.
Tel.: 07–467286.
Tel Beer Sheva is excellently sign-posted in English.

Introducing the Negev Highlands

Though the Negev is known to be hot, the highlands in its center are a cool surprise. Even in summer the weather here is quite pleasant, for the highlands rise from 450 to 1,000 meters above sea level.

Although in the past most Negev settlement was in the highlands, today the region is very underpopulated. It contains only one city, Dimona, the two small towns of Yeruham and Mitzpe Ramon and a few kibbutzim* and moshavim.*

The absence of modern civilization is, however, a blessing which has preserved many of the highland's fabulous natural attractions. Among them: three craters, unique flowers like the Yeruham iris and exceptionally beautiful riverbeds, canyons and desert springs.

Besides colossal natural sites, the highlands offer some of Israel's most outstanding national parks. Within their confines are the remains of four excavated ancient Nabatean cities; AVDAT, MAMSHIT, SHIVTA and Nitzana.

Vital Information
To reserve lodging, restaurants, activities, or arrange tours, call the Negev Highlands Tourism Reservation Center's toll-free number: 177–022–2646; or 07–588319 or 588290; fax: 588298.

Route No. 7: Beer Sheva to the Arava

Route No. 7
Beer Sheva to the Arava

*Route No.7 includes a dazzling array of wildflowers,
breathtaking craters, ancient and modern history
and the hairpin turns of the Scorpion Ascent*

Studded with stunning flowers in winter and early spring, the
Negev in season looks more like the Garden of Eden than a barren wedge
of land. Although the Negev has hosted some of the world's most
celebrated events, the region is so beautiful that you almost forget its
historical significance. One unusual trip through the Negev includes both
nature and history. It starts out south of Beer Sheva and ends on the Arava
Highway (90).

Begin on Highway 40 at Halukim Junction, just north of Kibbutz Sde
Boker. Turn towards Yeruham onto Road 204, drive about one kilometer,
and park off the side near kilometer marker 135. To your left you see Hurvat
Halukim, ruins of an Israelite fortress that are well worth a visit. Look for a
large white Antiquities Authority sign which relates information (in English)
about the biblical fortress.

King Solomon greatly expanded the Israelite Empire. The fortress and
settlement located at Halukim were part of his southern defensive system.
This included an oval-shaped citadel 23 meters long and eight casement
units built around a courtyard. Twenty-five private dwellings completed the
complex.

Follow the arrows along an excellent path that leads you through the
site. Among the ruins are the remains of a typical Israelite period house
and, on the top of a low hill, a tower. During the Israelite period this was a
small fortress; 1,000 years later the Romans constructed a tower over its
ruins. You can walk the Roman steps up to the "roof" for an excellent view
of the riverbed below and an unusually illustrative demonstration of
terraced agriculture.

Now continue on Road 204. You are traveling through a fertile valley
towards the development town of Yeruham. Crops thrive in the rich alluvial
soil, which erosive forces swept off the hills over the millennia.

As you approach kilometer marker 139, watch the slopes to your right to
see some strange-looking vertical rows. They are part of a scientific
experiment in the use of run-off water for agriculture. The experiment was

100

Route No. 7: Beer Sheva to the Arava

initiated after researchers discovered a curiosity which the Bedouin call *tulilat el-anav*, possibly part of a 2,000 year old grape industry.

A Roman papyrus found at the Nabatean*-Byzantine* city of NITZANA describes a system for using protective walls to cultivate grapes on the slopes. Possibly, Roman soldiers serving in the Negev brought to Israel a novel method for growing grapes.

Near the development town of Yeruham, at kilometer marker 149, you will see an orange sign pointing to the Sternbergia Nature Reserve. If you are touring in late autumn or early winter, follow the dirt road on your left to reach a nature reserve* literally bursting with glorious yellow-orange sternbergia blossoms. The road takes you through a valley to the point at which you leave your car. Flower-shaped signs lead you a few hundred meters to the reserve.

Without question the queen of Israeli wildflowers, sternbergia were considered extremely rare until they were discovered in dozens of isolated locations. Although sternbergia sites are only a few dunams in size, each separate spot contains over a hundred flowers clustered together and flowering within a period of several weeks.

Blooms resemble large bells and sport unusually attractive yellow stamens. During their fall appearance they have no leaves and burst full-blown out of the ground. What makes them especially appealing is their appearance in November, when other flowers are few and far between.

Return to Road 204 and drive to Yeruham. Turn right into the town (onto Road 225), then drive through an entrance lined with tall palm trees. A lovely park further into the city—Founders' Forest—was put up here in 1993 by the Jewish National Fund (JNF). The road continues through the industrial area of the city, then starts climbing the Hatira Mountain range. Eventually it moves into the BIG CRATER (*Hamachtesh Hagadol* in Hebrew). Turn left at the sign which reads "Mitzpor Har Avnun" to follow one of the British-made roads which crisscross this region. The Big Crater is located in the heart of an anticline, the kind of locale which often contains oil. During the 1940's the British paved these roads and marked them with barrels, while actively searching for the liquid gold.

When you reach the overlook, park and pile out of your cars. Then walk down the steps for a breathtaking view of the Big Crater. Approximately 12 kilometers long, seven kilometers wide and 400 meters deep, the crater is almost completely surrounded by mountains. Unusually large quantities of fossilized sea creatures can be found inside the crater,* which has not yet experienced total erosion. Quarries here have exposed excellent, clean sand which is used in the glass industry.

101

Route No. 7: Beer Sheva to the Arava

a sign on your right points to *Ma'ale Akrabim*—Scorpion Ascent. Turn in. This is Road 227.

On your way to the ascent you pass through the Yemin Plain. A huge, sandy area more than 100 square kilometers in size, the plain is located between the Hatira Mountain range (containing the Big Crater) and the Hatzera range (encompassing the Small or Little Crater).

In late winter and early spring the Yemin Plain is covered with an amazing variety of brilliant wildflowers. They vary from deep red bloodwort and blood-red buttercup (crowfoot) to orange marigolds and the brilliant purple of one of Israel's 50 species of milk vetch.

Look for light purple flowers called "stork's bill" because the fruit resembles a stork's head with a long bill. Each stork's bill blossom flowers for only a few hours; it opens in the morning, is pollinated, and then its petals drop off one by one. A patch of ground covered with purple-blue stork's bills in the morning will look almost empty in the afternoon.

So exciting is the contrast between the sand of the plains, and the blooms which burst with color from January to April, that you will stop time and again for a closer look. Brilliant red poppies are an especially astonishing sight.

Both sides of this desert road are lined with a species of flower called desert diplotaxis. A relative of the cabbage and the radish, this plant sports cross-shaped flowers whose bright pinkish-purple color can be seen from a great distance. When its leaves or stalks are torn, the plant smells and tastes very much like a radish. The sharp odor and taste are its protection against vegetarians such as insects, gazelles and goats.

Desert flowers of the same species may vary greatly in height, depending on the rainfall in each region. The diplotaxis is a good example of this phenomenon, for sometimes the blossoms are very low, and at others they tower above the road.

Portions of Road 227 are paved. Nevertheless, there are some curiously placed stones along the road: winter floods wash out the asphalt in the plains and the JNF filled the lowest depressions with these small rocks. Pass an orange sign pointing to the WADI YEMIN TRAIL. You will view the Yemin riverbed just before you begin climbing the Hatzera range.

Between a green sign to your right and another further up the road is a stone causeway. It was built by the British during their Mandate over Palestine to consolidate control of the southern Negev and Eilat. The British road led from Mamshit to the Arava and on to UM RASHRASH (now Eilat). Look for a stone curb lining both sides of the causeway. When Israel liberated Eilat in the 1949 Uvda Campaign, her Golani forces utilized this British-built road.

Route No. 7: Beer Sheva to the Arava

After crossing plains covered with naturally crushed stones known as hamada, you pass through a riverbed lined with acacia trees. This rather isolated and lonely wadi* is lovely in winter and spring, when flowering plants jut out of rock crevices and its slopes are covered with green foliage. The sweet-smelling white broom can be easily identified by its long, thin needle-like branches. Both the acacia and broom trees have romantic associations. According to an ancient Jewish custom, when a girl was born the family planted an acacia tree (for a boy it was a cedar). Years later, they would cut branches from these trees for the wedding canopy.

We were once told that Bedouin shepherds and shepherdesses get engaged with the help of the white broom. When a boy falls in love with a girl he has seen at a watering hole, said our guide, he leaves a knot of needles near the water to signal his intentions. If the feeling is mutual she adds a knot of her own. But if she doesn't like the fella, she unties the needles!

High on a hill to the right is a Roman outpost, called Tzafir Fortress (*Meitzad Tzafir*). It was part of the Roman defensive line, which began in Israel's north and included fortified posts on its eastern edge.

A fork in the road leads right to Scorpion Ascent, also called Scorpion Pass and, in Hebrew, *Ma'ale Akrabim*. But before you begin, make a short detour off the main road to a JNF observation point above the Little Crater (the sign reads "Little Makhtesh O.P."). Follow the road left for 700 meters, park and walk east about 15 minutes on a red-marked trail. It leads to a stupendous overlook.

From here you have a fabulous view of the Little Crater's unique topography: steep, straight walls 400 meters tall make a virtually complete circle. Its single opening is the narrow channel of Wadi Hatzera, which drains the crater. Since it is only four by seven kilometers in size, you can observe the whole phenomenon from where you stand.

Now return to the intersection and this time take the asphalt road to Scorpion Ascent. The road leads down into a riverbed where pink or red bloodwort covers the ground in winter and spring.

Before you begin the serpentine-like descent to the Arava, stop at a delightful overlook completed by the JNF two years ago, exactly 40 years after a horrific massacre took place at this site. An orange sign points to the overlook, designed to resemble Scorpion Ascent. Park your car, then follow steps carved into the twisting, turning slope. Relevant biblical quotes are written on the rock (in Hebrew). The first is from Numbers, 34: 2–4: "Command the Israelites and say to them: 'When you enter Canaan, the land that will be allotted to you as an inheritance will have these boundaries: Your southern side will include some of the Desert of Tzin

105

Route No. 7: Beer Sheva to the Arava

along the border of Edom. On the east, your southern boundary will start from the end of the Salt Sea, cross south of Scorpion Ascent.'"

The outlook's slope is covered with wildflowers in winter and spring, just like the landscape through which you have passed. Most prominent are desert diplotaxis and gacea.

During the biblical period, the Scorpion Ascent was the boundary between the Jews and the Amorites (Judges 1:36). Although it is uncertain whether the Scorpion Ascent you are about to descend is that mentioned in the Scriptures, the topography here has not changed over the years and there are few other options for trails in this area. New roads are often constructed on top of older paths.

The Scorpion Ascent was a vital link in the Roman Spice Trail connecting the Hatzera range with the Edom Mountains. Its execution required a grandiose operation typical of the Romans, and its remains are found just west of today's paved road. Although the natural incline here is 36 degrees, the Roman road rarely goes above 18. Roman engineers accomplished this feat by paving a road that winds its way up the hill, and by quarrying steps in the steepest parts.

The Romans constructed three fortresses to guard the road. Recent studies indicate that the citadels were built at the end of the third century, during the rule of Emperor Diocletian. The highest was Meitzad Tzafir, which you saw earlier. There was one in the middle and you will be visiting the lowest fortress, Rogem Tzafir, after your descent. All three were part of a chain of positions which the Romans established in order to fortify the road that led from Mamshit to the Edom Mountains.

In 1927 the British built a parallel road based on the Roman ascent, with 18 hairpin curves. This road rapidly descends 322 meters and you should check your brakes before heading downhill! The road—today's Scorpion Pass—connects the Arava Valley with the Negev highlands. About 20 meters further on is a monument to Israel's Engineering Corps, which improved and expanded this road in 1950. The monument looks like a chess rook, which is the symbol of the corps.

In the 1950's this was the only route to Eilat and was very dangerous to travel. Navigational problems were compounded by the constant threat of Arab assault. It took 24 hours to drive from Eilat to Beer Sheva!

The most vicious attack came on March 17, 1954. A busload of people celebrating the fifth anniversary of Eilat's liberation was ambushed by terrorists who had infiltrated from Jordan. Passengers and military escort alike were slaughtered. Only three people survived: the driver's five-year-old daughter, who was pinned beneath her mother's inanimate body; her small brother (who never regained consciousness and died many years

Route No. 7: Beer Sheva to the Arava

later); and a woman who was left for dead. (Fourteen years after the assault, Israeli army forces encountered and killed a group of terrorists. Among them was the leader of the bus massacre.)

Following the blood bath at Scorpion Ascent, the Israeli government decided to build a second road to Eilat. The result was a highway running from Mitzpe Ramon to Eilat, further from the border. It was completed in 1955.

From this vantage point there is a fantastic view of the Arava's swirls and depressions. You can see Wadi Tzin, the lush spring of EIN TZIN within the riverbed, the Edom Mountains and, standing tall and proud within a misty cloud, Mount Tzin.

Until recently Mount Tzin was considered one of the possible locations of Mount Hor, which the Bible gives as Aaron's final resting place (Numbers 20:22). Today, however, historians believe Mount Hor is in Jordan. And the mist surrounding the mountain, mystical as it is, is no more than dust from the phosphate mines nearby.

Mount Tzin is a table mountain, in which a soft lower level of rock is covered and protected by a hard upper level. The upper level is of hard limestone, atop crumbly clay. Since clay erodes faster than lime, the mountain is eaten from below. The result is this singular shape. Below

Rogem Tzafir guarded the bottom of the Scorpion Ascent.

Route No. 7: Beer Sheva to the Arava

Mount Tzin is a site more curious still: a large expanse of land chock full of smooth, oval rocks called "bulboosim."

The proximity of this "bulboose" field to the stunning, flat-topped mountain has sparked numerous legends. One Bedouin tale relates the story of a traveler who reached the city at the top of the mountain. When he asked the inhabitants for hospitality he was spurned and sent packing. This made the Lord angry, so He turned the city upside down, burying its people underneath. The "bulboosim," so they say, are the fossilized heads of these inhospitable city-dwellers.

Today, the "bulboosim" field is a nature reserve,* but it was discovered quite by accident during quarrying operations at Mount Tzin. As bulldozers reached an underground layer, they exposed hundreds of these peculiar rocks. Before this impressive and unusual phenomenon of similar-shaped limestone rocks could be destroyed, the Society for the Protection of Nature in Israel quickly concentrated them all in this one field.

Israel's "bulboose" field is the only one in the world where the rocks are pure limestone; elsewhere the stones are made of flint. The limestone is a very rare occurrence and at present there is no explanation for their formation.

Now it is time to descend. Count the curves as you plummet from a height of 402 meters above sea level to a mere 80. You can stop at the Roman Ascent Observation Point about 1.5 kilometers below the top of the pass, to observe Meitzad Tzafir to the west. Further down is a pile of stones—the remains of the middle citadel. And at the foot of the mountain is the lowest fortress, Rogem Tzafir. Stop the car when you reach the bottom, then turn around and gaze back up at the Scorpion Ascent.

Now drive several dozen meters further to an orange sign on the right which indicates Rogem Tzafir. Built at the time the Romans controlled the Negev, this fortress guarded the bottom of the Scorpion Ascent and was part of the spice trail that passed Petra and led to Ein Hatzeva, Mamshit, Hebron and Jerusalem.

Rogem Tzafir consists of two very well preserved buildings which have been partially reconstructed. Steps even lead up to a second story. Decorative chiseled stones line the outside of the fortress, while those inside the building are much less elaborate.

Across from the citadel ruins is a sign which points you towards EIN TZIN. Take a circular walk in the oasis, then return to your car and drive back to Road 227. Continue straight ahead and follow the signs for the Arava Highway (90). Turn right to connect up with ROUTE NO. 10, which ends in Eilat and offers a choice of exciting stop-offs along the way. Or turn left at the Arava Highway and head north by way of the DEAD SEA.

Yorkeam Spring (*Ein Yorkeam*)

Some desert spots are so magnificent that they take your breath away. In winter and spring Ein Yorkeam is one such site: a pool and riverbed enclosed within a glorious white canyon, Ein Yorkeam bursts with so many flowers that you wonder if you are really in the Negev!

 You can stop at Ein Yorkeam as you visit Scorpion Ascent (see ROUTE NO. 7). Or you can reach it from Yeruham, located 25 kilometers south of Beer Sheva on the Dimona-Sde Boker Highway. At the Dimona-Oron intersection turn right in the direction of Oron. Drive a few hundred meters to the sign that reads Ein Yorkeam.

Park here, then turn around to face a distinctive pile of stones. Called Meitzad Yorkeam, this was once a Roman fortress where soldiers stood guard over the springs. Now look for a green trail-marker and follow it 500 meters east until, to your surprise, you suddenly reach a rock formation atop a little stream. Move around the rocks to the left of the stream to find steps, carved out by the ancients so they could bring their camels to the water.

The green-marked trail leads right, to a waterfall. Caper plants peer from the crevices of this cool, shady spot, and there are many kinds of brush. Spring flowers include the fairly rare haelava toadflax, a stunning purple flower with yellow and white edges, whose blossom is reminiscent of the snapdragon.

As you walk, look for a thornbush. Shrikes utilize the plant's strong thorns for spearing the prey they carry in their mouths, and you may see beetles and other insects skewered on the tree. When hungry, the shrike returns to its thornbush "storehouses."

On the ground between the rocks are delightful white-blossomed androcymbium. And until the end of March you will see fields of minuscule yellow flowers with a long, long name—Aaronsohnia Faktorovsky —honoring not one, but two different Jewish scientists. One of them, Aaronsohn, was a renowned botanist in the early 1900's and one of the few Jews whom the Turks allowed to travel freely around the Land of Israel during World War I. His research served as a convenient cover for spying on behalf of the British, and the military information he supplied played a crucial role in the British conquest of the Negev.

Yorkeam Spring (Ein Yorkeam)

In winter fine muscari—*kadan* in Hebrew—is in bloom. Can you find stalks of little flowers whose bluish-purple bell-like buds drop downwards? Vaguely resembling the jars (*kadim*) for which they are named, the muscari are unusually attractive despite their size. Muscari have also been called "rain-bells," both for their appearance and because they blossom during the rainy season. Fine muscari closely resembles one of its brother species, "baby's breath," but the latter appears much earlier in the season.

There is a good reason why the flowers drop to the ground. Since they bloom during the rainy season, they must ensure that their pollen does not get wet and prevent the flower's reproduction. So they hang their heads, and rain falls only on the closed bottom of the flower while the protected grains stay dry.

Also blooming in winter are bloodworts, plants that enjoy the Negev's heat. Their distinctive pinkish-red petals seem almost transparent. The leaves are fleshy and tasty, but contain a high percentage of an acid that can be harmful if too much is eaten.

The channel is full of reeds: you can tell them from cattails because reeds have bushy, broom-like tops. Reeds grow incredibly fast—so rapidly that at one time they were used as instruments of torture. The victim was tied to a reed which, as it grew, painfully pulled him apart.

Tamarisks are often found in water and you will see them here, in the wadi. In fact desert tamarisks with their flexible branches are well adapted to life in the gullies, for less pliant trees are broken and bent by sudden flash floods. Tamarisks expel the surplus salt they absorb from the saline soil through special glands in their leaves. Excreted as a solution, the fluid evaporates. Crystals of concentrated salt collect on the leaves and then drop to ground. The soil under a tamarisk tree often becomes too brackish for other plants and may be completely barren.

Walk over to the dry waterfall. Underneath it is a spring, surrounded by fabulous rock formations. Enjoy a picnic, if you like, before you return to your car.

Vital Information

From Ein Yorkeam it is another 30 minutes on the green-marked trail to an overlook near Ma'ale Palmach, the "Palmach Ascent." For more information, see WADI YEMIN.

Springs and pools at Ein Tzin.

Ein Tzin

Ein Tzin

Desert oases are an enchanting sight and Ein Tzin, a lush refuge deep inside the Tzin riverbed, is no exception. Tall white cliffs surround the path through this unusually wide gully, which leads to masses of date and tamarisk trees, rush, reeds and other vegetation. The crowning touches are a spring and some sparkling pools of water.

Ein Tzin is located off Road 227, just north of Ein Hatzeva on the Arava Highway (see description in ROUTE NO. 7). After the turn (west), you will pass an orange sign leading to Ein Tzin. Follow the dirt road to a low stone wall and a parking lot. A circular walk to Ein Tzin takes about an hour and a half.

Although the trail is marked by black trail-markers, green-and-white arrows also lead you to the oasis and back to your car. As you walk towards the spring the Hatzera cliffs are on your left; you return on the opposite side of the riverbed.

Look for the common nitraria plant, almost two meters high. Its greenish-grey leaves are fleshy because there is so much water in this area, and they are easily identifiable because their asymmetrical edges look so unfinished. Nitraria bloom in winter. The flowers are white, with delicate yellow stamens. Birds delight in the nitraria's delicious-looking fruit; they digest the juicy covering and disperse the complete seeds in their droppings.

After the first rain you will see masses of flying ants—yes ants! While ants usually don't fly, at this season all the males sprout wings and mate with winged females. The phenomenon is known as "wedding flight," with the groom literally sweeping the bride off her feet.

The spring that fostered the lush oasis at Ein Tzin developed when rain water trickling through the ground was trapped in the aquifer.* Over the years, a strongly flowing river exposed a crack between the layers that caused the water to burst out of the rock.

Today, water used to wash the minerals in a nearby phosphate mine returns to the aquifer, and makes up part of the waters at Ein Tzin. Some effort is being made to alleviate future pollution, which could have dire consequences for the Arava.

Wadi Tzin is the second largest riverbed in Israel and after it rains in winter its flow is of incredible magnitude. Floods change the look of the spring and the pools, so to find Ein Tzin you have to search out the tall

Ein Tzin

palms. You can sit in their shade, then cross to the other side of the river to see the spring and pools. While Ein Tzin is known for its beautiful palm grove, it is especially enchanting because it contains flat white limestone surfaces studded with water-filled hollows. Do not drink the water, as inviting as it seems. To return to your cars, look for an arrow on the hill behind the spring.

Take a good look at the smooth stones on the ground. David used smooth rocks from a riverbed (though not from this one) to attack Goliath (I Samuel 17:40). They come in a variety of colors, and represent flint, lime and sandstone.

On your way back you will pass a spring called Ein Akrabim, for the Ma'ale Akrabim, or "Scorpion Ascent," nearby (see ROUTE NO. 7). However, today it is completely dry and you may even be unable to find it. Then cross back to the Hatzera cliffs.

Vital Information

Expect to get a bit lost looking for the oasis—you need a sense of direction as well as a sense of humor for this trip!
Hikers may swim in the pools but on occasion suffer from temporary skin discomfort after doing so.

Introducing Yeruham
THE CITY, THE TEL, AND THE NATURE RESERVE*

Your canteen is empty, your throat is dry, and you are dying for the sight of water. Suddenly, a lake appears in front of you, smack in the middle of your desert trail. Could you be suffering from delusions? Will this lovely, sparkling, WET mirage suddenly disappear?

Not if you are near Yeruham, a development town created in 1951 as one of many tent-cities in Israel for Jewish refugees from North Africa and Europe. Designed for miners who would hopefully dig for phosphates and other minerals in the Big Crater, Yeruham has only 8,500 residents, a revolving population and a soaring unemployment rate. Yet the normally obscure town reached national prominence in 1986, when a woman from Yeruham became the first female member of a municipal religious council in Israel. Her appointment sparked many debates regarding the role of women in the orthodox Jewish world.

> *You can fish at Lake Yeruham, view historical ruins and visit a stunning nature reserve all within a short distance of the town. Begin by taking Highway 40 south from Beer Sheva, then turn left onto Road 224 in the direction of Yeruham. The lake is immediately across from the town's southern entrance.*

Yeruham Lake was created by a dam built in the 1950's to retain flood waters for agriculture. At first the water flowed to Kibbutz Mashabei Sadeh. Later the kibbutz drilled for water elsewhere, and it was decided to use the lovely lake as a tourist attraction.

Before proceeding to the lake, stop at Be'er Yeruham. Known as *Bir Rahmi* to local Arabs, the well has canals so that three troughs can be filled for watering flocks. Some people identify this as the well which God showed Hagar when she "wandered in the desert of Beer Sheva" and "saw a well of water" (Genesis 21:14, 19). Others think it is at BIR ASLUJ— somehow holy sites have a strange way of multiplying!

An impressive Nabatean* fortress has been restored at Yeruham Park. You can reach the site by following the signs for archeological sites and looking for it on a hill to the left. Originally a caravansary for travelers between MAMSHIT and AVDAT, Meitzad Yeruham was built by the Nabateans in the first century B.C.E. and was inhabited for the next 600 to 700 years. It contains 100 dunams of land, spread out over the hills. The signs here—in

Introducing Yeruham

English—are unusually clear and include excellent maps. You will enjoy exploring fancy villas and other partially reconstructed buildings.

Now drive along the park's lake. When you reach the last curve in the road, you see the strangest-looking structure! The mayor of Yeruham wanted to put a pub inside the lake: this is part of what he wanted to move inside the water, along with the frame.

The slopes are covered with wildflowers in late winter and early spring, especially squill and asphodel. Both plants were apparently a major source of nourishment for monks in the Judean desert. They would dig up asphodel with a small trowel and eat the tuber.

If asphodel roots were not handy, the monks often ate wild onions—often identified as squill—instead. White squill flower from the bottom up, growing out of bulbs that store their nourishment underground. Harbingers of shorter days and more humidity in the air, they are the first blooms to emerge at the end of the dry, hot summer. Few animals will touch the white squill, for it has a very sharp, unpleasant smell. Only the gazelle bothers to nibble at its dark green leaves when they poke through the ground in early winter.

Finally, park and climb up the flint-covered hill. From this point you can see the whole of Lake Yeruham, one and a half kilometers in size and

The delectable Yeruham iris.

Introducing Yeruham

providing a welcome break in the desert landscape. Note the clouds and trees reflected in the water, which contains only a little sewage and plenty of fish (the lake is stocked with carp). You will see coot, freshwater ducklike birds with long-lobed, unwebbed toes, and hear their cries.

Stand, if you wish, on the bridge next to the dam. Although the dam was built with clay and is theoretically impermeable, Mother Nature can foil the best intentions. The water tamarisk trees that grow here penetrate through the clay and break the sealing at the bottom. So instead of considering them trees, the gardeners here call them weeds!

By the time you read this there will be lots more to do and see at the park. Every time we visit, something new has appeared—grassy slopes, pedal boats—who knows what we'll see there the next time we journey to Yeruham!

The Yeruham Iris

During the 1950's Israel's wildflowers—especially her irises—verged on extinction. Fortunately, the newly-emerged Society for the Protection of Nature in Israel carried out a fantastically successful campaign which taught the public to leave wildflowers in their natural settings. The stunning iris was chosen to be the SPNI's symbol.

From winter to spring, Israelis fill the nation's flower reserves, enjoying bright yellow sternbergia, blood-red tulips, anemone and various species of iris. The name iris is Greek for "rainbow," undoubtedly granted to the flower because the iris appears in such a wide variety of colors: from pink to yellow to deep purple to a speckled variety. You will see several species in the Negev, including the white and yellow Land of Israel iris, at Kibbutz BE'ERI. Found on the sand in regions which are not nature reserves, the purple Negev iris—endemic to Israel—may soon be extinct. The dark iris grows on chalky soil in the northern and eastern Negev. All of these flowers bloom in March, some begin in February, others last until April or May.

One of the most popular reserves in the country has been set aside for the delectable Yeruham iris, endemic to a small area near the town of Yeruham. A sign for the reserve is located on Road 204, 4.5 kilometers northeast of Yeruham between kilometer markers 158 and 159. The reserve is situated about a kilometer east of the road, but it is easy to find only during the season when the iris flowers (late February to early April).

116

Dimona

Usually dark violet in color, the Yeruham iris sometimes appears in brown or yellow. The colorful bottom leaf of each flower attracts pollinating insects and serves as their landing pad.

In season, this is a tremendously crowded site and Israelis come from far away to get a close look at these beautiful flowers. For many, the iris is more than just another pretty flower. It is a true and burning passion.

Dimona

Soon after Dimona was established, Jews from Morocco docked at Haifa. When told their destination was Dimona they were delighted, for Dimona in at least one Arabic dialect means "luck." Imagine their shock when they were bused down at night from Haifa and dumped in the middle of a desert. And when another group of immigrants arrived the next day, the "experienced" settlers from the first day rushed to the bus and warned the newcomers not to get off!

Founded in 1955 by 36 new immigrant families from North Africa, Dimona is inhabited, today, by 35,000 people. Among them are 2,500 Black Hebrews from the United States, and 8,000 Russian immigrants.

Within the city is a memorial to Moroccan Jews who tried to enter the country during the British Mandate, when Jewish immigration was severely limited. One ship sank en route, and 23 people drowned.

Israel built an atomic reactor near Dimona and fenced off the site. In an effort to keep the building secret, it was euphemistically called a "textile factory" for many years. Look for small holes along the fence when you drive along Highway 25 from Beer Sheva to Dimona. They permit animals to roam freely in and out of the enclosed area. Imagine—a fence built for security has inadvertently created a small nature preserve!

117

Route No. 8: To Mitzpe Ramon via Avdat

Route No. 8
To Mitzpe Ramon via Avdat

Route eight propels you through desert landscapes,
Nabatean caves and Avdat National Park.
Visit several splendid parks, the grave of a Nabatean king
and the tomb of Israel's first prime minister.
Also on this route are unusual roadstops, and a family walk
way off the beaten track

Begin at the southern tip of Beer Sheva on Highway 40 (also called Eilat Road). About seven kilometers south of Beer Sheva, little eucalyptus groves appear to the right. These are *limans* planted by the Jewish National Fund (JNF) in a low spot and irrigated only by the Negev's scanty rainfall. A special technique entails encircling drainage basins with partial or total embankments and planting trees inside. As a result the trees don't need any artificial irrigation; they provide shade and shelter near the road and grazing for sheep and goats during the dry season.

Because of an overflow system, once the drainage basin fills to a certain height water spills over onto the ground outside. And when water floods the area, the embankments are not endangered.

Local Bedouin have also begun building *limans*, for fruit trees like pomegranates, dates and almonds. They do not construct overflow canals, however, and their version of the *liman* lasts for only a short time. You will see a number of Bedouin encampments, complete with tin shacks and huts, along the road.

About 11 kilometers out of Beer Sheva, on a hill to your right, stands a phoenix-shaped memorial. This monument is dedicated to an Israeli brigade that was devastated but "came back to life." South of Ramat Hovav is an area in which the JNF planted trees on unstable sands in the 1950's. At the time, every winter flood washed a dunam of sand onto the road. Tamarisks are frequently used to anchor sand dunes because the branches themselves hold back the sand. And because tamarisk grow rapidly, they don't get buried under sand drifts.

While some of the trees didn't take, a number of tamarisks and eucalyptus put down roots up to 20 meters deep. These roots were able to

118

Route No. 8: To Mitzpe Ramon via Avdat

nourish the trees from the stable land beneath the sands. Water stopped filtering through the sands, and the sands stopped shifting.

Continue to Mashabim Junction, which is only a few kilometers east of three wonderful attractions: GOLDA MEIR PARK, MITZPE REVIVIM and BIR ASLUJ. The acacia trees you see were planted by the British during the Mandate period for political purposes: they wanted to keep the Bedouin off government land and this was one way of demonstrating public ownership.

Between Mashabim Junction and Telalim Junction is the Ramat Negev Information Center, set up by the JNF and open mainly on Saturdays and holidays. Next to it are a gas station, snack bar and bathrooms.

At Telalim Junction turn left and continue on Highway 40 in the direction of Sde Boker. You should be able to spot Kibbutz Sde Boker's green foliage in the desert sands to your left, only moments after you turn right at Halukim Junction. The kibbutz's most famous member was David Ben-Gurion, the first prime minister of Israel.

Directly afterwards, on your right, is a very special recreation site called Henion Haro'a, or "Shepherdess Park." It is named for Barbara Proper, one of the founders of Kibbutz Sde Boker. On September 23, 1952, less than six months after the kibbutz was established, the shepherdess was murdered by Arab terrorists as she guarded the kibbutz flocks.

What makes this particular picnic and play site unusual is its location both within and outside of a *liman*. You can climb the embankment around the *liman*, while examining the spillway created for the overflow from winter floods. Washingtonian palm, tamarisk, eucalyptus and pine shade the lovely park, which also has playground equipment and bathrooms. Through Sde Boker's pistachio orchards, on the slopes of a hill, is a memorial plaque for the shepherdess.

Almost directly across from the park is the entrance to BEN GURION'S DESERT HOME. About three kilometers further south you reach Midreshet Ben Gurion, which encompasses the SDE BOKER Society for the Protection of Nature in Israel Field Study Center, the lower entrance to EIN AVDAT NATIONAL PARK, BEN GURION'S BURIAL GROUND and the Negev's SOLAR ENERGY CENTER. All of these sites are described in detail in the following articles.

About eight kilometers north of Avdat National Park is the Wadi Havarim riverbed. Above the riverbed, but lower than the surrounding hills, stands a majestic water hole carved out of the rock. One of at least 120 cisterns built by the Nabateans,* the Havarim Cistern fills from an intricate canal system, which drains floodwaters from the hills as they pour down the slopes towards the riverbed.

You can visit this fascinating site by turning left at kilometer marker 128,

119

Route No. 8: To Mitzpe Ramon via Avdat

Route No. 8: To Mitzpe Ramon via Avdat

where a large sign reads "Hawwarim Cistern" (*Bor Havarim*). As soon as you've driven in, park. Then begin to look for a path on your left, which descends slightly to a patch of vegetation.

The Havarim Cistern was one of at least two reservoirs which provided water for the ancient Nabatean city of AVDAT. It was carved out of the chalky rock and has a supporting pillar; you can still see marks made by chisels during its construction. Water streamed down the nearby hills into Wadi Havarim below and canals diverted it into the cave. After a wet winter, the cave fills to overflowing. At other times—even in early spring—it may be empty.

The steps you descend were cut by the Nabateans and look just like they did 2,000 years ago. Note the enormous horseshoe carved into the stone at the top of the supporting wall. This is a *wassem*, a Bedouin sign of ownership. Poplar trees and bean caper plants grow above the reservoir.

Bean capers hail from the Sahara Desert. They grow well in the Negev's limestone, and are found next to rocky channels and slopes. Often hundreds of years old, the bean caper adapts nicely to long periods of drought. It gets its Hebrew name—*zugan hasiah* or "pair of the bush" —because its little hot-dog shaped leaves are found in pairs. The plants are 40 to 80 centimeters high with fleshy leaves; they develop well shortly after the first rain.

In dry years the bean caper grows only part of its leaves and may not even flower. If the drought is really severe many of its branches will dry out, and it can then survive until the next rain on minimal water. This is possible because each branch is connected to the roots, and the fact that one branch dries out has no effect on any other.

Back on the highway, watch the hills on your left to spot ancient AVDAT'S restored ruins. Look for a camel convoy stopping to rest on the top of the mountain. The convoy is a recent addition to the national park and so realistic you may not notice that it is a sculpture. In addition to visiting the ancient city, you can take an adventurous walk across from Avdat to yet another Nabatean creation, the Ramalia Cisterns which serviced Avdat. Drive to the national park and leave your car in the lot (you have to pay an entrance fee, so if you aren't planning to tour Avdat later on, leave your vehicle outside). Then, pack some water and get ready for an hour's easy trek (round trip) to a second, very different reservoir.

Cross the highway. About 100 meters north of the gas station is a rusty metal Hebrew sign that barely reads *Bor Ramalia*, or "Ramalia Cistern." It points to a path leading to the mountains across the highway from Avdat

Before you take the trail gaze toward the hills to try and find openings in

Fun on the slopes near Wadi Havarim.

121

Route No. 8: To Mitzpe Ramon via Avdat

the white rock at their feet. This is your destination.

Stroll as far as the fence which encircles a large empty site. It has been around for ages, and prevents you from crossing directly to the reservoirs. At this point stop and look to your right. You have been walking through loess* soil, of which dust is a major component. Note the weird mazes that water has created within the loess to your right; they are tremendous fun. When you (and the kids) have finished weaving through the mazes, continue towards the mountains.

Resist the temptation to shortcut through holes in the fence, as you may come out in the wrong place. Simply walk along it (the fence should be on your left). You will pass hairy leatherwood plants, used in the past for making rope.

Look for a beetle called *loessit*. Although black, it will appear to be the color of loess. When frightened, the beetle secretes a fluid which helps soil stick to its body as protective coloring.

All the grasshoppers jumping around on the ground may look the same to you, but some belong to the species called *hagav*, and others to the *hargol* family. You can tell the difference by their feelers: the one with the longer name has longer feelers. Only the male is capable of making noise. It does so by rubbing two small teeth located under one of its left wings, apparently to attract females. Some of these species are kosher (Leviticus 11:23) and Yemenite Jews even claim that they are tasty.

The spies sent by Moses entered Israel from the Negev. Believing the Jews were not capable of conquering Israel, they tried to dissuade the Hebrews from even making the attempt by describing the Canaanites as giants. The Israelites, they said, were like grasshoppers in comparison (Numbers 13:33).

Having detoured around the fence you should soon reach one of the channels belonging to Wadi Tzin. You will see caves, but no water holes, as the Nabateans did not want their reservoirs discovered. Once you have crossed the riverbed look for the openings which hide the water holes. During floods, water seeps inside. Caves to the south of you are still used by local Bedouin to water their flocks. If the pools are clean and contain water, you can take a swim; otherwise, just enjoy the climb and the cool afternoon breeze. Then return to your car.

Continue your drive on Highway 40, in the direction of MITZPE RAMON. We recommend you stay overnight in the city and enjoy its spectacular attractions (see SITE INDEX).

Ben Gurion's House

In May 1953 David Ben Gurion, Israel's first prime minister, visited a bare encampment in the heart of the Negev desert. He was enchanted by what he found there: a small group of young men and women were trying to create an agricultural settlement within the sandy, barren wilderness. Ben Gurion was so impressed with these youngsters that he resolved, then and there, to become part of the pioneer group. And, indeed, when he retired from the government six months later he joined the settlement.

For Ben Gurion settling the Negev was a mission of national, military and economic significance. Influenced by biblical passages describing the ancient Negev's fertility, he believed that the desert could flourish again. Since this area was the largest and least populous part of the country, Ben Gurion considered its development one of the greatest challenges of modern Israel.

In his will, Ben Gurion asked that his house be left as it had been during his lifetime. It is a simple home, painted several shades of green, and somewhat larger than others on the kibbutz* to enable him to receive heads of state and other guests.

Enter via the verandah, where the famous man often entertained. Then walk into the living room, noting in particular the corner where he would chat with visitors. A photograph taken in 1966 shows that the room has remained unchanged. While the furniture is quite simple, exquisite gifts include a Hanukkah lamp whose candleholders are shaped like Maccabean soldiers. Look for the map of pre-1967 Israel. How enormous the Negev is compared to the rest of the country!

Move on to the great man's bedroom. He and his wife, Paula, had separate bedrooms: Ben Gurion slept only three hours a night and kept the light on the rest of the time, in order to read.

Inside Ben Gurion's closet are his clothes: a khaki shirt, an army uniform and one good suit. The only picture in his bedroom was of Mahatma Ghandi. Ghandi's non-violent methods of protest were an inspiration to Ben Gurion, although he felt they would be ineffective against the Arabs. A huge globe in one corner of the house was a gift from General Omar Bradley.

The most impressive room is the library, which contains over 5,000 books. Ben Gurion understood nine languages and was an avid reader with a voracious interest in subjects ranging from judo and yoga to geography, history and philosophy. A vast number of volumes are on biblical subjects

Ben Gurion's House

for, although wholly secular, Ben Gurion considered the Bible his nation's history. It was Ben Gurion who made Bible studies mandatory in Israel's schools.

On the desk are quotations from the Bible. One is the prophecy that "The Lord shall comfort Zion: He will comfort all her waste places; and He will make her wilderness like Eden, and her desert like the garden of the Lord; joy and gladness shall be found therein, thanksgiving, and the voice of melody" (Isaiah 51:3).

Vital Information
Sun. to Thurs. 8:30–15:30, Friday & holiday eves 8:30–14:00, Sat. and Jewish holidays 9:00–14:30.
Tel.: 07–558444; fax: 560119.
Ask for special brochures in English with activities for the whole family.

Ben Gurion's Burial Ground

Did Israel's first prime minister asked to be buried in the Negev, instead of in Jerusalem alongside other heads of state, only to be near his beloved kibbutz of Sde Boker? Perhaps he hoped that his callers would feel the Negev desert's mighty pull as they experienced its vast and awesome beauty. For visitors paying their respects at the graves of David and Paula Ben Gurion can't help but be touched by at least some primitive longing for the desert.

The national park which houses the Ben Gurion tombs stands against the backdrop of the starkly beautiful Tzin riverbed. At sunset incredibly brilliant colors light up the sky: fiery red, bright crimson, an achingly purple magenta, all lasting far longer than they would in most other parts of the country.

Superbly designed and executed, the park is worth a visit on its own merits. The path slithers hither and yon, like the channel of a riverbed. Lining the trail are stones reminiscent of the rock layers which form the Negev's hills and mountains. And the desert landscaping, amid the rocks and stones, is graceful and serene.

Many believe that the modern State of Israel would not have come into being had it not been for David Ben Gurion. Born in Russia in 1886, he moved to pre-state Israel when he was 20 and worked in pioneer agricultural settlements. After the Turks expelled him from the country during World War I, he helped form a battalion of Jewish volunteers who served in the British army.

As director of the Jewish Agency from 1935, Ben Gurion played a key role in the development of Israel. On the eve of the British withdrawal from Palestine in May, 1948, Jewish Agency leaders met to discuss whether the Jews should declare a state. Many feared the tiny new country would be immediately overwhelmed by the threatened Arab invasion and favored establishing a new mandate under the United Nations.

It was Ben Gurion who cast the decisive vote for statehood. He served as the country's first prime minister and its minister of defense from 1948 to 1953 and again from 1955 to 1963.

Vital Information
The entrance to the park is clearly marked on Highway 40, south of Kibbutz Sde Boker.
The park is open all day. There are bathrooms near the entrance.

National Solar Energy Center

If you plan a visit on Saturday call first, and you may be able to view an audio-visual display in English, by Ben Gurion's tomb. Tel.: 07–565717.

National Solar Energy Center

With ecology and pollution such important contemporary issues, scientists are looking for a "clean" and independent source of energy. The sun is the most abundant source of energy on earth: the amount of sunlight that hits earth daily is more than 35,000 times the annual electric needs for the entire planet. But how to harness this vast source of energy, without spending too much money?

In the Negev the sun shines almost every day (over 3,000 hours of sunlight per year), making this the obvious region for conducting research on solar energy. You can visit the Solar Energy Center at Sde Boker to see new innovative ideas in solar energy research.

The tour includes an explanation of the site, a wonderful audio-visual show on energy through the ages, and the systems so far developed in Israel.

Vital Information
Although the center is not set up for individual visitors, people who show a real interest are welcome. Often you get your own personal tour; otherwise you can be attached to a group.
Sun. to Thurs. 8:30–15:30. Entrance fee.
Tel.: 07–555059; fax: 555060.
The audio-visual presentation is available in English, Hebrew, German, French and Spanish.

Ein Avdat National Park

Deep within the desert riverbed of Wadi Tzin is the magnificent gorge called Ein Avdat. Only two kilometers long and amazingly narrow, the stunning canyon is home to ibex, fat sand rats and rock doves. And although spotted only rarely, a desert leopard often hangs out behind Ein Avdat's enormous cliffside boulders.

Nature lovers who visit Ein Avdat walk right through the riverbed, dry unless floodwaters are flowing through its channel. Fantastic rock formations and thick river foliage add a paradisiacal touch to shimmering pools. The pools were formed after millennia of floods and erosion and are filled year round by underground streams. You can sit alongside a large pool—or perhaps meditate on the bluffs, as monks did long ago.

To take an enchanting walk through the canyon you must begin at the bottom entrance to Ein Avdat. Bring two cars, so that one will be waiting at the end of the hike, further south. The relatively simple trip takes almost two hours and ends with a steep climb up rock steps to the top of the canyon.

If you have only one vehicle or have trouble hiking, take an easy 15- to 30-minute walk to the spring. Then return to your car and drive to the observation point at the top. See Vital Information for an alternative: a longer and more difficult circular outing.

You can reach the lower parking lot and canyon walk by driving through Midreshet Sde Boker and go down the road that leads to the canyon. Leave your car in the lot.

As you enter the canyon look for a model of Ein Avdat, cut into the rock. The model includes the road you traveled as well as the canyon's three springs: Ein Avdat, Ein Mor and Ein Ma'areef. Note how the canyon cuts through the Avdat Plateau.

Within the riverbed you will be walking along Ein Mor, a layered spring* whose name means "bitter" in Arabic. In winter, water drips from one pool down to the next, and the moisture in the ground provides a congenial habitat for many desert plants.

Surprisingly enough, next to this tiny spring there is an Atlantic pistachio tree. It is very rare to find trees of this kind at such a low altitude—only 350 meters above sea level—for they usually grow at double this height. Atlantic

127

Ein Avdat National Park

pistachio can survive on as little as 200 millimeters of rain per year and still produce fruit.

Although most Middle East pistachio nuts come from Iran and Turkey, pistachios were once cultivated in the land of Israel. In fact, Genesis 43:11 reads: "Then their father Israel [Jacob] said to them, 'Put some of the best products of the land in your bags and take them down to the man [Joseph] as a gift—a little balm and a little honey, some spices and myrrh, some pistachio nuts and almonds.'"

The Hebrew name for this tree, *ela*, means "goddess." In biblical times, this was one of Israel's most common trees. The fact that it lives for up to 800 years and can regenerate from its stump was seen as a symbol of immortality by the ancient Semites. Consequently, Canaanites and some Israelites worshipped the pistachio tree as a goddess.

On the left, past the pistachio are boulders which fell from the cliff walls. The darkest rocks are travertine, formed when water runs over limestone for long periods of time. A large cave on the right of the canyon was formed in a karstic* process, indicating that water ate away at the rock.

Ein Avdat's soil and water are slightly saline and the canyon's plants have accommodated to salty conditions. The saltbush has adapted especially well; tiny hairs on its leaves absorb the salt and then fall off, allowing the plant to survive. Salt colors this green plant with a silver sheen. Saltbush leaves are tasty and we read in Job that they were food for the "haggard and hungry" men who roamed the wastelands. "In the brush they gathered salt herbs, and their food was the root of the broom tree" (Job 30:4), and indeed saltbush is still an important edible plant for both people and animals.

Near the saltbush plants in the riverbed look for dens belonging to fat sand rats. These rodents apparently have very high blood sugar levels and eat saltbush to balance their metabolism. Fat sand rats have four teeth—two upper and two lower. If they don't wear them down by constant nibbling, the teeth continue to grow—and grow, and grow. The bottom ones eventually extend upward and can enter the brain, killing the rat.

Because the sand rat is so chunky scientists added the adjective "fat" to its name. It weighs about 165 grams and its fur is the same color as the ground where it spends its time. The fat sand rat's den is interesting, for it contains a variety of rooms, sometimes built in stories! Its enemies are mammals, snakes and birds of prey.

About five minutes into the riverbed, you will see to your right what looks like a natural amphitheater: rows of limestone with layers of dark flint. Because it is so hard, flint helps slow the erosion of the limestone and

Ein Avdat.

128

Ein Avdat National Park

Ein Avdat National Park

provides a striking contrast to the light color of the lime. As you go deeper into the gorge, the walls on both sides seem to grow taller and taller and you may feel you have begun to shrink. The canyon narrows and you hear the sound of water. Any bent-over foliage you see was probably damaged in winter floods.

Ibex often roam the canyon. They have grown quite used to people invading their territory and you can watch them clamber along the sides of the cliff. Their muscular bodies and short legs are well adapted to life in the hills. The ibex has a special groove in its hoof which makes cliff-climbing easy; mountain climbing shoes are designed according to the ibex hoof.

Fabulous rock steps and structures have been carved by erosive elements, particularly water which wore down the rock. On the cliffs to your right you can see where water trickles through the cracks, forming travertine and making it easy for foliage to grow. Black stripes along the cliff sides and on the steps hewn by the water look painted but are really a very thin layer of flint.

Cross the water along a small dam, which ends in a natural pool filled by a waterfall. This pool is the main attraction at Ein Avdat and is worth a stop. It was built by Kibbutz Sde Boker in 1955 so that despite their desert habitat they would have a water hole for swimming. Today the kibbutz has its own modern swimming pool.

Walk back across the dam. If you are ending the hike at this point, go back to your car. Otherwise, climb the stairs on the left, which will bring you to the top of the waterfall. Keep to the path, and be careful not to dislodge stones. In the past hikers below have been injured by falling rocks.

Above the water are crags full of little niches which make the cliffs resemble giant dovecotes. And, indeed, rock doves and pale crag martins build homes here, above the water. Other birds inhabit the canyon as well: predators like the griffon, Egyptian vulture and buzzard, which enjoy the excellent protection afforded by the cliffs. The impressive Egyptian vulture was a symbol in Egyptian hieroglyphics. When it spreads its wings in flight, you will be startled by the contrast between its light-colored body and head and the dark edges of its wings.

At the top of the waterfall you see even more flowing water. Keep on climbing, to the right of a grove of Euphrates poplar trees. Found across Asia and all the way to northwest Africa, this type of tree has taken root in only four Negev locations—yet another indication of a once wetter and colder climate in Ein Avdat. Euphrates poplar are especially beautiful in autumn, when they turn yellow before shedding their leaves.

For a lovely side trip, leave the path and continue along the left side of the pool, following the gorge as far as you can, then return to the grove.

130

Ein Avdat National Park

Savor its pastoral scenery, then continue along the path up its stairs and ladders. The walk to the top is about 20 minutes from the grove, steep but not difficult. Along the left side of the cliff are caves that were used by Christian hermits in the Byzantine* period.

The idea of monks living a life of prayer and contemplation far from civilization began in Egypt and Syria in the fourth century, and a few decades later the movement spread to this area. Often, the holy men lived in small communities removed from the vices of the city. Others chose to be totally alone in more remote desert spots. The ascetics who lived in this gorge were from the Nabatean-Byzantine city of AVDAT, only a few kilometers away by foot.

Some of the soft limestone cliffs contain caves, prepared by the monks who cut into the stone. In several are small rooms and shelves for personal belongings. Inscriptions carved in the walls include prayers for salvation to Jesus and Theodore. Theodore was the patron saint of Avdat and one of the churches there is named in his memory. A branch of the trail leads to several of the caves.

At the end of this walk you come to the upper parking lot, bathrooms, a Bedouin tent (and hopefully a second car). Continue straight along the side of the riverbed for about five minutes, to an observation point. The path is marked with the orange and blue colors that signify the Israel Trail.*

As well as a spectacular panorama, you will be able to observe an interesting geological phenomena. Notice how the riverbed turns sharply to the right: this is where one riverbed "captured" another. Millions of years ago Wadi Habesor flowed on a northern course to the Mediterranean. Later, the Syrian-African rift* developed a new river, Wadi Tzin, and its waters began to cut in the rock towards the west. Here, at the T-junction in front of you, Wadi Tzin broke into Wadi Habesor and changed its course 90 degrees, so that it flowed straight to the Dead Sea.

It is possible to cover all of Ein Avdat even if you have only one car. This option adds an hour and a half to your hike and is too hot to take in summer. It is suitable for older children and fairly good walkers.

To take this outing, park in the lower parking lot. Then follow the trail through Ein Avdat and climb all the way to the top. On your immediate right when you get there, just below the upper parking lot, are remains of a Roman fortress. With the canyon below you to the right and the fortress on your left, begin the walk back to your car. The trail you are taking is not marked and is not much of a path but it is easy to follow for you walk on a plateau above the canyon. Take advantage of the many places where you can get a good look at the gorge below, but watch your step when you do so!

Ein Avdat National Park

After about half an hour of walking, you will clearly see the lower parking lot below. About 100 meters past the lot, the plateau above the cliff begins to descend. At the point where shiny white limestone is exposed in the rocks to your left, look right to see a gully leading to the park. Natural rock steps on your right take you in the correct direction and you should look for the easiest way to climb down the cliff—a bit to the left of the gully as you descend.

If you only have a short time, or if you want to enjoy the scenery without walking, view Ein Avdat from an overlook at the upper parking lot. The entrance is about seven kilometers south of Midreshet Sde Boker on Highway 40. You will immediately come face to face with the stupendous gorge described above.

Vital Information

Sun. to Thurs. & Sat. 8:00–17:00; Fri. & holiday eves 8:00–14:00. From Oct. to March the site closes one hour earlier. Entrance to the national park is up to an hour before closing time.

The entrance fee at the lower parking lot includes the upper overlook as well.

Tel.: 07-555684.

Bathrooms and water are available at both the upper and lower parking lots.

Sde Boker Field School

The Society for the Protection of Nature in Israel's Sde Boker Field Study Center is the last word in inexpensive comfort. The field study center also boasts a snake house and Bedouin exhibit, mainly open to groups taking part in SPNI vacations. Visiting individuals and families are welcome to participate when the groups tour these special attractions: ask about the possibility when you register for your room. Guided tours are generally in Hebrew.

The Snake House

Most snakes (and the rodents at Sde Boker's reptile house) are active at night. During the day they hide away in underground burrows or expertly camouflage themselves, and it is hard to spot them while you hike. At Sde Boker you have the opportunity to examine an extensive collection of reptiles up close and to learn how they live.

Of the world's 2,500 species of snake, 38 are found in Israel. Eight of them are venomous; six of these eight poisonous snakes inhabit the Negev.

Snakes can be divided into three categories according to how they kill their prey. There are venomous ones, semi-poisonous snakes and those which kill without venom. Non-poisonous snakes have teeth which curve inward and have no poison. These snakes sometimes coil around their victims and squeeze them to death. They may bite their prey on its windpipe and hold on until it suffocates, or simply squash their unfortunate victims with their weight.

Venomous snakes, on the other hand, have two large fangs which they fold into their mouths when not in use. When they sink these fangs into a victim, venom rushes through hollow grooves in their teeth and sends the prey a powerful injection.

Semi-poisonous snakes can also deliver a fatal bite, but they have to work harder than their more venal brothers. Because their teeth are smaller and set far back inside their mouths, semi-venomous snakes must bite extra deeply and wait for several minutes until their poison drips its way from these back fangs into the victim's body.

Snakes are active only 10 percent of the day, for besides mating once a year they do little but hunt for food one a week, then eat and digest their prey. The rest of the time they sleep. Unlike humans, who have a stable body temperature, snakes (and other reptiles) must rely on external factors to warm themselves enough so that they gather the strength to function.

133

Sde Boker Field School

Called cold-blooded because they need to sit in the sun or on a hot rock to raise their body temperature, reptiles cool off when they get too hot by lying in the shade or slithering through water.

People usually laugh when nature guides demonstrate how a snake's tongue darts in and out of its mouth. But to a snake this is no laughing matter. The snake has very poor eyesight; its eyes are covered with a transparent film, and it lacks both lids and lashes. What it does have is a wonderful sense of smell, and by flicking its sensitive tongue in and out it picks up scent from the ground. That's how it knows when dinner is near.

Next to each cage is a description and photograph of the snake. Because there are stools for the smallest children, they can watch the snakes from just the right vantage point while guides point out some of their characteristics.

The Talmud* relates an occasion when people rushed into Rabbi ben Dosa's house of study and told the learned man that a poisonous snake was on a rampage. The rabbi went to the entrance of the snake's hole and blocked it with his foot. The snake bit him and died. Rabbi ben Dosa carried the snake back to the house and study and exclaimed, "it is not the snake that kills, but sin!" The story concludes with the expression "Woe to the person bit by a viper, and woe to a viper which bites Rabbi ben Dosa."

In contrast to similar-looking snakes in northern Israel, black Negev snakes can be highly dangerous. The black desert cobra puts on a show, making a whooshing noise and puffing up quite impressively, a bluff when it senses danger. Its dark color lets it roam freely at night, both outdoors and within the dens and burrows of potential prey.

The guide may take out a slender whip snake. Guests are invited to hold and pet the snake, and to enjoy the feel of twisting it around in their hands.

Stuffed mammals in the collection include the lynx, hedgehog, ibex, wolf and porcupine. From the window display it is easy to examine the muscular legs of the ibex. These enable him to skip up mountains and walk along the cliffs.

Vultures are also represented in the stuffed wildlife collection. They have big strong beaks, so tough they can even bite through a camel's leathery skin. But vultures have to stick their heads way inside a carcass to get at its meat, and if they had feathers on their necks this would be uncomfortable, to say the least. So vultures have "lost" their feathers and sport bare necks. Called *nesharim*, in Hebrew, their name comes from the Hebrew word *nashru* or dropped off.

Sde Boker Field School

The Bedouin Exhibit

The delightful Bedouin collection at Sde Boker was contributed by the Netzer family of Kibbutz Ramat Yohanan. The donation was made in memory of son Yitzhak, killed during his army service.

Take off your shoes before entering. Observe the traditional tent, divided into male and female sections. On each side a large photo depicts daily life for the relevant sex, and on display are the tools and utensils typically used by each gender. Guests at a Bedouin encampment are offered tea called *shai jabel*. It has to be brewed until it is "so red you can't see a mountain through it."

Tea you may drink until your thirst is quenched; coffee is valuable and not given as freely. You get three glasses: one for *kef* (enjoyment); one for *def* (guests); and one for *sef* (sword, or defense). Bedouin men begin the coffee-making process whenever a new guest appears in the tent or when they expect company. Hosts offer only a third of a cup of coffee to each guest; if the cup is full it signifies that they have had their fill of you and your presence is unwanted. Cups are refilled twice.

The coffee ceremony takes a long time. First, coffee beans are roasted. Then they are poured into the mortar and pounded with a stick, making beautiful music. When the beans are thin, they are placed in a special kettle called a *bakrash* and set on the fire to brew.

In the women's section of the tent a huge pot of rice is generally on the fire. This is where the ladies take care of the children and weave rugs and tents. Your guide will probably demonstrate weaving techniques.

Exhibits on the other side of the little museum feature agricultural tools, musical instruments and the different uses of Bedouin livestock. Especially interesting are photographs of the transition made by Bedouin Negev from tent to cabin to villa.

Avdat National Park

The ancient city of Avdat now has an exciting new look. Not only has much of this magnificent Nabatean* center been restored, but the site was recently embellished with playful, humoresque scenes. "Nabatean caravans" are visible from as far away as the main road between Sde Boker and Mitzpe Ramon, and provide travelers with a hint of the excitement in store at Avdat National Park.

Founded in the fourth century B.C.E. as a small Nabatean inn, Avdat's history revolves around cycles of prosperity and destruction. In the beginning, Avdat's inhabitants offered services to caravans traveling along the trade routes. Avdat thrived and expanded until the year 103 B.C.E., when Alexander Jannaeus (Yannai), King of Israel, conquered Gaza and disrupted the spice trade. Avdat was abandoned.

Years later, the city was rebuilt by Nabatean King Avdat II. During his reign (30 to 9 B.C.E.), the Nabateans began the transformation from traders to farmers. Avdat, however, was soon to be destroyed again—this time by non-Nabatean Arab tribes in the first or second century C.E.

The Nabatean population, with its distinct architectural style and religion, came under direct Roman rule in the year 106. A few centuries later, now controlled by the Byzantine* Empire, the people of Avdat accepted Christianity and the city reached its peak of size and prosperity. During your visit here, you will see early Nabatean, Roman and Byzantine remains and witness how the locals adapted to vast changes in religion and culture. Avdat was finally deserted during the Moslem conquest in 636. Modern excavations and restoration began in 1958 and creative frills were added in the 1990's.

Begin by driving to the upper parking lot next to the camel caravan, stopping along the road at the mausoleum. This is a large stone tomb which you reach by walking along a dirt path. As you enter the burial cave note the design cut into its lintel. It depicts the sun and the moon, objects of worship in ancient times.

The room may give you an eerie feeling, for the walls are lined with horizontally cut burial niches similar to beds. This third century mausoleum may be the burial site of King Avdat II, who was revered as a god.

From the burial cave, return to the car and park in the upper lot. Begin your tour of the city with a Roman tower from the third century. Although there was a Roman camp at Avdat and the observation tower was built dur-

Picturesque view below ancient Avdat.

Avdat National Park

Avdat National Park

ing the Roman period, Avdat at this time was inhabited by a mixed Roman-Nabatean population and it isn't clear who designed and constructed the tower and the city. Steps probably led to a second story, for the tower was 12 meters high.

Here, as in other Avdat structures, you will find that the stones which face the street are nicely hewn, while the inside walls, covered with thick plaster, are not. White plaster on the upper level dates from the Byzantine period, whereas the colored plaster with geometric designs is from an earlier era. Look for pieces of wood in some of the cracks: the Nabateans were terrified of earthquakes and hoped this would make the walls more elastic. You are viewing wood that is over 1,700 years old!

Avdat's original tower was preserved up to the roof. From here you have a wonderful view of the acropolis, the high portion of the city. Important both for military and religious reasons, it was the site of the Nabatean temple to their pagan god, the place where the Romans built a fortress and the Byzantines their churches.

After Avdat became part of the Roman Empire, the Nabateans incorporated the beliefs of their new rulers into their own religion. Some inscriptions refer to Zeus/Avdat, the Nabatean king who was later worshipped as Zeus (the Greek-Roman god) as well.

Follow the arrows and stroll through the city's main street, where the walls have been only slightly reconstructed. Like other Nabatean cities, Avdat was designed to collect every drop of water. Rain accumulating in the stone-paved streets flowed along an elaborate drainage system, to be stored in family cisterns or a central cistern.

The structure with graceful arches may have been a Nabatean stable, as there is a horse trough nearby. Modern-day camels—made of metal—give the stables a light touch.

Now the arrows lead you to a beautiful winepress. Around the press itself are several compartments. Each farmer would place his grapes in baskets in the "waiting room" until it was his turn to pour them into the vat and tread on them to extract the grape juice that became wine. The juice drained through a hole into a vat below. Remaining pits and peels were squeezed with the screw press to create other products: fertilizer out of the peels and dye from the pits. Two ceramic jugs were found here—perhaps buyers tasted the wine before they purchased it.

So far, five wine vats have been uncovered in Avdat, and more have been found in other Nabatean cities. The hot desert sun was excellent for ripening the grapes and the juice was stored in underground caves in controlled, cool temperatures. Since wine is prohibited to Moslems,

Avdat National Park

Nabatean wine manufacture apparently ceased after the Moslem conquest of Israel.

Enter the acropolis, which contained both a fortress surrounded by a wall and an area of worship. The fort had its own system of collecting and stockpiling rainwater—in an enormous cistern with a capacity of some 200 cubic meters. Saltpeter for curing meat was found in a natural cave within the fortress. There was also a military base whose remains can be seen below. None of these defensive measures, however, was sufficient to protect Avdat during the Moslem conquest. Its churches were torched and the city deserted.

Begin with the fortress, which included a huge courtyard. An enormous underground cistern is carved out of stone. A pillar holds up the ceiling of the cistern and you can see plaster inside, which sealed in the water.

Guards stood watch in nine rooms along the wall. Through several of its openings you have a picturesque view of the hills below.

Move into the church precinct, the square between the northern and southern churches. Probably this was a busy plaza, full of shoppers and merchants.

Avdat has two large Byzantine churches standing in close proximity. The southern church is named after the martyred Saint Theodore and there is a model to help you visualize this and other period houses of prayer. Note particularly the proportions that you see in the model. What remains standing on the grounds today are columns about half the height they were during the Byzantine era. Next to one of the pillars is a round decorative stone, the "preaching stone" from which church fathers delivered their sermons. On each side of the apse is a separate room. One was a dressing room; in the other priests prepared the bread and wine.

The bones of holy fathers are considered sacrosanct and were buried inside the church. Look for the marble covers which top graves containing bones.

There were enough believers in Avdat to support two separate churches. As you walk towards the northern church, look for round holes in the ground. To level the ground of the acropolis the Nabateans drilled holes, stuck wooden beams inside them, and poured water on top. The wet wood expanded and cracked the rocky ground, creating blocks of stone which were removed for use in construction. Then the ground was smoothed down.

Before entering the northern church stop at a wonderfully preserved gate, which was once part of a Nabatean temple. The stone altar from this temple, where animals were sacrificed, has remained. Blood would drip

139

Avdat National Park

from the altar into the carved basin at the end: look for tiny canals on the rock.

The Nabatean temple wall was incorporated into the northern church. The inscription on the lintel is from 268 C.E. (162 of the Nabatean year, which began from the Roman conquest in 106 C.E.).

It is likely that the region's bishop officiated in the northern church. Three stairs in the apse were the base of a special chair for the bishop. The priests sat in a semicircle behind him.

Excavators found a marble relic box shaped like a sarcophagus on the site. There was a small hole in its cover through which oil could be poured over the relics, and then collected in bottles, or with cloth, for worshippers to take home. Most Byzantine churches had holy relics related to the life of Jesus or the saints. Often these were buried in the church in a coffin-shaped box or sarcophagus. These relics added to the importance of the church as did the graves of priests, monks and martyrs buried within its confines. Worshippers and pilgrims would descend to the room where the relics were kept.

Because Byzantine churches were built to impress the pagans and help convince them to convert, great sums of money were invested to create splendid buildings. Exquisite marble and cedars of Lebanon, unavailable in

Avdat's churches were built on the acropolis.

Avdat National Park

Israel and brought from afar, adorned the churches. Inside the northern church you will see another atrium, a basilica-style hall and pillars. Here, decorative pieces of stone holding up the roof's wooden beams still remain. Wander through this splendid house of worship and examine the inscriptions and decorations. Inside one of the side rooms is a gorgeous window with beautiful frames, perhaps the place where holy articles were stored.

Find the baptismal font. After the pagan Nabateans came under Roman influence during the Common Era, they converted to Christianity. Here you see a large marble-covered cross, a baptismal font for adults, and a smaller one with marble-coated lining for babies.

Next to the baptismal fonts is a balcony from which you can see Avdat's residential area on the slopes below. Across from you is Ramalia, and you can also view the road from SDE BOKER and MITZPE RAMON, leading to EILAT.

As you will see, much of the city of Avdat has not yet been excavated. Look for the dirt outline of a perfect square, 100 by 100 meters with clear rows dividing the square. This was the "cavalry base" where Nabatean soldiers and their camels were stationed. In the late Roman period this camp was dismantled and its stones used to build the Roman fortress above.

Descend stairs that take you to the lower city, but remember you will have to come back up to your car. Better still, send a volunteer to bring your car to the middle parking lot, and have him meet you at the living area.

Look around as you walk down the hill. Four hundred caves have been discovered on this slope, some of them residential and others used for burial. It is estimated that several thousand people once lived in the city. Avdat was very crowded and the caves were terraced up and down about eight floors, so that space could be used efficiently. People first dug their caves, then the better-off added porches in front.

A brown arrow leads you left to a cave entrance. Walk through, taking note of the cave itself and the storerooms, until you reach the more interesting portion of the site. If you find the correct spot a light turns on and metal figurines demonstrate the room's use as a storehouse. Further inside, in the Yekev ("wine") Cave, you will see exactly how wine was stored. Nabateans crawled inside through tiny openings carrying jars brought directly from the Avdat winepress, and left them here for the wine to ferment.

Gracing the entrance is the head of a bull. Rings in the ceiling were clearly used for hanging food—dried fruit, for example—which rodents couldn't reach. One of these rings is decorated with a cross. The bull was a symbol of Zeus whereas the crosses are obviously Christian. Perhaps this

Avdat National Park

combination illustrates, again, that even after the Nabateans accepted Christianity their earlier beliefs remained.

Outside again, follow the arrows into another house, with an unusually large outer porch. You will see a trough and a drainpipe in the yard, then view rooms that served as kitchens and living rooms. Walk down a few steps to your car.

A splendid bathhouse, located next to the gas station at the bottom of the hill, is currently being restored. It wasn't easy to build a bathhouse in the middle of the desert; this one required a well over 60 meters deep, whose water was brackish and could not be used for drinking or agriculture. Bathers who frequented the bathhouse passed through a series of pools whose waters ranged from cold to tepid. Bathers ended their dips in the steam room and hot bath.

Vital Information

Sun. to Thurs. & Sat. 8:00–17:00; Fri. & holiday eves 8:00–15:00. From Oct. to March the site closes one hour earlier. The entrance fee includes a pamphlet.

Tel.: 07–550954

At the entrance are a gas station, restaurant and bathrooms. There are no bathrooms in the upper city.

Mamshit National Park

Unlike Israel's five other Nabatean* cities, Mamshit was situated well away from the famous SPICE TRAIL. Despite its seemingly out-of-the-way location, however, its inhabitants were extraordinarily wealthy. One house at Mamshit was over 1,500 square meters in size—and even the poorest family could boast a dwelling of at least 500 meters. Some people were so rich they apparently "forgot" where they hid their money: archaeologists found an incredible hoard of over 10,500 silver coins in one of the homes!

The city may have been off the Spice Trail, but the people of Mamshit dealt in commerce just like their fellow Nabateans. Mamshit was an important crossroads along trade routes leading towards the Dead Sea and the Arava. It was too hot to live in the Dead Sea Valley and no cooler in the Arava, so Nabatean merchants built their homes at a comfortable location several hundred meters above sea level. Nearby Dimona, seven kilometers to the west, occasionally shines with snow in winter.

Today Mamshit is a well-organized national park, easily accessible from Highway 25. A path within the once-booming city leads through churches, a bathhouse and exquisite villas decorated with mosaics and frescos.

Before you enter the city walls, not far from the entrance to the park, look right to see the stone remains of an ancient inn where camels and their drivers once spent the night. Mamshit and other cities profited from tourists, but preferred to have them, and their animals, outside of the city.

Camels drink enormous quantities of water and there are very few water sources around Mamshit. The Nabateans solved this problem by building dams along the adjacent riverbed: one reservoir held some 10,000 cubic meters of water! The caravansary and a Roman-style bath house are clear evidence that the people of Mamshit were able to provide abundant supplies of water in the desert.

You will notice both in the gate and throughout the city modern metal and wooden lintels. According to an international agreement, archaeologists may reconstruct ancient sites only when they are absolutely certain as to their original appearance. Mamshit was apparently destroyed during the Moslem conquest in the seventh century and abandoned for the next 1,300 years; moreover the Ottoman Turks used stones from the city to construct modern Beer Sheva. Therefore no one really knows what

143

Mamshit National Park

Mamshit looked like and archaeologists used iron and wood, instead of stone, to remind us that this reconstruction is only an educated guess.

Enter Mamshit through the gate in the city walls, intended not for defense but merely to separate inhabitants from the nomads who wandered around outside. Look closely at the ground to see where ancient wheeled vehicles cut grooves in the rock.

In another break from the traditional pattern, Mamshit began with a scattering of lavish houses, large villas built by rich traders. Stables within some of the houses had exactly the same function as the two-car garages of today. Floors were covered with wooden panels brought from afar, indicating that trade was well developed. Yet unlike other Nabatean cities, which grew ever more wealthy, Mamshit went from riches to rags.

Follow the arrows leading to the palace. A cistern carved into the road in front of the palace remains from the original Nabatean city. Along the houses are drainage canals, meant to collect every possible drop of rainwater from rooftops and streets for storage in reservoirs throughout Mamshit.

As you explore the palace, look for a piece of the original wood on the threshold of one of the rooms, an indication that the climate here is extremely dry (if it were humid, the wood would have rotted and disintegrated). Niches in walls here and throughout the city may have held Nabatean deities.

Mamshit's houses were one to two stories tall, and each contained a side tower with staircase unique to Nabatean architecture. You can climb many of the staircase towers, but the tower with the best view belongs to the large building which probably housed the local governor, located just behind the palace. From the top of this building you get a panoramic look at Mamshit and can see how it was spread out along the hills. When you descend, examine the walls inside. One of them is covered with the original Nabatean plaster.

Now stop in at one of Mamshit's two churches. When residents converted to Christianity in the fourth century, they had to find room for churches in a city that was already bursting at the seams. There were no pagan temples to transform into churches, and one inhabitant had to tear down part of his home to make room for this Christian house of worship. Consequently the entrance does not face due west, as is common in Byzantine churches.

It took a lot of money to create an elegant house of worship and mosaic floors are very rare in the Negev churches. Yet this church, named for a donor called Nilus, included a mosaic floor decorated with representations of birds, baskets of fruit and geometric designs. Unfortunately the floor was

Mamshit National Park

recently destroyed by vandals; it is currently being repaired by Italian experts. Enormous wooden beams were imported from other countries, as was the decorative Italian marble.

Two rooms flanked the apse. In one priests prepared the wafers; in the other they donned their vestments.

Continue along the wall, and peek over the side for a view of the magnificent riverbed that lay below the ancient city. Because the riverbed passes through a sandy area, the industrious Nabateans periodically cleaned out the reservoirs. More recently, the British built a dam for local Bedouin, based on the Nabatean-Roman design. But since they didn't maintain the pool, it clogged with sand and is no longer in use. Palm trees grow nearby, evidence that the water table is close to the surface.

Now enter the second house of prayer, called the Church of Saints and Martyrs. In the rubble, archaeologists found two containers filled with the bones of saints. Worshippers poured oil into the box through a small hole.

To make room for this church, Mamshit residents filled in part of the riverbed. Again, topographical considerations rendered it impossible for the entrance to face the west. Notice the unusual baptistery,* probably used at first for converts. Shaped like a cross, it had a deep section for adults and a smaller recess on the side for infants.

Mamshit's residents were extraordinarily wealthy.

Mamshit National Park

Part of the marble partition in front of the apse has remained as it was for almost 2,000 years. Crosses were commonly carved into church floors but, in 427, church leaders decided to forbid this practice. Apparently this church was built before the ruling. We don't know for certain, however, as not all communities abided by the new law.

A large, modern edifice on a hill sticks out like a sore thumb. Once a British police station, it is currently being transformed into a "Nabatean" restaurant. Ironically, the ancient Nabatean kitchen which lay underneath was destroyed during construction.

Now stroll over to Mamshit's largest private dwelling. Although the building is not marked from the outside, as you go in you see a sign that reads "the house of the frescos." This is where Mamshit's most exciting finds were made, among them an enormous hoard of Roman coins from the third century, hidden beneath a stairwell. In one of the rooms you will see a pair of roundish Nabatean capitals, one with a human face and the other with the face of a bull. And behind a locked door on an inaccessible wall (you have to look through iron bars) is an ornamental fresco depicting mythological and sometimes erotic scenes.

Inside the house is a large stable with troughs. Perhaps horses were so expensive that people preferred to keep them safely in their homes!

Private indoor plumbing was rare in Israel at this period and one unique aspect of this house is a bathroom and changing room supplied with water from a special pool. In a Talmudic* source which discusses the meaning of finding something "good," some rabbis suggested that the "good" discovery is a nice house while others contended it means a good wife. But the rabbis who wrote the dissertation concluded otherwise. They decided it meant having a bathroom close to your house.

You will see market stalls with thatched roofs. A few archaeologists suggest that these were actually the small rooms of a monastery.

As you exit the city look for a large Roman bath, and the pool where its water was stored. The pool was fed by water collected in the city and covered to prevent evaporation.

Outside Mamshit and not yet open to the public is another unusual find: a Nabatean cemetery whose graves were built in the shape of underground rooms. Archaeologists found gold jewelry in the graves. Like the Romans, the Nabateans would put a coin in the mouth of the deceased as payment to Charon, the guardian of hell.

Vital Information

Sun. to Thurs. & Sat. 8:00–17:00; Fri. & holiday eves 8:00–14:00. From Oct. to March the site closes one hour earlier. Entrance fee. Tel.: 07–556478.

146

Route No. 9: Sinai Border Scenic Drive

Route No. 9
Sinai Border Scenic Drive

*Route No. 9 includes a visit to the Nitzana Border Crossing,
a scenic drive, two ancient Nabatean* cities, and
several charming picnic sites in the desert.*

In 1994 rain fell so heavily in Israel's south that during one
24-hour period 90 millimeters flooded the northern Negev. Water pelting
onto Revivim Bridge gushed atop the main highway and the road collapsed.
A waterfall running from the former road dashed to the riverbed below. As
a result almost a dozen supporting arches from a bridge built during the
Ottoman empire—previously completely covered with debris—were
exposed to view.

Travelers driving from Beer Sheva south on Highway 40 can now observe
these newly-revealed arches. The supports are part of a thoroughly
delightful route from Beer Sheva to Israel's border with Egypt at Nitzana,
and finally to Mitzpe Ramon. Plan to spend an entire day on this route.

Exit Beer Sheva going south on Highway 40. If you can't find a sign for the
highway, make sure you are on the Eilat Road (*Derech Eilat*). Look left to
see a Turkish-built bridge; you will be following Turkish-built embankments
and bridges all the way to the Israeli border.

Before World War I the Turks ruled what is now Israel, and Egypt was a
British protectorate. On the eve of the war, both sides prepared for the
battle in Sinai and the Negev. The Turks hoped to transport military
equipment and personnel to Sinai by rail, so that they could attack the
British along the Suez Canal. Because the Turkish line reached only to
Nablus, it was quickly extended all the way to Nitzana.

But the Turkish train never reached Suez City, for the British conquered
Sinai and halted its construction. Thus the Turkish railroad operated only
until 1917, stopping after the British conquest of the Negev. While the tracks
are desolate today, had they been completed the Turks may have taken the
Suez Canal and drastically altered the outcome of World War I.

Every time the railroad crossed a river, the Turks built a bridge. The
bridge spanning Wadi Revivim, to your right immediately south of Mashabim Junction, sported 23 supporting arches. Only three were visible until
the immense floods of 1994, after which 11 more arches were exposed.

147

Route No. 9: Sinai Border Scenic Drive

Pass the Ramat Negev Information Center. Open mainly on Saturdays and Jewish holidays, it was built by the Jewish National Fund (JNF). Even if it is closed take advantage of a snack bar, gas station and bathrooms.

At Telalim Junction continue straight onto Road 211 towards Nitzana. Drive four kilometers to a sign that reads "French Commando View Point." Turn right, then continue left on a dirt road for about 200 meters and park. You have reached Atmille Hill.

Atmille was a well-fortified Egyptian outpost in the Negev. On December 26, 1948, as part of the Horev Campaign to liberate the Negev, Battalion Seven of the Negev Brigade attacked and conquered the outpost. Jewish volunteers from abroad who came to fight for Israel in 1948 were under the command of a Frenchman, Teddy Eitan. Eitan had been a French commando in Algeria and the group of volunteers attached to the Negev Brigade became known as the French commandos.

An Egyptian counterattack on the outpost forced the French commandos to retreat. The wounded were left under one of the railroad's little water-overflow bridges. At dawn, when Israeli soldiers recaptured the outpost, they discovered that Egyptian troops had murdered all of the wounded during the night.

Now walk up the steps to Atmille Hill, today a very special memorial. Positions rimmed with sandbags still lie on the top. Every few meters, a marker bearing the name of a fallen soldier breaks the sandy monotony of the desert. Even if you can't read their names and countries of origin you will be saddened by the soldiers' youth. At the end of the memorial is a circular observation point, with maps and a Hebrew illustration of the battles fought at this site.

The same turnoff you took to reach Atmille Hill leads to an experimental farm where scientists are conducting research on an enormous body of underground water. The problem is that the water contains 2,300 milligrams of salt per liter, over four times the quantity fit for agricultural use. The experimental farm is run by Yoel de Malach, one of the original members of Kibbutz Revivim (see MITZPE REVIVIM).

About 23 kilometers past Telalim Junction, you will see a green sign on your right and an orange sign pointing left to Hurvot SHIVTA. It is eight kilometers to the ancient Nabatean city.

Visit Shivta, then return to Highway 211 and continue driving southwest. Past the turnoff for Ketziot you will see the tiny village of Kmehin ("truffles") to your right. Make a mental note of the turnoff to Nitzana on your left, then continue straight ahead. A few dozen meters further is a small JNF picnic area with a sign that reads "afforestation with brackish water." It has picnic tables, lovely wildflowers, eucalyptus trees and Washingtonian palms.

148

Route No. 9: Sinai Border Scenic Drive

    Throughout the Negev, and even on the hottest summer days, you will see Thai workers whose faces are covered by stocking caps. We were told that Thais keep their faces covered to prevent a suntan, for in Thailand brown faces are the mark of poor people who must work in the fields.

    You are about to visit a crossing on Israel's frontier with Egypt. The border itself was determined in 1906, when the Turkish Empire was crumbling and Britain was a rising star. At the time the Turks ruled the land of Israel, including half the Sinai Peninsula, and England controlled Egypt.

    Britain's main concern was to protect the Suez Canal and she considered the Sinai an important part of its defense. After some clashes with Turkish forces England rushed warships to the area and threatened war if the Turks did not comply with British demands for more territory. Turkey capitulated and it was agreed the border would be a straight line stretching from Taba to Rafiah. Having conducted geological surveys in Sinai, the British knew where its water sources were located. Thus, when a joint Turkish-British team set off to mark the border, the British fooled the Turks and made a few bends in the "straight line" that included these vital sources. The British joked that the bumps in the line were the fingers of Winston Churchill, holding the ruler when he drew the line on the map.

    Ninety border stones were put up to mark the 1906 border, which

A 3,000 year old Israelite cistern.

Route No. 9: Sinai Border Scenic Drive

stretched from the Mediterranean to the Gulf of Eilat. In 1949 this became the cease-fire line between Israel and Egypt; during the Sinai Campaign* of 1956, Israel conquered Sinai and the border disappeared—until the following year when international pressure returned the peninsula to Egypt. From that time on, the border was guarded by United Nations forces.

Prior to the Six Day War,* President Nasser of Egypt demanded that the U.N. forces evacuate Sinai. They left immediately and were replaced by the Egyptian army in May, 1967. During the Six Day War, which broke out on June 5, Israel took the Sinai and the old border was forgotten.

According to the 1979 peace agreement between Israel and Egypt, the old Turkish-British border, bumps and all, was restored. A joint team of experts from both countries worked on determining the old line. This time disagreement between the two countries concerned the very last marker. Where, exactly, did the border end in Taba? When the issue reached international arbitration, the authorities ruled in Egypt's favor.

Continue on Road 211 to the terminal. There are four places to cross into Egypt: Taba is for tourists; Netafim services the armed forces; Rafiah—and Nitzana, which you have reached—are designed for commercial use. You will probably see Egyptian trucks unloading goods into Israeli trucks and returning to Egypt, and vice versa. On your left is a portion of Peace Forest, a JNF project with a different flavor. The JNF hopes these trees will one day be part of a green stretch continued by the Egyptians well into Sinai. These particular trees are irrigated with the saline water discovered in the underground reservoir mentioned previously.

The Society for the Preservation of Nature chose this site to celebrate its 40th anniversary in 1994. The theme of the international gathering was "nature has no boundaries," and the guest of honor was the Dalai Lama—Tibet's spiritual leader and winner of the Nobel Peace Prize.

Nitzana is an opening into the Sinai Peninsula, a valley through which it is easy to enter or leave Israel. Indeed, three times in recent years this was the point where Israeli forces broke into Sinai: in the War of Independence,* the Sinai Campaign and the Six Day War.

Israel's western border with Egypt includes a superb scenic route between Nitzana and Mount Harif. The border today is calm and the main security problem is smugglers. The road opens an hour after dawn and closes an hour before dark; your drive will take about an hour.

First follow a little side trip to Tel Nitzana, Be'erotayim-Ezuz and a Turkish railroad embankment. Finally, connect up with the prettiest portion of the border route and continue south to Mount Harif.

Go back to the intersection leading to Nitzana (and Be'erotayim Park). Pass Nitzana Youth Village, founded in 1987 by left wing politician Luba

150

Route No. 9: Sinai Border Scenic Drive

Eliav to realize his concept of modern Zionism. The village hosts youngsters whose parents have remained abroad—among them young Russians and Ethiopians. During their stay at the village boys and girls carry out reclamation projects of different sorts, learning to irrigate with both fresh and saline water.

Continue until you reach Tel Nitzana, two kilometers past the intersection—look for it on a hill to your left. You turn towards it at a large white Hebrew sign. The bumpy, rocky path barely seems to be a road, but it really does lead to the ancient site! In winter, wildflowers add charm and color to the route.

Although the Tel Nitzana region seems totally wild and untouched, in Byzantine* times it was a major tourist center. Christian pilgrims on their way to Mount Sinai and travelers from Egypt to the Holy Land stopped off at Nitzana, one of six Nabatean cities in the Negev.

This is the only site in the Negev where archaeologists have found a large number of papyri, well preserved by the dry desert air. The documents include literary and theological sources, such as a Greek dictionary to Virgil's Aeneid, parts of the Gospel and 195 non-literary documents covering many aspects of everyday life: financial contracts, divorce, property, military matters and taxes.

Like most of the other Nabatean cities, Nitzana was established along the SPICE TRAIL around the second century B.C.E. At its peak in the sixth century C.E. it contained 116 homes and about 1,500 people. The church leaders ran the city's religious and secular life from the acropolis which overlooked the city, and the riverbeds below provided water for agriculture.

Following the Moslem conquest and heavy taxes imposed by the Arabs, the town was gradually deserted. The water system fell into disrepair and families apparently packed up one by one and left. By the end of the ninth century this formerly prosperous city was totally abandoned and neglected.

The Egyptian army attacked Israel on two fronts in the War of Independence. The bulk of the army went along the coast towards Tel Aviv, while some troops entered Israel here and continued to Jerusalem (Kibbutz Ramat Rachel). After the war, Nitzana was the meeting place for Israeli and Egyptian officers that supervised the cease-fire agreement. When Israel evacuated Sinai in 1956, the Turkish buildings were blown up to prevent terrorists infiltrating into Israel from using them for cover.

Lock your car and walk up to the tel.* Although this is a national park, Nitzana has no entrance fee and there are no closing hours—or bathrooms. Nevertheless, there are some signs to help you find your way along.

Begin in the main complex, on your left. Standing next to the sign "Fifth Century Byzantine Fortress," look down to the right to see a recently

151

Route No. 9: Sinai Border Scenic Drive

uncovered Byzantine church. You can easily identify the basilica style and the apses by its rows of columns.

Now walk through the fortress gate. The fantastically well-preserved structure you see is from the Turkish period and served as a Turkish-German hospital during World War I. The stones are in secondary use, taken from the fortress. On both sides of you are holes—perhaps cisterns, or rooms where the roofs have collapsed. This fortress was the headquarters of a military unit called the "Most Loyal Theodosians," Byzantine soldiers who patrolled the land by camel and received a regular monthly income from the Byzantine imperial treasury. In an area that often suffered from drought, this regular guaranteed income was an important element in the town's economy. However, when Emperor Justinian I reached an "everlasting peace" in the year 532 he stopped payment to the soldiers. Thus peace brought unemployment, and not prosperity, to Nitzana.

Continue through a perfectly preserved arch to reach the northern church, complete with apses, a central hall and a baptistery.* At one end of the church is a very large cistern, to catch rainfall.

Some of the Nabatean cities had to change the city plan in order to build churches where none had existed before. In Nitzana and AVDAT, however, pagan temples adorned the highest point in the city and it was easy to find a place to build the church: the Nabatean temple was simply destroyed and replaced with a Christian house of prayer.

Although the church housed a monastery, the monks did not spend a life of contemplation away from the city. On the contrary, from papyri found here it is clear that the monks were the city's rulers. Similar to other churches, this one is designed in the basilica style, with a baptistery and a room dedicated to saints.

As you walk back to your car, pass the Turkish-German hospital and continue straight ahead to the ruins of the southern church. Because the walls were taken apart by the Turks very little remains. You can, however, see a portion of the apses. Built outside of the city wall, the church was dedicated to Mary.

Back on the excellent paved road, continue towards Be'erotayim. A strange sight in the Negev desert is a *tukul*, or Ethiopian hut, put up by youngsters at Nitzana Youth Village next to a grove which contains the seven species used to describe Israel in the Bible (Deuteronomy 8:8).

And again, you see the Turkish railroad embankment. You are next to the railroad station built by the Turks in 1916. Locals worked at the train station, which was also a military base for the Turkish-German army. The large edifice was the water tower which serviced the trains.

Route No. 9: Sinai Border Scenic Drive

When the road forks, turn right to the *hursha* or grove. Eventually the road passes through a hill, a crossing carved out by the Turks so they could lay tracks at this spot. Then you emerge, to find you are on top of a Turkish bridge, above the small channel of a river. Drive to the end, then walk back under the embankment to see the bridge's perfect arches.

When you reach the Be'erotayim picnic area, turn in. The trees were planted by (Jewish) graduates of the Mikve Israel Agricultural School, recruited into the Turkish army as gardeners, during World War I. Now the JNF takes care of the beautiful trees and play equipment. Most of the trees here are fast-growing giant tamarisk. You may have to hunt a bit to find the park's excellent bathrooms.

After the War of Independence the Nitzana region was demilitarized, and in 1956 a *Nahal* (army) settlement was established to guard and farm the spot. But conditions here are difficult and the settlement was abandoned twice. Five families re-established it in 1985. Both the Hebrew word *Be'erotayim* and the Arabic *Birim* refer to the regions two main wells.

Return to the road and continue south. Immediately past Be'erotayim, the road becomes extremely uneven and although it is only three kilometers to the excellent paved border road, it may seem a lot longer.

Now begin the scenic route. Turn left, and you will be driving south along the border. Egypt remains due west during the entire drive and her landscape looks so much like Israel's that you wonder why it was divided in the first place. Remember, however, that the border was created so Britain would have Sinai—and its water sources.

The border road on the Egyptian side was completed in 1991 and more or less parallels the Israeli road. But what a difference in style! Israel's byway was designed by the Nature Reserves Authority and blends with the landscape. Thus as you approach the mountains, looking straight ahead, the road seems to disappear. Egypt's route was built on a straight line, and necessitated ramps and other territorial concessions. It is used only by the army and is of little interest to Egyptian tourists. The purpose of the mound on your right is to prevent car thieves from smuggling stolen cars into Egypt.

Look for a sign that says "Aleph Bet 37." On the fence beyond the sign you will see a triangle with a funny top. This is one of many border stones which accompany you on your ride. These were put up after Sinai was transferred to Egypt in 1982 and replaced the Turkish border stones.

Little huts are located at intervals along the road on the Egyptian side of the border. Unlike Israel's troops, who ride in jeeps, the Egyptian soldiers patrol on foot and these are their bases. You will see the Egyptians trekking along as you drive by. Ascend into the hills. Passengers should turn around and look behind them to see where they've been, for the scenery is

153

Route No. 9: Sinai Border Scenic Drive

enchanting. On your left, about two-thirds of the way up the mountain, you will spot a patrol road used by Israel before 1967.

Stop at the Sheluhat Kadesh Barnea Outlook. This delightful project, created by the Jewish National Fund (JNF), includes panoramic stone maps.

One indicates the patrol road, Yair Way, named for Yair Peled. After the War of Independence, in 1948, the Negev became part of Israel—but only in theory, for it was the Bedouin who ruled the desert. They sporadically raided Israeli settlements and even murdered some civilians. In 1953, paratroop patrol commander Yair Peled began paving a jeep road through the Negev. His example attracted others, who joined him in literally digging a road here with their own hands, despite seemingly insurmountable conditions. The dirt path was an important element in patrolling the border.

But the Bedouin were unable to share the desert and in the late 1950's they killed the heroic Peled. That was the last straw for the Israelis, and the Bedouin involved in the murder were forced out of Israel.

From this observation point you have an excellent view of the Egyptian and Israeli roads, each on its own side of the border. As you can see, both are located in a valley between two sets of mountains.

As you continue, Wadi Nitzana is on your left. Note how the Israeli road

Sunroses in the Negev highlands.

Route No. 9: Sinai Border Scenic Drive

follows the wadi while the Egyptian seems to struggle with the landscape. They may have the right idea, however: during floods the Israeli road gets washed out and the Egyptian one doesn't.

Now to the extraordinary Mount Horsha Observation Point, from which you have a view in every direction. Stand at the sign that says "Barnea Plateau," looking down over an area rich in remnants of civilization that date back 90,000 years. Below you is a huge Bronze Age burial field, full of cairns—tumuli from around 2900 B.C.E. Tumuli usually consist of large stone circular structures filled in with smaller rocks. You may have noticed tumuli along the hilltops previously, for this region contains one of the biggest tumulus collections in the Negev, several hundred in one field. It is assumed that these are the burial sites of nomads brought to this collective burial ground some 5,000 years ago.

As you look ahead of you from your vantage point on Mount Horsha, you can see Wadi Horsha down below. Find an easily visible trail on Jabel Tawill—two mountains left of the highest peak. A border stone is located there—between an Israeli and an Egyptian outpost.

Move on to an overlook above Kadesh Barnea, a green patch signifying an oasis which should have been in Israel but is one of the "bulges" on the map. This may be the biblical Kadesh Barnea where some of the most important events in ancient Jewish history took place. The name, which means "holy," implies it was an important religious site. While Moses sent spies to prepare for the entry into Israel, the Jews camped at Kadesh Barnea. This is where Miriam (Moses' sister) died and the fateful site where Moses lost his temper, struck the rock and was given the ultimate punishment; he was barred from entering the Promised Land. His brother Aaron died nearby and the high priesthood was passed on to his son (Numbers 20).

Take a look at the hill across the road as you walk back to your car. These perfectly "hewn" stones were naturally created: temperature differences caused cracks in rocks at weak points.

Continue on the winding road, enjoying the lovely scenery. All of this beautiful region is part of the Negev Highlands Nature Reserve. On your ascent of Mount Harif, you can peer down into the Sinai Mountains. Just before kilometer marker 210 is a sign that reads "45." Stop your car a moment and look in the distance to find the actual border marker: to its left are remains of tumuli.

Between border stones 46 and 47 is a red-and-white monument, a memorial for two pilots. It consists of remains from an airplane that crashed during training. If you stop here a moment you will be able to see straight into Egypt—in fact you are actually standing on its edge. Enjoy a great view

155

Route No. 9: Sinai Border Scenic Drive

of Egypt's Mount Harif. The mountain looks like a dome—inside it there is a *machtesh* (crater-like formation caused when the middle of a mountain collapses).

You may have noticed that altitude affects the region's vegetation. The drive began at about 350 meters above sea level where most plant life is located along the riverbeds. Now you are some 900 meters high, enjoying a cooler climate, and the vegetation covers a much wider area.

Straight ahead into Egypt, on the horizon, is Jabel Onega or the "Mount of Pleasures." According to legend, a certain Bedouin whose wife was indifferent to conjugal delights hosted his other women on Jabel Onega.

Rising some 500 meters above the plains of Sinai, to the south, is a striking mountain called Jabel Arif a-Naka. This is probably one of the landmarks of the southern border described in the Bible (Numbers 43:3–5).

Your ride on the border road is almost over, for at Mount Harif Junction you turn left onto Road 171, in the direction of MITZPE RAMON. Before you reach the city, however, you will pass Hemet Well (*Bor Hemet*), the wonderful LOTZ CISTERNS (*Borot Lotz*) and MITZPE AROD.

About 16 kilometers after the turn to Borot Lotz look for the orange sign leading to Bor Hemet, on your right. This is a water cistern built during the Israelite period. Park, walk down a few dozen meters to the left and then up the first small hill. Within its confines is a reconstructed water cistern. Without cisterns like these, the Negev could never have been settled.

Now continue driving east towards Mitzpe Ramon. In spring you will be accompanied by brilliant red tulips. Eventually you reach Ruhot Junction, a T-intersection where a right turn leads to Mitzpe Ramon and Eilat, and whose left turn goes to Beer Sheva. However there is not a single sign to point out directions. You will see, however, an orange sign that says "Visitor Center," to the right (Mitzpe Ramon).

Vital Information
Begin this route early enough in the morning so you take the scenic border drive at midday when you can clearly see both sides of the border.
Don't get out of your car when following the scenic border route because the ground is checked periodically for footprints.
Bring loads of water.
With the exception of the End of the World Restaurant at Qetziot Junction, you won't see any eateries or gas stations until you reach Mitzpe Ramon.

Shivta National Park

The ancient Nabateans* were originally nomads who roamed the desert. Yet over the centuries they built six towns in the Negev wilderness: Rehovot, Nitzana, Halutza, MAMSHIT, AVDAT and Shivta. Because Shivta escaped destruction during the Moslem invasion and only later fell into disrepair, many of its houses, churches and streets are partially intact and the city is quite well-preserved. Most of the ruins you will see at Shivta are Byzantine.*

Shivta has been cleaned and prepared for visitors but only somewhat restored. Its very informality is what makes this Nabatean-Byzantine ruin so special. As you walk the streets looking for the intricate water system, churches, troughs and the winepress, you can let your imagination run wild.

To reach Hurvot Shivta, or the "Shivta Ruins," follow Highway 40 south of Beer Sheva, then continue straight on Road 211 when 40 swerves to the left. About 23 kilometers past Telalim Junction is a sign leading left to Hurvot Shivta. The road narrows and there are frequent potholes. Don't let other signs sidetrack you; bump along until you reach the site. Do not stray from the road, as it passes near a firing zone.*

Look for birds and animals along the roadside—especially the little owl, which blends almost perfectly into the landscape. It is often seen standing on telephone poles and electric wires, as well as atop rocks near the road. A tiny raptor which successfully hunts insects and mice, the little owl was the symbol of Athena, goddess of wisdom in ancient Greece. The Greek name—nocturnal Athena—reflects the fact that the little owl is a night predator.

After driving about eight kilometers you reach Shivta National Park. Built as a small farming community in the second or first century B.C.E., the town was transformed into a large and flourishing Byzantine city hundreds of years later. The Nabateans converted to Christianity and remained in Shivta for many centuries, disappearing from history after the Moslem conquest. Today's Bedouins sometimes trace their line to the Nabateans.

The first house in Shivta, on the far right, looks too modern to be part of the ancient settlement. Actually, its owner was an archaeologist named Colt, the son of the famous arms manufacturer, who constructed it in 1935.

Shivta National Park

Under the rubble are some fabulous mosaics "borrowed" from the ancient site. Outside the house, over the entrance, you will find a very strange mixture of letters. The inscription was Colt's way of writing "this is the house of Colt" in what he considered Nabatean style.

In sharp contrast to the straight avenues typical of Byzantine cities, Shivta's streets and plazas are crooked. At first archaeologists thought this indicated that the city was unplanned. Closer examination showed that the many streets and plazas were carefully designed, but water, not aesthetics, was the planners' main consideration.

Shivta's signs are very misleading, when they appear at all. But the site is small enough that you won't get totally lost and we suggest you simply wander around and try to find the places we describe. You will be walking in and out of ancient churches, Nabatean-Byzantine dwellings and a government mansion.

Raising horses, especially for racing, was an important source of income here as well as in other Nabatean cities. As you roam around, look for a house with its cistern and original arches still intact. A well-preserved staircase in the middle of another room probably led to a second story. Try to find a stone gutter directing water from the roof to a cistern in the courtyard. Troughs next to the outer walls are the clue that horses were

Three Byzantine churches were built in Shivta.

Shivta National Park

indeed stabled here. A few were tied to a stone protruding from the wall.

The Nabateans learned to collect and hoard every drop of the desert's precious water. Rain water was directed along the streets into two large pools and wells. The pools held over 1,500 cubic meters of water. Shivta residents were required to maintain the pools and, indeed, documents discovered here state that "so-and-so fulfilled his obligation of cleaning the pool."

Near the pools is a large building with about a dozen rooms covering 400 square meters. Shivta's houses were built of three different kinds of sandstone, the harder rock serving as the foundation and two softer rocks used for the walls. A double sandstone wall, sandwiched around rubble for insulation, kept the houses cool in the summer and retained heat in winter.

Three Byzantine churches were built in Shivta and still stand today. One contains a baptismal font, probably used in converting Nabateans and other locals to Christianity. It is not clear why Shivta needed three large churches. Perhaps the city served not only its permanent residents but also local tribes that had converted. Possibly converts were displaying loyalty to their new faith by constructing so many houses of worship.

You can't miss the southern church, reached after you pass two beautiful Nabatean reservoirs. Note the rounded step at the elegant entrance. The structure is divided into three parts, similar to other fourth-century Byzantine churches. Two rows of columns lead to the main altar and apse; side apses contained hair, clothes and other artifacts belonging to holy martyrs.

What was perhaps a waiting room, complete with benches, is located outside the chapel. Note the baptismal urn, whose steps are shaped like a cross. At that time, adult converts stood in water up to their waists; the smaller baptistery was for babies. It was covered with marble slabs and you can see holes left there from the nails. When the Moslems built a mosque adjacent to the church they were careful not to damage the nearby baptistery. Scholars see this as evidence of peaceful relations between Christians and Moslems in Shivta.

Scenes from the New Testament were painted on the church walls. These pictures were still visible when the legendary Lawrence of Arabia surveyed Shivta in 1914. At a later stage the church's walls were paved with marble.

As you walk further into the city, on a path to the right of the church, you pass through a large square. Way at the end stands what was the highest building in town—probably the governor's mansion. Beyond the mansion is the northern church, which also served as a monastery. The round "bench" in the middle was a permanent platform holding a straw basket, and a

Shivta National Park

monk who sat here during prayers. Congregants considered this monk especially holy and, as they walked in, dropped presents into the basket.

Although this was the main public chapel, the monks had their own house of prayer next door decorated with lovely mosaic designs. Next to the monks' chapel is another baptismal urn.

The northern church was built in the sixth or seventh century and was the last to be constructed. Its lintel had Greek letters within a circle. The lowest two letters were alpha and omega, the first and last letters of the Greek alphabet. They refer to the New Testament verse: "[I am the] Alpha and the Omega, the First and the Last, the Beginning and the End" (Revelations 22:13).

Outside the chapel is a courtyard, the atrium, which measures some 500 square meters. Non-Christians who came to church were prohibited from entering the sanctity of the church until after conversion and stood in the atrium. A small piece of marble near the altar is all that remains of the Italian marble that once covered the wall.

Look for another church, a workshop and the northern winepress. There are three winepresses in town, but this is unique because it does not have a storage area. It might be that storage room in the other presses belonged to different people, whereas this press was operated by monks who had communal property and wouldn't need individual storage space.

One of the houses on X Street (if the sign is still there) is almost complete. Inside are arches and beautifully chiseled rocks; outside look for decorations.

Look for a wonderfully preserved winepress and two pools for draining wine. Grapes were placed in storage, nearby.

While walking around Shivta, watch for insects and reptiles in the dusty ground. You may see an elephant beetle among the ruins—a beetle with a tiny trunk coming out of its snout. When frightened, it turns onto its back and plays dead!

Vital Information

There are no set hours or entrance fee. There are also no bathrooms—you get what you pay for!

In late 1995, vandals destroyed many of the lintels, blocking rooms within the churches and homes. The National Parks Authority hopes to restore as much of the damage as possible. At some time during 1996 the site will be temporarily closed for repairs. For further information call the NPA's southern district office: 07–469981 or 467286.

The Lotz Cisterns (*Borot Lotz*)

In early spring, the otherwise desolate Negev highlands seem to explode with dazzling blossoms. To enjoy their most spectacular colors and striking hues visit the Lotz Cisterns, about half an hour's drive from MITZPE RAMON. Built by the Israelites almost 3,000 years ago, the water holes of Lotz continue to collect rainwater flowing off the mountains. During the season, flora of all kinds cluster around them *en masse*.

Seventeen Israelite cisterns have been uncovered to date, along with fascinating remains from a 3,000-year-old house. Nature and history lovers who take an easy, circular jaunt around the Lotz Cisterns encounter striking flowers, interesting reservoirs and exciting ruins.

It all began when King Solomon opened up trade with the Queen of Sheba. Solomon constructed fortresses along the main roads to protect merchant caravans and, in the wake of these military outposts, civilian centers developed in the Negev. Although a number of such farming communities were later destroyed by the Egyptians, King Uzziah subsequently had them rebuilt. The Bible describes this restoration of the Negev: "He also built towers in the desert and dug many cisterns" (II Chronicles 26:9–10).

The Lotz Cisterns (called Luz Wells on some signs) are easy to find. From Mitzpe Ramon, take Highway 40 towards Beer Sheva (left). Drive five kilometers to Haruhot Junction and turn left (Road 171).

As you ride you will find the air getting progressively cooler, for you are climbing up to the highlands, between 900 and 1,000 meters above sea level. Although you are passing through a seemingly dry and barren desert, magnificent wildflowers line the highway as you approach the cisterns. Savor the sight of the glorious sunrose, in shades ranging from yellow to pink to fuchsia to deep red. Each shrub bears flowers of a different hue.

Other enchanting blooms include the pink stork's bill, a pincer-shaped purple milk vetch, and a green and yellow species of the same plant. Look for variations on the intricate, multipetaled oyster flower, bright yellow Damascene picris, and furry, wrinkle-leaved sage. Because this sage's buds are so woolly, the plant has a whitish tinge. Shiny moricandia line the path and there should even be bright red, wild tulips. Gillyflowers sport long, lilac-colored flowers with wrinkly edges and emit a delicious smell during the morning and evening hours.

161

The Lotz Cisterns (Borot Lotz)

Turn at the sign for the cisterns and park in the lot. Near the low walls you may find dark red Arabic poppies, which grow only in desert mountains. While most people associate poppies with opium, no narcotic can be derived from the Israeli species. This is, after all, the holy land!

Your walk will take you two to three hours and bring you back to the parking lot. If you want to finish earlier, leave the path at the point suggested in the text, follow the jeep road and return. Several trails and signs lead to red-marked paths beginning at the lot. The one we recommend is next to the bathrooms and you walk to the southwest.

Stunning flowers line your path as you stroll into a sudden patch of river foliage that hints at nearby water. And indeed, if you continue, you will run right into one of the area's prettiest water holes.

Israelite settlers obtained water for drinking and irrigation through sophisticated systems which demonstrate they were well acquainted with the region's geology. When it rained, water rushed down the mountain slopes and streamed into otherwise dry riverbeds. The Israelites diverted rainwater into an intricate system of canals and on to special pools adjacent to huge pits. From there, it flowed directly into these reservoirs.

While some Israelites dug their pits out of hard limestone rock, the family near this first water hole used a practical knowledge of the soil and created their water storage more easily, from loess. When it rains, loess absorbs water, then its granules puff up and create an impermeable layer; the second time the heavens open up, water remains on the surface. Thus with every additional storm the water diverted from the canals accumulates into a loess pit. And by the time winter is over, the reservoir is full.

At this cistern you can clearly make out two smaller pools, where water was strained before it entered the main reservoir. Sediment, leaves, stones and dirt remained behind and only clear water entered the stone-lined pit.

Note the belt of foliage around the reservoir. Nowadays the cistern dries up in summer, but 3,000 years ago it was probably covered, keeping the water cool and the plants from photosynthesizing, growing and reproducing. In winter, there is an added attraction at the Lotz Cisterns. All kinds of birds migrating from Europe to Africa stop here for a drink!

Across from the cistern is a wooden sign with microscopic letters that reads "the ancient Israelite house." Walk behind it up the hill and to the left; you will notice boulders scattered around as you approach. Here you will see remains of a house built by early Jewish settlers, a dwelling left untouched for over 2,000 years!

Most Israelite homes were constructed in a design known as "four chambered houses." Such houses contained three parallel rectangular rooms with one perpendicular chamber at its head. Here the longer room

162

The Lotz Cisterns (Borot Lotz)

is divided in two and may have been used for storage. These remains help determine who dug the wells and when. Since the house is in typical early Israelite style, experts assume that the wells were dug at the same time.

Stand near the house and gaze towards the path: you will see terraces and lush ground to your right. These agricultural sites, begun three millennia ago and left unused since they were abandoned, were built on small river channels. Rainwater would soak the top layer, then dribble to the next.

Under each planted fruit tree (almond, olive, carob—food which could be easily dried and stored), the Israelites dug a pit which served as a miniature reservoir. Behind this area is a field studded with trees, a modern-day experiment in desert agriculture.

The period when the Israelites inhabited this region was a prosperous one. But after they were forced out (perhaps during the Babylonian conquest in 586 B.C.E.) this part of the Negev highlands remained deserted.

Return to the water hole and turn right so that you are walking east along a narrow, stone-lined path (below the jeep trail). You will be next to a little ravine; from the flowers and shrubs you can see that water flows here during winter rains. Look for exquisite, tall yellowish-brown asphodeline, or Jacob's rod. Asphodeline are found solely in areas that are dry, rocky and

Dazzling blossoms at Lotz cisterns.

The Lotz Cisterns (Borot Lotz)

mountainous, and only for two months of the year.

When the path splits go right, and you will stumble onto another water hole almost completely covered with foliage. There are openings from two little reservoirs as well—be careful not to fall in! This is the second kind of cistern, carved out of solid rock. Return to the stone-lined path leading around the hill (look for the red trail-markers).

By now you will have realized that where there is thick, lush foliage you are likely to find a cistern. Reservoirs dug out of limestone have another giveaway: bald-topped hills, the remains of rock and soil which piled up as farmers carved their cisterns. Although the path stops suddenly you should see a naked hill a few dozen meters in front of you. This, of course, is another water hole. Continue walking—you will again run into the trail. A bit to its right is a huge, flowering white broom and a reservoir.

A yellow-flowered bladder-senna tree stands close by. Some Bedouin at St. Catherine's monastery in Sinai believe that Aaron's staff was made out of its branches although the Bible clearly states that the staff came from an almond tree (Numbers 17:8). If you look carefully at the strange yellow blooms you will notice two eye-like circles near the top of the flower. These attract insects which land on the flower's "nose," their weight pressing on the "mouth." When the "mouth" drops, the hind end of the insect is covered with pollen, to be taken to the next flower it visits.

Try to find an agama, a well-camouflaged little creature. Despite its protective coloring the agama is easy to catch for, unlike lizards which defend themselves by running away from their enemies, the agama lies still and hopes it blends with the background. Fortunately for the agama, there is at least one local resident not remotely interested in capturing her species. Because many Moslems believe its back-and-forth movements ridicule their manner of prayer, they hate the creature and tend to ignore it like the plague. But the little agama is, in fact, rather cute.

The canal parallel to your path is another sign that you are nearing a reservoir, for rain rolling down the hills was diverted into just such channels. After this cistern you will cross a riverbed full of red, white, pink and yellow flowers, ascend a hill and walk down into a wadi covered with rich, green plants. Climb the next slope and turn right (follow the red marker).

Continue, looking for a stone in the middle of the path with two painted red trail-markers. One of them points in the direction of a 3,000-year-old threshing floor; the other to the continuation of the trail.

Take a detour to the threshing floor. Beautifully preserved, and left as it was for millennia, this floor was used for storing grain and for separating the kernels from the chaff. Farmers would toss the wheat into the air and let

164

The Lotz Cisterns (Borot Lotz)

the wind blow away the chaff. This process, along with other types of agricultural work, is used as a metaphor in the Bible. King David wrote that "the wicked are like the chaff, blown away by the wind" (Psalms 1:4).

Back to the stone and the path. As you pass through another small riverbed you will see a lot of white wormwood. This strong-smelling shrub is the most common plant in the Lotz Cisterns region and is mentioned no less than eight times in the Bible as a symbol of bitterness. "For the lips of a strange woman drop as honeycomb...but her end is as bitter as wormwood (Proverbs 5:3). Animals avoid this species because its volatile oil is bitter.

Used in folk medicine for stomach pains and toothaches, wormwood can grow in places where less than 100 millimeters of rain falls each year and is thus very common in the Negev. It has other characteristics that make it well adapted to the desert: the wormwood's winter leaves give way to far smaller summer leaves in order to conserve water, and each of its branches is sustained by an independent root. In this way, even if some branches die, those that were able to find water survive.

It's hard to see the trail here—look for a tall antenna and walk in that direction. At the far edge of the hill, red trail-markers point to the right. They lead to a huge tamarisk tree growing inside a cistern. Above and beyond it, near the sign for "the Tamarisk Hole," find the trail-markers and continue. Cross a wide, exposed hill to reach a beautiful Atlantic pistachio tree. Hundreds of years ago the whole area was covered with these lovely trees, but that was in a colder era and now only a very few are left.

You will note a sphinx-like mountain protruding from the hills to your right (north). This is called Rosh Elot, and adventurous hikers can take a two-hour trail that leads to the mountain and eventually back to the parking lot. Those who do so will stumble upon the largest concentration of Atlantic pistachio trees in the Negev.

To continue on the regular path, cross the jeep tracks and then look to the right of the trail to find rocks covered with dark brown fossils. When the Negev was under water some millions of years ago, stones and creatures from the Dead Sea sank to the bottom and were covered by a layer of lime.

Walk up the hill, then follow the dirt road to return to the parking lot.

Vital Information

This site is a nature reserve.* The walk is circular, about four kilometers long and marked with red trail-markers.

The Lotz Cisterns are delightful from mid-February through March and pleasant even when the rest of the country is sweltering in a heat wave.

Campgrounds include bathrooms, water, and walls to keep out the wind.

Do not swim in the reservoirs or drink their waters.

Arod Observation Point (*Mitzpe Arod*)

Have you walked through the incredible LOTZ CISTERNS to the north of Road 171? Now you are ready for another Negev wonder, the biggest *machtesh* (crater*) in the world. RAMON CRATER, created over time after the middle of a mountain ridge was eroded, is a smashing formation 40 kilometers long and up to 10 kilometers wide. One end is shaped like a heart (a mountain in the middle keeps it from having straight edges) and the other like the tip of that very same heart.

You have a superb view of this marvel from Mitzpe Arod, an observation point located exactly above the crater. It lies off Road 171, almost directly across the street from the Lotz Cisterns. Turn in, then continue straight (south) to Mitzpe Arod on an excellent dirt road.

Park in the lot, then walk up to the lookout. This is the western end of the *machtesh*, the beginning of all the tributaries which flow into the Ramon River. Below you are two basalt hills—Karnei Ramon and Mount Arod. The black basalt rock which contrasts sharply with "natural" desert colors indicates past volcanic activity.

Before you return to your car, look around on the mountain top for the rare wild rhubarb plant. Wild rhubarb, which flowers in spring, is endemic to Israel and appears only in the upper Negev mountains. It is a strange-looking thing; a miniature plant with tiny round red fruit and an absolutely gigantic leaf on its bottom. A medicinal plant, wild rhubarb is used primarily as a diuretic. Bedouin drink it in tea; you may have eaten it in rhubarb pie.

Introducing the Negev Craters

Just when you think you've seen almost everything this country has to offer, you stumble into the Negev—and discover something new! A triangle on the lower half of the Israeli map which receives less than 200 millimeters of rain per year, the Negev boasts colored sands and nocturnal animals, wide open spaces, lush riverbeds and painted rocks. It also possesses a marvel unique to the Negev and the Sinai Peninsula —craters* of the kind known by the Hebrew term *"machteshim."*

The Negev has three large and two tiny *machteshim*. According to the most commonly accepted theory, they were formed by a special kind of erosion which began millions of years ago, when the whole area was covered by an ocean. A gigantic mountain ridge, its top made of hard limestone, protruded from the water and was exposed to harsh erosive forces.

Wind and water cracked the limestone and moisture seeped into the fragile, crumbly sandstone beneath. Over time the top layer was completely destroyed. The middle was exposed and easily washed away, and only the hard limestone sides remained. These, too, were partly eroded, leaving prehistoric layers open to view. How awesome it is to realize that when you walk inside of a *machtesh*, you are actually standing on the top of what was once a mountain!

Imagine the mountain ridge as a gooey chocolate-covered marshmallow treat. Pretend you have scratched away the chocolate covering with a fork, then taken a bite out of the top and spooned out the middle. You will have created your own tasty *machtesh*!

Machtesh Ramon is the largest of the three big Negev craters*: it is 40 kilometers long, two to 10 kilometers wide and 300 to 400 meters deep. This is the only site in Israel whose exposed rock layers form a vast geological window dating back over 200,000,000 years. Special in other ways as well, this crater probably has more varied scenery per square meter than any other natural region in the Negev.

Nature-lovers can hike through two of the three largest *machteshim:* RAMON CRATER and the BIG CRATER with its splendid colored sand. If you want to try trekking in the Little Crater call the Nature Reserves Authority or a local Society for the Protection of Nature in Israel field school to check whether the trails are open. Stay out of the craters during heavy rains!

167

Big Crater Walk

Despite its name, the Big Crater is not the largest of Israel's three major *machteshim*. It was first charted in 1942 by a group of palmachniks* who named it the Big Crater only after discovering a smaller one, later on. Unaware that there was a third, even larger crater near today's Mitzpe Ramon, they simply named them by size: the Big and Little Craters.

A climb up and down the slopes of the Big Crater is the perfect outing for early spring, when the air is still cool and the desert bursts with multicolored blossoms. Although it is preferable to have two cars for this family walk, it can be accomplished with only one (see Vital Information).

Begin your trip by driving to Yeruham, a development town located 25 kilometers south of Beer Sheva on the Dimona-Sde Boker Highway (Highway 204). Turn in at the sign leading to the Big Crater and follow Road 225 to a large sign which points left to Mitzpor Har Avnun. Drive to a lovely overlook and park at the large green sign.

You are now on the western slopes of the Big Crater, gazing at its eastern side. The crater is approximately 12 kilometers long, seven kilometers wide and 400 meters deep. You should be able to view much of it from this point, noting how it is completely encircled by mountains.

Millions of years ago a crack apparently appeared in the top of a mountain in Hatira Ridge, where the crater was formed. Rain slowly penetrated to the base of the mountain; when it reached the bottom sandstone level the hill crumbled. Thus the Big Crater is actually a mountain which disintegrated.

The colored sand you see in the distance—which will be far more visible and vibrant later in the trip—results from minerals combining with its sandstone. Such colored sand lies under all mountains in the area but will be exposed only if they, too, collapse. Now return to the main road.

From the Big Crater sign where you originally turned in, (the entrance to Yeruham) it is 13 kilometers to the area's only eucalyptus tree (on your left) and behind it, mound upon mound of multicolored sand. This is the only site in the crater from which you may remove the sand. Leave one car in the

Big Crater Walk

 parking lot, then drive on just a bit to the Dimona-Oron Junction. Turn right on (Road 206) in the direction of Oron: you are outside the Big Crater and, to your right, can see its tough-looking walls. A few hundred meters further on, turn left at the sign that reads "EIN YORKEAM."

Park your second vehicle here. The pile of stones you see is Meitzad Yorkeam; almost two millennia ago they were part of a citadel that controlled an important road. You can visit Ein Yorkeam, a shaded underground spring, by following the green trail-markers east.

Now return to your vehicle, but only to take water and snacks. Then look across the highway at Hatira Ridge. On the right you see the peak of the mountain, which you are soon going to climb.

Cross the Dimona-Oron Road (206) to the black trail-markers and follow them along the dirt path in the direction of the ridge. Note the milk vetch, a plant whose puffy fruit is filled with air. You will also see tiny muscari in two shades of purple.

The trail leads to a tunnel, under the railroad tracks. You emerge next to a flint covered mountain. Climb straight up to a shady overhang where there are lots of blooming campion. Above you are angled markers, indicating you continue up and to the right.

Called *snapir* in Hebrew ("fin") because that is the mountain's shape, the path you are on is challenging but not overly difficult. From the peak you can gaze straight down into the colored sands. Then, once you've rested and feasted on the magnificent view, follow the black markers down the mountain and into the crater. On the way you will pass a great observation point and, right below it as you continue your descent, a fascinating wall made completely of fossils. At one point, near the wall, you may need some help.

Near the bottom you will be walking right through colored sand. The whole area, especially down where you left one car, is strange and surrealistic. Watching the kids collect their sand right beyond the eucalyptus can give you the sense of being part of a Disney movie, or maybe a Smurf cartoon.

Vital Information

The hike takes three to four hours, but it may take several more to tear your children away!

If you only have one car available leave it at Meitzad Yorkeam. Then take the hike, collect colored sand, and walk back to your car on the road—about two and a half kilometers.

Wadi Yemin and Wadi Hatira

Wadi Yemin and Wadi Hatira

So many sites have been developed in the Negev that it is becoming increasingly difficult to find raw natural scenery through which to hike. Nevertheless, a number of stunning trails remain.

One such five-hour route runs through two riverbeds which have been left untouched, except for trail-markers and a man-made rope-and-ladder ascent along one of the cliffs. The riverbeds are Wadi Yemin and Wadi Hatira, on the outskirts of the Big Crater.

To take this hike, take two cars to Yeruham, a town located 25 kilometers south of Beer Sheva on the Dimona-Sde Boker Highway. You will be leaving one at Ein Yorkeam and the other at the beginning of the trail.

As the road through Yeruham descends towards the BIG CRATER, look for the observation point called Mitzpor Har Avnun on your left. When you get there, park and pile out of your cars. From here, take a good look at the Big Crater.

About twelve kilometers long, seven kilometers wide and 400 meters deep, this interesting natural phenomenon is almost completely surrounded by mountains. Unusually large quantities of fossilized sea creatures can be found inside the crater,* which has not yet experienced total erosion.

When you reach the Dimona-Oron intersection turn right in the direction of Oron: you are now outside of the Big Crater and to your right can see its tough-looking walls. A few hundred meters further on turn left at the sign that reads EIN YORKEAM. Leave one vehicle here, then return to the main road and head right towards Dimona. Turn right at an orange sign leading to Ma'ale Akrabim (Scorpion Ascent), then continue for a little over three kilometers to the sign for Wadi "Yamin" and Wadi Hatira. This is where you leave your second car.

You are standing at the beginning of the Yemin riverbed, which is covered with soft sand. This is because the first portion of the riverbed drains the entire Yemin Plateau, an area formed when sand transported here from Saudi Arabia settled between the two mountain ranges of

---
* This crack is very slowly turning into a canyon.

Wadi Yemin and Wadi Hatira

Hatzera and Hatira.

Because the plateau (and thus the riverbed) are so sandy, animal tracks are unusually easy to spot. You may discover tracks belonging to lizards, beetles, and gazelles. Desert gazelles are swift runners which communicate by using colors provided by Mother Nature. When danger threatens, and the gazelle is forced to flee, its dark tail waving across its white rump beams out a clear signal from afar.

A nimble creature, the gazelle was chosen as the symbol for Israel's speedy mail service. Historically, gazelles are also a symbol of beauty. Ancient Jewish sources refer to the Land of Israel as the land of the gazelle.

Gazelles rest in the shade of the acacia tree during the hot noon hours, but are active the rest of the day. They do not have to drink water because the foliage they eat, especially in the riverbeds, provides them with sufficient fluids. A favorite plant is the acacia tree, which supplies gazelles with 70 percent of their diet. But they also thrive on squill and oleander, which are dangerous to humans.

Look for hyena tracks, easily identifiable because the animal's front legs are bigger than its hind legs. Hyenas sometimes weigh as much as 40 kilograms and are the desert's largest predators. They travel great distances in search of food, and their highly developed sense of smell helps them to sniff out carcasses from afar.

See if you can find a nest on the sand built by a *devora banait admonit,* loosely translated as the "reddish builder bee." Made of sand and mud, a builder bee's nest is round and slightly larger than a ping-pong ball. Inside the nest are little cells which the bee fills with a special food made of pollen and honeydew. After laying an egg in the chamber, it seals the room with mud and straightens out the entrance.

Before the Syrian-African rift* changed the geography in this part of the world, huge rivers flowed through the Negev from south to north (instead of west to east, as they do in the Negev today). One vast stream gushed through this ravine, leaving masses of sand, stones, shells and debris in its wake. Clumped together, these are called conglomerate and they line both sides of the riverbed. Since the conglomerate—sometimes dozens of meters high—has been partially eroded over time, we can assume that in their heyday the rivers were immense.

Throughout this riverbed, and the wadi you will visit later, large bushes of white broom may be in flower. White broom adapts wondrously to the desert. Among its several amazing mechanisms is a double set of roots—long ones to absorb water from deep within the ground in summer, and horizontal roots which hold onto maximum flood waters in winter.

Wadi Yemin and Wadi Hatira

Like many other desert plants, the white broom can discard some of its branches while they are still connected to the shrub and thus consume far less water. Although the dead branches don't come back to life, new ones replace the old.

Dozens of empty snail shells next to a hole in the sand indicate that you have discovered the den of a spiny mouse, a little rodent which dines on *escargots*. But since hikers are not the only creatures that can find its home—raptors looking for prey can locate the den just as easily—the rodent has developed a crafty means of survival. True, it cracks its shells at night, when it is harder to find, but this is no defense: the raptors then simply wait till morning. So smart spiny mice take dinner in a special "shelling station." When sated they return to their burrows, some distance away.

Natural rock steps make a short descent fairly easy. At the bottom you turn 'round to find you have walked down Wadi Yemin's first dry waterfall. Further on there is a large recess which may be filled with water from winter rains—as well as a striking natural rock gate topped by a boulder just waiting to fall!

An astonishing long wall covered with red and yellow illustrations that resemble prehistoric drawings is part of a natural phenomenon which has not yet been fully explained. Immediately past the colored cliff is a giant, almost vertical sand dune which will provide energetic hikers with some exhilarating fun.

To the untrained eye, the attractive bright yellow broomrape in the riverbed looks just any other like flower. Actually, broomrape is a parasite which feeds off of other desert plants. It is usually found near silvery orache (saltbush), sprouting from seeds it disperses nearby and spreading roots like tentacles to penetrate the roots of unwilling host plants.

Follow the green trail-markers along the left side of the riverbed, which has cut a canyon through stone. The path then takes you over the wadi to the other side, past clusters of acacia and tamarisk trees. You may spot a gorgeous colored bird hiding among the branches. Truly splendid, this is a male redstart on its way back to Europe after wintering in Africa. It flaunts a long rust-colored tail, black cheeks and throat, and white forehead. The haunting sound of its cry fills the gully.

If, so far, the walk has been pure nature, you are now going to glimpse a view straight out of Genesis. The path leads you along a limestone slope peppered with sea fossils from an earlier era, and steers you to a starkly beautiful waterfall which will elicit gasps of excited pleasure. Except for what natural forces have wrought, absolutely nothing seems to have changed here since the Creation. When you stop at the edge of the cliff for

Wadi Yemin and Wadi Hatira

Wadi Yemin and Wadi Hatira

a better look, be very, very careful!

Climb the hill and walk around the slope on your side of the deep wadi. After a fairly difficult descent, you will be stopped momentarily by a large crack in the wall between you and the rocks ahead. It stretches all the way down to the riverbed and is undergoing the long, long process of becoming a canyon.

Still to come is a long hike through Wadi Hatira and an extremely challenging ascent up a cliff. This is the time for those who are tired, or have only one car, to retrace their steps and enjoy the scenery from the other direction. Those who chose to continue will cross the crack and descend to the riverbed between the impressive walls of the wadi, past great boulders thrown every which way.

Eventually you reach the point at which Wadi Yemin flows into Wadi Hatira. Take the right fork and climb up to another wonderful view of fantastic boulders and plentiful foliage: so many rivers drain into Wadi Hatira that the ground here fairly bursts with shrubs, plants and flowers.

The next stop is the most exciting—and the most difficult. Called *Nakeb el-Yehud* in Arabic and *Ma'ale Palmach* (Palmach Ascent) in Hebrew, it entails a challenging climb up a cliff next to a dry waterfall 80 meters high.

Nakeb el-Yehud was first scaled in 1944. Palmachniks* undergoing arms training found it prudent to conduct exercises deep inside the virgin desert, far from the eyes of the British colonial rulers. Aware that they were being closely watched on one specific trek across the desert, a group of soldiers decided to vary their route. The young men and women blindly followed their scouts to a magnificent, sheer, dry waterfall with no way out.

Too embarrassed to return and admit defeat, the soldiers searched fruitlessly for an easy way up. In the end they took out axes and ropes and carved holes in the rocks. Then they stuck stakes inside, and pulled and pushed each other to the top.

Once they'd made it, so goes the story, they walked to Ein Yorkeam to find several wide-eyed Bedouin wondering at their appearance. When they pointed in the direction of the waterfall the Bedouin cried *"Ya'Alla, nakeb el-Yehud!"* ("the way of the Jew"). And that is what the cliff wall is called to this day.

Even with an iron ladder set up about 200 meters from the original ascent and ropes to help you up, some hikers will find the climb difficult. When you've finally reached the top, instead of relaxing, increase your vigilance: ahead of you is a dangerous cliff.

Once on the top look for a leopard trap, probably several hundred years old. Bedouin would tie bait here, usually a kid, to a stone placed vertically

The brilliant broomrape is really a desert parasite.

175

Wadi Yemin and Wadi Hatira

inside the trap. When the leopard crawled inside, the stone snapped shut, trapping it and giving hunters the chance to stab the poor animal.

After an easy 30-minute walk above the lovely riverbed (which includes one large rock with huge, imbedded shells), you come to the intriguing naturally carved rocks and canyons of Ein Yorkeam. A watering hole for traders along the Nabatean* spice route, Ein Yorkeam consists of a series of crevices. Some contain water, and you can take a refreshing swim.

Carved stone steps on the northern side of the riverbed are close to 2000 years old and provided camels—and their masters—with a means of getting close to the water below. Along the steps look for drilled holes in the rock. Rocks were quarried here for the desert sculpture that you will see above RAMON CRATER. Ten minutes later you reach the parking lot and the remains of the fortress which controlled the byway, Meitzad Yorkeam.

Vital Information

Ideally, you should have two cars for this six- to seven-hour trip. If you have only one, leave it at the entrance to the trail and return at the point indicated in the description.

This is a firing zone,* and although on Fridays and Saturdays you take the trip with no fear it is sometimes closed to hikers during the week. To find out what's happening on the day you plan to hike, call the Sde Boker Field School before setting out (see IMPORTANT PHONE NUMBERS).

Wadi Hava

Wadi Hava lies deep in the wilderness that is Israel's central
Negev. Thirty-five kilometers in length, Wadi Hava begins slightly north of Mitzpe Ramon and reaches to the Tzin Valley. Portions of the wadi form a natural border between the Tzin Valley and the Avdat Plateau.

For millions and millions of years, rainfall and floods cut through the chalk and limestone around the Avdat Plateau. They created Wadi Hava and a number of dry waterfalls within its channels. Eventually the plunging, pounding water of the falls eroded backwards and formed the sensational 80-to-150-meter-high walls which surround the ravine.

What makes Wadi Hava such a thrilling site for a hike are the breathtaking canyons which surround parts of the ravine. And in addition to spectacular rock walls and formations around the riverbed, the wadi boasts a large natural hollow which is filled with water all year round.

We debated long and hard before deciding to include Wadi Hava in this book. First and foremost, you need a car with four wheel drive or a high-bottomed vehicle to even attempt to reach this riverbed and you may waste precious time looking for the beginning of the trail. The trip is quite difficult, and even dangerous to undertake if you aren't a good hiker. Besides, Wadi Hava is located in a firing zone,* so you can hike only on Fridays and Saturdays.

Yet Wadi Hava is so special we decided it couldn't be left out. This is the kind of natural site in which you may never encounter another living soul—with the exception of birds, ibex and gazelles. Wadi Hava is truly nature in the raw.

You must begin very early in the morning, as it takes six to eight hours to follow a circular path through Wadi Hava, and it is another 90 minutes by car to and from the point at which you begin your hike.

To reach the starting point, take Highway 40 to Nafha Junction, between Sde Boker and Mitzpe Ramon. Turn at the Hebrew sign to the memorial (gal ed) and Wadi Hava. Drive 2.8 kilometers, then head sharply to the right at the sign that reads "four wheel drive only" (4 X 4) and "firing zone" (shetach esh) in Hebrew. With luck (ours had run out), there will also be a sign pointing to Wadi Hava.

A poorly paved road turns into dirt; follow it in and out of riverbeds along a black-marked trail (up-to-date marked-

177

Wadi Yemin and Wadi Hatira

trails map #15, road 17084). The first marker is on your left, 500 meters along the trail. After driving 12.5 kilometers you will see an angled black trail-marker pointing to the right. When you have gone 13.7 kilometers you will see a fork in the road: continue straight ahead.

You reach your destination after driving a total of 16.1 kilometers. Look for a pole with signs leading to Wadi Hava (blue-marked trail) and Hurvat Sharav (red). Park next to the pole, cross the road, and follow blue trail-markers down to the riverbed. When you get there, turn left.

Your hike begins above the canyon. Across from your cliff, on the other side of the twisting, turning gully below, is a second mountain wall. Strange echoes are produced by any noise you make as sound waves bounce from one side of the ridge to the other: on our trip, our poor dog went wild trying to chase the children's whistles—she just couldn't figure out where they came from! Perhaps this is why the riverbed is called *Wadi Hava*—Wadi of the Winds (or Spirits) in Arabic.

You will be stunned by immense rocks perched on the bluffs and standing in the riverbed, the result of tremendous Negev floods. Often they are tipped onto their sides or lie at an angle; a few appear to be just waiting to topple down on your head. Pass a boulder which the Sde Boker Field School uses when it takes hikers out for cliff gliding (rappelling). They tie the rope through a natural hole near its edge.

A blue arrow marked "to the recess" (*lagev*, in Hebrew) points you on a detour off the path to the left, so that you are walking inside the stunning gorge that you saw from above. A tree, very rare in the Negev and called the "young sycamore fig," stands alone inside the wadi. This tree originated in East Africa and moved to Israel together with its pollinators. The pollinators, however, did not survive and the tree can reproduce today only with human intervention.

The prophet Amos gathered sycamore tree fruit until his first revelation from God (Amos 7:14). Wadi Hava boasts one of only two young sycamore figs in the entire Negev. Large caper plants jut out of rocks on both sides of the gully and if you come in late winter you will see them in flower.

Eventually you reach a dry waterfall, 10 meters high, one of three in this part of the riverbed. Below it is a large water hole, six to seven meters deep and about 15 meters wide. It was formed over the years when gigantic rocks were hurled down the fall's sharply angled descent. As more and more rocks hit the deck, they carved out the pit.

Wadi Hava is nature in the raw.

Wadi Hava

Wadi Yemin and Wadi Hatira

Because it is constantly in shade, the water here is unusually chilly and very little evaporates in summer. Still, the hollow depends somewhat on rainfall to keep it brimming. One of the boulders which tumbled from the top of the cliff over the waterfall is stuck, just now, between two canyon walls.

A swim in the hollow is cool and refreshing, and swallows and pink rose finch fly overhead. When you finish, and as you backtrack through the ravine, note some gigantic, especially hard limestone rocks. Little prisms sparkle in the sun from within the cracks: this is quartz, formed by hardened, molten silicon.

Wadi Hava is dry most of the year. After it rains, however, and especially after a flood, its channels and little hollows fill with water. In winter and spring you will find lots of tiny pools in the wadi, and perhaps spot some tiny creatures called *shatgavim* inside. The word combines the terms for "sailing" and "back"—and, indeed, they do their own version of the backstroke.

Some of the fields on the side of the wadi are speckled with black stone, sometimes black mixed with bronze. This is flint, about 35 million years old (as opposed to the approximately 60 million-year-old limestone and chalk which characterize the Avdat Plateau and thus the wadi which runs along its sides). If you are hot, look for little pools hiding under boulders, and you can have a desert water fight!

Prehistoric man fashioned the first tools out of flint, which is extremely sharp. On one of our trips the guide asked for a junior volunteer with long hair. When a young lady with flowing blond tresses said she was game, the guide slashed away at her mane, slicing off a strand with one quick flick of the wrist. She added that baby boys were circumcised with flint in the olden days—"Zipporah took a flint knife, cut off her son's foreskin" (Exodus 4:25).

Incredibly large boulders, some lying on their sides and others apparently about to fall, line your path. A special, overhanging rock forms a low chamber, the kind of place where a desert traveler might spend the night.

As you walk through the ravine or along the cliffs, you see some strange stripes inside the rocks. Although they look suspiciously like Negev dikes (lava which gushes out of the soil and hardens vertically inside of rocks), they are actually crushed sandstone and pebbles swept here during floods and now stuck inside the limestone.

Shiny blue-and-red-veined stones may surprise you, as well. Bright colors result when minerals are exposed to the air after rocks are washed by the wind and rain.

Wadi Hava

What looks like tar on the ground and on some of the stones is actually oil. Wadi Hava passes near the government oil pipeline used until 1973 to transfer oil from Eilat port to the Ashdod refineries. A few decades ago, the line burst near the canyon and oil poured down the cliffs. Flood waters at about the same time spread the oil around the hills and left oil spots in the ravine.

Pass the boulder that led to the hollow, and continue following blue trail-markers through the riverbed. Soon you reach an easy patch where you walk between white broom trees and other foliage. Then you approach a waterfall, 10 meters high. Below it are the tamarisks that indicate water. Descend to the left of the waterfall.

Did you bring a picnic? If you want to wash up first, use one of three plants that are good for making desert soap: saxaul, anabasis and *hamada*. Anabasis—called *yafruk*, from the Hebrew word for joint (*perek*)—has no leaves, and is made up of separate branches attached to the stalk. Crumble the branches, add water and *voila*—real, cleansing soap!

On our hike we saw a great many ibex, which scattered to the cliff heights at the smell and sight of our gentle dog. You may see gazelles, distinguishable because they are smaller than ibex and their horns are straight and short. Gazelles run swiftly along the plains, while ibex prefer the cliffs. The reason for this difference in venue has to do with their need for defense: ibex can outrun their enemies as long as they are on the rock walls. Gazelles, on the other hand, flee better on level ground.

A fiercely territorial creature, the agile gazelle marks its boundaries with permanent dung and urine stations. An invading gazelle which ignores this claim must be prepared to lock its sharp, powerful horns in battle!

Participants taking the field school's courses on survival in the desert are taught to find water by looking for ibex trails. Ibex must come down from the cliffs to drink twice a day, and where ibex trails meet you can generally find a water source.

Eventually you reach the waterfall near Hava Springs, 40 meters high, and carved out of hard limestone rock. Climb down the cliff, to the left of the waterfall, to the springs at the bottom. You will be walking atop loosened boulders, which tumbled down the slopes during earthquakes in late 1995.

Look for travertine, or river stalactites. Travertine is limestone sediment left on riverbanks after the water has receded. Underground springs keep the area wet all year long and trickles of water drip continually over the steep slopes onto riverbed foliage. The process takes hundreds of years, but once plants have been covered with travertine they suffocate from lack of oxygen. Then they rot, crumble and disappear, leaving behind formations in

Wadi Yemin and Wadi Hatira

the shape of the flower, leaf or, as here, intertwined tree roots. Now head towards the rock walls called the "northern crevices."

It is unusual for the sides of a canyon to begin a slow slide towards the wadi and create crevices tall enough and just wide enough to walk through, but Wadi Hava has them in several different places and these are not only the most spectacular, but absolutely unforgettable. You walk through fabulous rock formations, and end up in a sort of den surrounded by canyon walls. All around you are rocks with faces and all kinds of shapes—a veritable sculpture garden!

To get there you continue walking through the canyon. As you walk the gorge gradually widens out and you should stay on the left side of the wadi. After you have gone about two kilometers, a channel to the left will run into the riverbed. Turn left into the channel, walking northwest, and begin an ascent. Follow the blue trail-markers so directly into the cliff that you may wonder exactly where you are headed! They take you into the crevices, where you twist and turn in the cracks and finally exit on the other side.

Now walk on the plateau above the cliffs about another two kilometers. The path leads to a fantastic vantage point from which you can see the wide valley created by Wadi Tzin. To the north is the Hatira range with the cock's comb at its peak (see RAMON CRATER), the Hatzera range and the phosphate fields of the Oron factory. To the east of Mount Tzin is the Scorpion Ascent and a cluster of mountain ranges. To the west is a path which leads from the Tzin Valley to Hurvat Sharav. Follow that path, along blue trail-markers, to Hurvat Sharav. Then let red trail-markers lead you back to your car, another half an hour.

Vital Information

Part of the route goes through an army training ground, so hike there only on Fridays and Saturdays.
Don't forget to stock up with lots of water!
Do not take this trip unless you have a compass, an up-to-date marked-trails map (#15), a spare tire, and an excellent sense of direction!
Begin this hike very early in the morning so that by dusk you are well out of the desert.

Introducing the Sites in Mitzpe Ramon

Not long ago we visited Mitzpe Ramon at dusk. The skies were grey and from the city's PROMENADE it was too dark to see fabulous Ramon Crater. Nevertheless a Japanese tourist ran here and there with his camera, taking pictures in a mad rush. Puzzled, we asked the tourist what in Heaven's name he was shooting in the dim evening light. Waving his arms wildly, he exclaimed in staccato tones of excitement: "True nature, true nature! Here no people! There no people!"

Israel's Negev is famous for its colors, winter wild flowers and geological formations. But most of all it is characterized by its wilderness, by kilometer after kilometer of empty space.

Situated above stupendous Machtesh Ramon, the little town of Mitzpe Ramon was created in 1954 when Israel paved a road to Eilat through the crater.* The town, whose name in English means "Ramon Overlook," is located in the Negev highlands, about an hour's drive south of Beer Sheva.

For years Mitzpe Ramon suffered from chronic unemployment and hundreds of dwellings remained empty. Recently, however, the situation has improved. With construction of the Ramon Inn, an elegant hotel, tourism has picked up. There is other industry, as well and one factory makes its living on air—*luftgesheft* in Yiddish. It actually produces compressed air!

Mitzpe Ramon boasts Israel's largest nature reserve* and most of the region has remained untouched. This happy state of affairs has had an important by-product, for the country's main telescope is located in Mitzpe Ramon, where the desert air is not affected by city lights. Unfortunately, the observatory is not open to tourists.

No matter which way you look, there is an inspiring sense of distant time at Mitzpe Ramon. As you descend into the crater you walk backwards to the beginning of time. You see rocks dating, perhaps, to the Creation. At night, you gaze at stars shining in the crystal-clear air whose brightness originated many light years ago.

Ramon Crater has so many unique sites that you could, and probably should, spend several days exploring the area. In this section we suggest that you begin at the VISITORS' CENTER and the adjacent HAI RAMON. The following chapters describe in detail two journeys into the crater, one by foot and private car and the other by jeep. Then enjoy the sites nearby which include the PROMENADE, DESERT SCULPTURE PARK, Alpaca Farm, and Desert Archery.

Mitzpe Ramon Visitors' Center

Ramon Park encompasses a million dunams of land, including Ramon Crater and the surrounding Negev Mountains. Within its borders are geological formations unparalleled elsewhere in the world—and over a thousand different kinds of desert vegetation!

Before you begin exploring any of the craters you may want to spend some time getting acquainted with the Negev. You can do so by stopping in at the Mitzpe Ramon Visitors' Center, an architectural gem situated on the edge of Ramon Crater. Through the picture window from the center's rooftop observation deck you have a stupendous view. This panoramic lookout really lets you feel the crater's enormity—and magnificence.

Near the entrance is a satellite photograph of Israel. You can identify Ramon Crater within the photo because it is shaped like a heart, the differing colors signifying varying altitudes. At your request, staff from the Nature Reserves Authority, which operates the center, will use a huge colored model to explain the crater's geography and geology.

A fascinating audio-visual production describes the formation of the Negev in general and the creation of its craters in particular. It also illustrates the history of settlement in the Negev, flashes photographs of stunning desert flowers, and offers an interesting segment in which you learn to identify animal tracks.

The center's splendid photography collection includes a picture of the male imperial sand grouse, which goes into water reservoirs during hatching periods, absorbs water in its feathers and carries moisture to its young. Learn how prehistoric man lived in the Negev and see a model from the later Israelite period as well.

Hebrew and English written explanations are in big, bold, easily readable letters. The audio-visual presentation is available in several languages.

Vital Information

Open every day 9:00–17:00. Entrance fee. We recommend you buy a combined ticket for the Visitors' Center and the BIO RAMON (HAI RAMON).
The center is wheelchair accessible.
Ask when the audio-visual program will be played in your language.
Free travel pamphlets and Negev touring information are available at the desk. You can purchase maps at the desk, as well.
Tel.: 07–588691; fax: 588620.

Bio Ramon (*Hai Ramon*)

When Jacob blessed his sons, he noted that "Dan shall be a serpent by the roadside, a viper along the path, that bites the horse's heels so that its rider tumbles backward" (Genesis 49:17). Perhaps he was referring to Field's horned viper, a snake which breathes very hard when it feels threatened and which scholars believe was the symbol of the tribe of Dan.

Field's horned viper is short and thick, with horns over its eyes. Its venom is dangerous to humans, but before it bites it sounds out a warning by breathing very loudly. This snake is very common in the Negev and you can get a close-up look from a safe distance at the Hai Ramon in Mitzpe Ramon.

Established by the Jewish National Fund, the Nature Reserves Authority and the Mitzpe Ramon Local Council, the 11-dunam complex is run by the NRA. Visitors the to Hai Ramon can observe dozens of species of plants and animals unique to the region, many of which they may have never seen before.

The Hai Ramon is divided into two parts. An outdoor area looks so natural it's hard to believe that the scenery has been especially created for the complex. Desert loess, hamada, sand, cliffs, riverbeds and even a small spring have all been reproduced to demonstrate the relationship between plant environments, the flora which thrive in them, and animal life.

Because most Negev animals and insects are active only at night (or are expert at hiding) many people never get to see them. The second part of the Hai Ramon—closed and semi-open enclosures—provides visitors with a good look at nocturnal or hidden animals.

You will find the enclosures large and their conditions similar to those in nature. And so that the experience will be educational for you and not harmful to the animals, small mammals, insects and reptiles are rotated so none are held too long in captivity.

Black beetles (called *shah'oriyot* from the Hebrew word for "black") are not only the wrong color for the desert, but their body area is relatively large. Nevertheless they are diurnal creatures, adapting to the heat by waking up with the sun and gathering dew before it evaporates. They collect the liquid in slits on their backs and then run away to hide while it is still cool. Black beetles have unusually long legs, which keep their bodies from touching the blazing sands.

Cold-blooded reptiles are active during the day, when the sun's heat makes it possible for them to move. If you visit the Hai Ramon in the

Bio Ramon (Hai Ramon)

morning, you will see them warming their bodies under the small slices of sun which enter their enclosures. They are fascinating to watch, for they stand like statues to conserve energy—or climb on top of one another if competition for the sun becomes too fierce.

Chameleons, however, are solitary creatures. You will probably see one walking carefully away from the crowds, even checking that there is no one about to annoy it, as it climbs a solitary tree.

A skink called a sandfish seems to be swimming under the sand. Its feet are shaped like shovels on a bulldozer scoop so that it can push the sand around, and it seems to be rowing underwater. Skinks' upper lips cover their bottom ones, so sand doesn't get in their mouths when they move.

Especially interesting is the Sinai agama, which has long skinny arms and legs and lives in cliffs and other high places. In order to flee from a hungry bird it jumps from rock to rock (or tree to tree) somewhat like a kangaroo. Sinai agamas use their colors to talk. Males protect their territory by turning the front of their bodies a bright blue color—a flag warning other males against invading their domain. Females are a dull brownish-gray, but when ready to mate two orange stripes appear on their backs. Their heads turn blue after mating, signaling the males that they are temporarily indisposed.

Unless you do a lot of desert hiking you may not see the dabb-lizard, Israel's second biggest lizard. Despite its wicked-looking tail, the dabb-lizard is a vegetarian which eats masses of plants, and stores water and nourishment in its body for use later in the season. Plants are scarce in the desert and the dabb-lizard has to travel long distances from home in order to pick up a meal. Fortunately, it can run quickly enough to escape its enemies.

Desert monitors spend almost their entire lives inside dens and are rarely seen by humans. The NRA's compromise with nature was to give them living quarters which provide the shelter they would have underground but with glass sides so that they can be observed by visitors. Both the dabb-lizard and the desert monitor use their tails as defense against enemies. You can watch reptilian predators feast on birds, lizards, snakes and other hapless victims.

Six diurnal snakes have spaghetti-like bodies which enable them to move very fast, crucial for animals exposed to danger during the day. Unlike most other snakes, these have fabulous eyesight and can spot enemies which are a long distance away.

See if you can find the lesser cerastes viper, which hides under the sand and is very hard to spot in nature. Look for a perfectly-shaped "S" in the sand: maybe you'll get lucky! Male and female hunters use a special trick to capture prey. They hide way underground, then push the tiny black tip of

Bio Ramon (Hai Ramon)

their tails above the sand. Lizards approach the tail, thinking it is a worm: the snake then jumps out and bites its latest quarry. If you have managed to locate one, you see that its head is under the sand with only its eyes sticking out.

Also represented in the Hai Ramon are nine very dangerous snakes, including the Ein Gedi mole viper. As there is no antidote to its poison, almost every bite means certain death. Its teeth are so long that it can't open its mouth and extend them out straight: instead of pushing them forward, the snake swings them to the side. Fortunately, the snake is rare, and therefore its human victims are few.

Clifford's snake is harmless. To protect itself, it pretends to be a ferocious creature and in fact has a triangular head like the more lethal variety. When it feels threatened it begins to move, and this causes the blotches on its body to look frightening.

You will see several fat sand rats in outdoor enclosures. These large, fleshy rodents build their homes under plants, generally the anabasis and saltbush. The roots help to hold the soil in place and keep the fat desert rat's favorite foods readily available. Fat sand rats are the only animals that feed on saltbush, and they can consume five times more concentrated salt than we humans. You can watch them run out of their dens, take a piece of saltbush and dash back inside.

Vital Information
Sun. to Thurs. 8:00–15:00; Fri: 8:00–13:00; Sat: 9:00–16:00. Entrance fee. Tel.: 07–588620, 588691.
Information is available on placards located on the enclosures. If you have additional questions about an animal, ask the NRA personnel.
During holidays there are usually hourly guided tours.

Ramon Crater (*Machtesh Ramon*)

When you drive from Mitzpe Ramon in the Negev to the southern city of Eilat you pass through the biggest crater* on earth. The ride is absolutely spectacular, especially in late afternoon and early evening when the sky is changing hue.

On your left side you can almost touch the black and white marbled cliffs which form the crater's northern border. Directly below you on the right lie its strange looking multicolored sands and spiral shapes.

Machtesh* Ramon is 40 kilometers long and two to 10 kilometers wide. Shaped like an elongated heart, it was formed hundreds of millions of years ago when the ocean that covered the Negev began to move north.

At that time, the crater was a hump-shaped hill. Water and other climatic forces slowly and steadily flattened the curve on top. Much later (a mere 5 million years ago), the Arava rift valley was formed and rivers changed their course. As they did so, they carved out the inside of the crater.

Folk legends offer another explanation for the creation of Ramon Crater. Once upon a time, they relate, the Negev contained a proud and cocky mountain who liked to boast that nothing in nature was stronger than he. And he challenged one and all to prove him wrong.

First came the ibex, whose horns practically snapped after he butted them against the mountain's hard rock. The mountain shook with laughter at the ibex's predicament and, as he did so, a crack began forming on the top of his head.

Next came the vulture. His proud curved beak almost straightened as he pecked his hardest against the rock. When the mountain again rocked with mirth the crack grew just a little bit bigger.

Little rain drops were the last to try. Creeping through the crevice they reached the mountain's soft sandstone heart. They washed the sandstone out of the mountain and left a big, empty hole inside. Once again the mountain shuddered with laughter. He cried, "You may be able to touch my heart but you can't hurt the rocks outside!" But even as he spoke his laughter weakened the rocks around the crack, so that they collapsed and fell into the cavern. Water washed all of the debris out of the mountain and left it entirely empty, a topless shell. Water had overcome rock, and Ramon Crater had come into being.

The *machtesh* lay along the ancient SPICE TRAIL, a trade route used by the Nabateans* 2,000 years ago. But other travelers passed through the crater

188

Ramon Crater (Machtesh Ramon)

long before the Nabateans. The severe challenges which faced these travelers ranged from dehydration, to illness, to death by marauders.

Those who died on the road were buried under mounds called tumuli, built of similarly shaped flat stones. It is thought that much later, after the bones had dried, traders repeating the journey would collect them and bring them home for burial near their native villages. There are hundreds of such tumuli all over the crater area.

It would take several days to explore all of the crater by foot. Alternatively, try the day tour suggested below, hiking from the top of the crater down to its depths and continuing by car to some of the *machtesh's* most sensational sights. You need two vehicles for this family walk.

While the hiking portion of the trip takes at least four hours and includes a trek over some very rocky terrain, the descent is gradual and suitable even for people who are afraid of heights. Still, if you are not up to the hike or have only one car, you can begin where the hiking part ends—at the remarkable "Carpentry Shop"—and drive to a small spring and a 2,000 year old inn.

Before you begin the cliff-to-crater hike, leave one vehicle within the crater. Follow the Mitzpe Ramon-Eilat road (Highway 40) from the city into the crater—along Ma'ale Ha'atzmaut. Turn right at the sign that reads "Haminsara, Carpentry Shop" two kilometers from the bottom of the descent. The road leads directly to the parking lot where you leave your car. Take the second vehicle to the town's attractive youth hostel and park it in the lot.

Right next to the hostel is a lovely PROMENADE which leads around the crater's cliffs and provides you with a splendid view of the colored sands below. The promenade ends with a large stone sign in Hebrew that leads to the "scenic trail" and a second sign in English closer to the crater. Keep walking towards the crater, to a trail-marker with orange and blue intertwined angles. Part of your hike is through a portion of the much longer Israel Trail* (designated by the angles) and is also a nature path signified by green trail-markers. During your walk the trail may seem to disappear: if it does, just search for one or another of the markers.

Now begin walking into the crater, along wide natural slabs of limestone. Look for marine fossils (there are hundreds of them strewn around), proof that the land was once submerged under the ocean. Do not remove fossils or anything else on the trail as this part of the crater is a nature reserve.*

You should also be watching for snakes, porcupine quills, centipedes and all kinds of animal droppings. Ibex droppings show you what the animals had for breakfast: ibex are vegetarians and when the droppings are

189

Ramon Crater (Machtesh Ramon)

broken in two you see only plants and seeds. A hyena's droppings are white from the calcium in the bones of their prey.

When you walk through fields in northern Israel you expect to see lots of flowers. Here, deep inside this desert crater, each delicate bloom is evidence of the magical adaptation of nature's creations to the arid Negev climate.

From the desert diplotaxis with pink or white petals around a yellow center, to the lavender-veined moricandia with a wavy green middle, each flower you see here is exquisite. So are the rocks you tread, which at one point turn a dozen shades of yellow. Peeking among the stones are lots of silvery orache (saltbush). In late summer or early fall you may find dark lavender flowers among the salty green leaves.

You will almost certainly see the multistalked, bluish-white bean caper, a succulent which stores water in its Mickey Mouse ears. It has also learned to remove its ears in summer and direct their water to the main stalk. In addition to water, the ears also contain poisonous oxalic acid to keep desert animals from drinking up the plant's supply of liquid.

At the end of the descent continue left (northeast) in the direction of little black hills, along the green-marked trail. Soon you should be walking along the edge of your first black hill (to your right). This is not a volcanic

"The ibex butted his horns against the mountain's hard rock."

Ramon Crater (Machtesh Ramon)

mountain, although the volcanic Giv'at Ga'ash was once active here in the crater. Instead this hill and others like it are limestone covered by basalt, or hardened lava, spewed here by Giv'at Ga'ash.

To your left on the mountainside is a beautiful exposure of rock layer from the period of the crater's formation. The path (note green markers) takes you into a tiny riverbed among clusters of the lemon-colored Negev sunrose, so called because its flowers open at sunrise. Look for bright purple globe thistles along the path. These are mentioned in the Bible. "Like a lily among thorns [thistles] is my darling among the maidens" (Song of Songs 2:1).

As you walk through the gully you see a strange basalt wall, where the rocks resemble long rounded tubes. Past this wall, which is on your left as you follow the riverbed, the paths split in two. On your right is a boulder marked with the arrows of the Israel Trail; that trail leads towards Shen Ramon ("Ramon tooth"). Green trail-markers point you to your destination, the Carpentry Shop.

Across from the boulder is a dark red wall. The soil is actually red clay, and because it dries oily skin it is said to be excellent for acne-suffering adolescents. A famous cosmetic company was denied access to this material to protect the nature reserve. The Nabateans used this clay, together with sesame oil, to paint their pottery. When baked the colors are very durable.

You should be able to spot a green marker at the top of the clay hill. Climb up and look across the plain to another green marker in the distance: the crater's cliffs should be on your left. Keep going northeast towards the riverbed.

All along your route you will see dwarf oxeye plants growing close to the soil. Dwarf oxeye has its own internal rain clock. It conserves its seeds until rain falls, when it slowly opens its shell to disperse them. If you see dwarf oxeye on your travels (but when you are not in a nature reserve), imitate rain by putting the dry-looking flower in your mouth or pouring water on top and watching it pop open.

The trail leads out of the gully, up a hill and then down into the riverbed. Eventually you come to a dark sandy path. Across from you, way in the distance, you will spot a flattish black mountain with a little white trail and railings around the top. This is the Carpentry Shop.

Follow the boulders down the hill and you will again hit the riverbed. You are now deep within the crater, walking in yellow clay. This contains a mineral called limonite, used in the past to produce colors, and in the present by forgers who want their pictures to look antique.

191

Ramon Crater (Machtesh Ramon)

There may be animal tracks on the trail. You can easily recognize those of the hyena, for its footprints are uneven. Hyenas have long front feet and short back feet, making it easier for them to drag their prey away from the scene.

Your route is an enchanting one. The rocks you see are spotted with ochre and beige, and when they break into smaller stones over a wide field it looks as though someone came through the gully with spray paint. Right before you begin to climb a low hill, see if you can find a furry plant called wrinkle-leaved sage. In winter and early spring its flowers are a ravishing shade of purple. Continue in the direction of the hills.

Previously, you saw only single flowers or tiny clusters of plants. Now the riverbed you cross contains row upon row of purple, pink and yellow flowering bushes and plenty of flourishing saltbush. Saltbush leaves are delicious and made up part of the staple diet of desert monks during the Byzantine* era.

It once happened that Maccabee King Alexander Yannai conquered 60 towns in the wilderness. On his return he rejoiced exceedingly and assembled all of the sages in Israel. Then he said, "Our forefathers ate the salt plant when they were engaged in the building of the Temple; let us too eat the salt plant in memory of our forefathers." So the salt plant was served on golden tables and they ate (Kiddushin 66a). Rabbis interpret the passage as follows: the Jews were poor, because they had given all their money to the Temple. Alexander Yannai wanted to eat the saltbush in celebration of the riches and success that God had granted the Jews.

If you cross the gully and walk towards the nearest antenna, you will see the Carpentry Shop to your right, where you left your car.

Get a drink, then begin the easier portion of this excursion. Start by taking the 20-minute circular trail from the parking lot to the strange collection of rocks sometimes called the *nagaria* and sometimes the *minsara* ("prism.")

At the bottom of the path you will find a big box of stones. These are pieces identical to the larger prisms on the hill above and here called by their correct geological composite: quartzite with patina. Some of these stones are in the touching tank for you to feel. Please leave the others alone.

Unlike most rocks in the crater, the strange rectangular pipes on the hill are made of sand, the same kind found at the seashore. This is the only place in the world you see prisms made of heated sand that turned into liquid. In cooling, the molten mass naturally formed rectangles and hexagons, losing no space in the middle. Look for signs explaining this unique phenomenon.

192

Ramon Crater (Machtesh Ramon)

Back in the car, continue five kilometers further south along Highway 40. Stop in Wadi Ramon, which extends through the crater for about 30 kilometers, and enjoy the riverbed walls' pretty colors.

Then go left towards Be'erot Camping Ground and the Saharonim Plateau. The campground was put up by the Nature Reserves Authority and has barbecue pits, shelters and bathrooms so that you can comfortably stop for a picnic or pitch a tent for the night. Continue until you reach the sign for Ein Saharonim; turn in and park in the lot.

At 480 meters above sea level Ein Saharonim is the lowest spot in the crater and contains its only natural water. Most of the year you have to dig a bit to get to the water but in winter there is plenty above ground. Note a very strange gigantic piece of rock in gorgeous hues that is tilted on its side. You may see ibex, which come here often to drink. The water is brackish, however, and not for human visitors.

On a hill on the other side of the parking lot stand the ruins of a large stone structure, Khan Saharonim. Nabatean traders and their camels spent the night at the inn before continuing on to Gaza port.

The caravansaries were built 35 kilometers apart, the distance one camel (and the people walking alongside) traveled in a day. They were set up as rooms around a central hall, which housed the merchants and perhaps some of the camels. Note the bathtubs, where tired and dusty travelers could freshen up.

Now you have finished your day in the crater. As you drive back towards Mitzpe Ramon enjoy the scenery from this direction. The colors are tremendous!

Jeep Trip Through Ramon Crater

With their scooped-out centers and encircling cliffs, Israel's three largest Negev craters* strongly resemble mortar bowls in which grains are pounded with a pestle. The Hebrew word for mortar is *machtesh** and, say many nature guides, that's why the craters have become known as *Hamachtesh Hagadol* ("the Big Crater"), *Hamachtesh Hakatan* ("the Little Crater") and *Machtesh Ramon* ("Ramon Crater").

Unlike the rounded Big and Little Craters which really do look like mortars, Machtesh Ramon is stretched out and narrower at one end. Two valleys, separated by a mountain at its head, give the crater the elongated heart-shape you see on satellite pictures of the *machteshim*.

While roads have been paved and paths prepared for tourists through much of Ramon Crater, there is still plenty of wilderness left. Probably the best (and certainly the easiest) way to see hard-to-reach crater sites is by jeep. One such trip includes a roller-coaster ride to delightful Wadi Nikarot. Seventy kilometers long, Wadi Nikarot begins in northern Sinai and runs towards the Arava Valley, ending at Ein Yahav. A number of tributaries drain into Wadi Nikarot, which swerves in and out of Ramon Crater.

Erosion has gouged out softer portions of the rock and left rows of fascinating overhangs. Their cracks and crevices hint at the wadi's English name of "Grotto Riverbed."

A number of the crater's black hills—Giv'at Ga'ash and Karnei Ramon—result from a long-ago volcanic eruption, when lava quickly cooled in the open air and turned into basalt rock. The granite hill called Shen Ramon, however, is different. Made of magma which hardened while still underground, and later shot up through cracks in the earth's surface, it becomes visible as you approach the southern wall of Ramon Crater.

Shen Ramon ("Ramon tooth") has sharp edges and a rough look which result from erosive forces over the millennia. Perhaps because it is black against the creamy southern wall of the crater, Shen Ramon resembles a rotten tooth in an otherwise healthy mouth. (Or perhaps its name comes from the fact that it looks just like an incisor!)

You will probably visit an astonishing ammonite wall—an entire hillside made of ammonite fossils. Ammonites were spiral-shaped sea creatures who lived under water 50 to 90 million years ago. They ranged from the size of snails to that of tractor wheels. Each ammonite resided within one square of its shell. Like a submarine, it expelled the water from its shell to

Jeep Trip Through Ramon Crater

ascend; to descend, it refilled. And to propel itself left and right it shot out a jet of water.

Your jeep will probably stop at a mound whose sandstone was once subject to tremendous heat. If you dig in the red, powdery ground at its feet you are in for a surprise, for a few millimeters beneath the surface is a rainbow of pretty colored sand. The different turquoise, yellow and red shades were created when the sandstone oxidized with various metals and minerals.

A number of dashing black-and-white birds fly through the crater. Topped by a white cap, the mourning wheatear has black cheeks, throat, chin and upper wings and a contrasting white belly. There are 11 species of wheatear in Israel; you can identity the mourning wheatear by a flash of white on its wing when in flight. It is this spot that gave it its Hebrew name: *sal'it livnat kanaf*, or "white wing." Mourning wheatears are territorial creatures which live in pairs and may want as many as 150 dunams for their living space! To stake a claim the male climbs onto a high rock and sings a special song. Meals consist of insects and crumbs of leftover food.

You may see some Asiatic wild asses—also called onagers—in the crater. Until they were reintroduced by rangers from the HAI BAR NATURE RESERVE, the ass was extinct in Israel. Identify the onager by a dark brown

Some people walk into the crater—and others rappel down the cliffs.

Jeep Trip Through Ramon Crater

stripe from tail to head.

When God created the world, He took care to provide for every single animal, including the ass. "They give water to all the beasts of the field; the wild donkeys quench their thirst" (Psalms 104:11). The onager's need to drink at least every 36 hours was the cause of its demise, despite the Lord's divine plan. Man hunted onagers recklessly during the 19th century, destroying the creatures when they came to drink. As a result, wild asses became extinct in Israel and in many other places in the world.

After a thrilling ride you may find yourselves on Mount Gevanim ("Shade" or "Diversity Mountain"). Because of its height—650 meters above sea level—you have a wonderful view of the crater, including Elbow Mountain. This is a table mountain, a hill left standing alone after everything around it was swept away.

Table mountains acquire their shapes over time as soft edges are eroded by the elements; the rest remains because of the hard flint covering which protects much of the chalk below. A second section of the "elbow" which gives this particular mountain its name is visible from a different angle. Next to Elbow Mountain is Backward Mountain, which leans 180 degrees towards the north instead of south like the rest of the crater wall in this part of the *machtesh.*

From your vantage point you will also see the Ardon Valley, sporting "negative" dikes: empty stripes between dark grey layers of stone. Negative dikes form when hot magma from within the earth's belly slowly rises up in a vertical plane through horizontally layered sandstone and bakes both its sides. Eventually the dried magma becomes weaker than the baked rock and, in time, erodes away.

Look, as well, for the "oil pipe route," a road paved in 1957 to transport oil from Eilat to the Mediterranean Sea. Part of the route from southern Eilat to Ashkelon can be seen in many parts of the crater. The oil pipeline, which follows the easiest topographical route, is very similar here to the path of the SPICE TRAIL.

The dirt along the oil pipe route looks as if it were dug yesterday. In sharp contrast to the Galilee, where the natural vegetation will grow over a damaged spot quickly, in the desert the slightest damage to nature creates a scar that remains for decades. Even biodegradable products like orange peels will remain intact and detract for years from a region's natural beauty. That's what makes nature preservation particularly important in the Negev.

Below the mountain is a colorful riverbed, Wadi Gevanim, and another called Zohalim ("Reptile") Valley for the giant lizard fossil that was discovered within. In one especially pretty spot there are red and white

Jeep Trip Through Ramon Crater

marbled rocks, formed from red and white sandstone which have been pressed together over time.

The numerous umbrella and twisted acacia trees in the wadi, their long roots soaking up underground water, originated in Africa. They weren't blown here by the wind nor planted by man, but arrived via birds and animals who eat their fruit. Acacia can only reproduce from seeds in these creatures' droppings.

Prickly thorns keep most animals from eating directly from the tree, and gazelles and birds who find acacia fruit particularly tasty prefer to get it from the ground. Their digestive juices are wonderfully adapted and serve a double function: they melt the seed's shell and at the same time kill off a deadly worm. So crucial is this animal-tree connection, that when hunters in the 1940's slaughtered huge numbers of gazelles the number of acacia was drastically reduced as well.

Only camels and goats ignore the acacia's thorns and munch right from the tree. Unfortunately for them, the thorns excrete a liquid which warrior ants consider a delicacy. As a result, when the animal takes a mouthful of fruit, the pain from their pinches and bites far outweighs the anguish produced by the thorns!

Spiny burnet is another prickly plant common in the riverbed. Soldiers use this low shrub to prepare excellent springform mattresses. All they have to do is cover it with canvas and settle down.

Saharonim Ridge is a steep and narrow mountain range which is part of the crater's southern wall. A spectacular panoramic view takes in a rich mass of fabulous multicolored hills in dozens of shades of bronze, red, beige, yellow, green, grey and black. You may reach the mountain at dusk, just about time to bid farewell to the Negev and return to home base.

Vital Information

To book jeep tours, call the Negev Highlands Tourism Reservations Center, at 177-022-2646 or 07-588319.

Promenade Along the Crater

In addition to its natural marvels, Mitzpe Ramon offers visitors a man-made wonder called the Albert Promenade. Constructed by the Jewish National Fund, the promenade offers a stupendous view of Ramon Crater, a strange balcony and some extraordinary statues. So delightful is this promenade that the JNF was awarded a special prize for its design. It is located across from the Mitzpe Ramon Visitors' Center, and right next to the town's excellent youth hostel.

Architect Zvi Dekel attempted to make a connection between the city's glorious panorama and the monotonous stone apartment blocks which face away from the view. To do so, he used statues made of the same stone employed in constructing the homes.

One sculpture made of local stone resembles a dolmen, a prehistoric megalithic structure consisting of two or more vertical stones and a horizontal stone lying across the top. Another statue strangely resembles half a face, whose one eye looks very much like Ramon Crater.

If you look at the real crater* below, you will see black spots that appear to be mushrooms. These result from a natural phenomenon called laccoliths, when magmatic material spurts up from within the earth. Upon reaching a space between layers it spreads out, like a mushroom. Erosive forces in the crater removed the layer on top of the magmatic mushroom, so what you see is what has remained after erosion.

Very close to the youth hostel is the "bird balcony," our favorite part of the promenade. Walk onto the patio, which hangs above the crater, and you will see it from the perspective of a bird. Occasionally, you will find that you are higher than the birds and can watch them flying below your feet!

Desert Sculpture in Mitzpe Ramon

The Jewish National Fund's extraordinary Desert Sculpture Park was born in 1963, when a group of foreign artists landed at Ben Gurion Airport. They were driven to Haifa, picked up rocks from the city's quarries, and then joined Israeli artists at Mitzpe Ramon. Two decades later initiators of the park decided that in phase two artists would use only local material.

Desert Sculpture in Mitzpe Ramon

Today the park—greatly enriched between 1986 and 1988—includes some outstanding sculptures. All are located either on the edge of the Ramon Crater or across the road on the slope of a hill. In front of each work of art is a low, modest plaque stating the artist's country of origin and name.

Because the sculptures themselves have no titles, you can call them whatever you want. Our favorite is a piece we labeled "Window to the Crater," which seems to change form depending on where you are when you walk or drive through the park. Get there by turning into Ma'ale Noah at the entrance (or exit) of Mitzpe Ramon.

Introducing the Arava

The Negev is a land of great contrasts. From the cool Negev highlands, 1,000 meters above sea level, you can quickly descend to the Arava. Hot and barren, it lies about 400 meters below sea level and is the lowest place on earth. The border between Israel and Jordan runs along its eastern edge.

A narrow strip eight to 10 kilometers wide and 175 kilometers long, the Arava stretches from the Dead Sea all the way down to Eilat. It was fashioned as part of the Syrian-African rift, a gigantic fault line running from Turkey to Uganda. Incredibly intense tectonic forces pushed the ground down—creating the Arava—and at the same time raised mountains parallel to the rift. The mountains of Edom on the rift's eastern side are especially striking, for they rise steeply to a height of up to 1,500 meters.

Although often called wasteland, the sand and rocks of the Arava contain a plethora of desert creatures and foliage. All have adapted well to the intense heat, lack of water and high salinity of the soil. Flowering desert plants include the bean caper, which kills off some of its own stems so that others may benefit from the region's meager rainfall. White broom has needles instead of leaves, where it snugly stores its stomata. From afar, the leafless silk vine plants look dead, but they bloom in spring with deep red flowers.

Dabb-lizards live in Wadi Bitron, at Shezaf, and in other parts of the Arava. Although they resemble crocodiles, dabb-lizards are far from green. In cold weather the lizards turn dark grey, which helps them soak up sunshine; when it is hot they become a dull yellow color. Because the liquid in the plants they eat is sufficient for their needs, dabb-lizards can get along without any water at all. Burrows a meter deep and five meters wide provide them with plenty of shade during hot summer days.

Ant lions—insects the size of dragonflies—also flourish in the Arava. You can see where they live by watching for little cone-shaped holes in the sand. The holes are perfect for catching dinner, since unsuspecting ants walking on the surface tumble inside and can't get out.

Try to visit the Arava near sunset. Across the Jordanian border, the Edom Mountains glow with a reddish glint that reflects gloriously onto the Arava sands.

What makes the Arava especially enchanting are its unique geological formations. The Dead Sea is one of them—and so are the adjacent badlands where erosion of the soft marl rock has created a landscape that

Introducing the Arava

resembles the surface of the moon. Enjoy the view from Mount Sodom, an entire mountain composed of salt. Or climb Mount Tzin to see a field of *bulboosim* below. (Read the chapter called ROUTE NO. 7 to see what *bulboosim* are!)

Rivers that ran down from the highlands formed beautiful canyons that today are marked as nature trails. Walking through Arava canyons, you may see dry rivulets resembling stalagmites, where water pours over the cliff walls during winter rains.

The road down the Arava Highway, which we call Route No. 10, is lined with fascinating sights. Among them: an animal reserve (Hai Bar) and the ancient copper mines at Timna. Along the highway you will see markers that seem to make no sense. These are gates to measure the water level. Despite minimal precipitation (70 millimeters in the north to only 10 millimeters in the south), when rain does fall here it comes in storms that cause tremendous floods. Now you will better understand the verse in Psalms: "Return us to Zion O Lord, like streams in the Negev" (Psalms 126:4).

While the border with Jordan is calm, we do have a serious problem in the Arava. Speeding or sleepy drivers consistently cause tragic accidents despite the fact that the highway is generally a straight and excellent road. Take advantage of the many stopping-off places to relax during your drive.

Route No. 10: The Southern Dead Sea to Eilat

Route No. 10
The Southern Dead Sea to Eilat

*Ancient history and unique natural sites—
with a rest stop at a brand-new desert oasis*

At first glance, Israel's Arava region appears to be no more than a long, narrow belt of arid land. Yet this geographical lane may have played a major role in the history of the human race. Many anthropologists believe all *Homo sapiens* have their roots in Africa, and migrated north to Europe and Asia by way of the Arava.

Route No. 10 takes you south on Highway 90, commonly called the Arava Highway, from the southern Dead Sea to Eilat. If you are coming from Arad after following ROUTE NO. 6, turn right on the Arava Highway and you will begin traveling south.

The Bible uses the word "Arava" for a desolate area (Jeremiah 50:12),

Sapir Park—an oasis in the desert.

Route No. 10: The Southern Dead Sea to Eilat

and it has become the modern name for the narrow band between the Dead Sea and Eilat. Isaiah predicted that at some future time the barren strip was destined to flourish (Isaiah 35:2). Could he have foreseen the contemporary plan to dig a canal from Eilat to the Dead Sea? For in the future there may be a water canal parallel to the highway.

Water flowing downhill can be used to generate hydroelectric power and to replenish the sea's rapidly evaporating waters.

The project is complicated, however, because the route is not all downhill. Although Eilat is at sea level and the Dead Sea 400 meters below, there is a 225 meter peak above sea level in the middle.

Just past Zohar Junction, on your right, the Wadi Hemar Reservoir contains three million cubic meters of water. During heavy rains in 1992, the reservoir overflowed, spilling onto the highway and demolishing a section of the road.

On the drive south, you pass caves that were once part of the DEAD SEA WORKS. Originally built at Kalia, further north, the Dead Sea Works moved to its present site in 1934. Colonel Cave, for example, is where the laborers cooled off and watched movies in the 1940's. Don't explore the caves, as they have been known to collapse.

About a kilometer north of the Dead Sea Works—between kilometers

The pink canyons at Timna Park.

Route No. 10: The Southern Dead Sea to Eilat

193 and 194—a red-marked trail leads to the Amiaz Plains. Turn in and drive on a bumpy dirt road for about 2.5 kilometers to an intersection at the entrance to the plains. If you are planning to take the one-hour circular family hike through the Flour Cave, turn left and stay on the red-marked road another four kilometers. Stop at the parking lot near the cave.

The trail to the Flour Cave is not marked, but you stroll straight ahead through an enchanting ravine for 10 to 15 minutes. Enjoy the elegant swirls on both sides of the gully. While sedimentary rocks normally form nice, even lines, here the stone is very soft and flexible. Over time, geological pressures have bent the rock rather than broken it and created some truly amazing designs.

A large natural archway to your right is the entrance to the cave. It is marked only with a small wooden sign in Hebrew and an arrow. When you enter, you will discover that the flour cave is actually a tunnel, formed when water seeped in through a crack extending along its roof. After taking a few short steps, look back towards the entrance for an eerie sight. Then walk through the dark tunnel to its end, and exit with a short climb back to ground level.

Imaginative hikers endowed the tunnel with its enticing name of "Flour Cave." Wondering why? Then examine your clothes when you leave the cave. They are covered with the chalky white powder which rubbed off on you as you walked through.

Once outside, you should be able to see your car about 800 meters to the south. If you happened to tie a red piece of cloth to the antenna, it will really stick out!

Travelers skipping the flour cave walk who nevertheless want to see the view from Mount Sodom should continue straight ahead. A blue-marked trail leads to a black-marked trail, where you turn right and ascend a bumpy road to the mountain. Stop wherever you like to enjoy the scenery.

Mount Sodom is actually a ridge of salt, 11 kilometers long and two kilometers wide. Below a thin crust of ground are three kilometers of salt. Today this high salty mound is some 650 meters above the Dead Sea and still rising at the rate of 3.5 millimeters a year.

Although you can stand on the mound and enjoy a tranquil view of the Dead Sea, Lot's wife wasn't as lucky as you. When she disobeyed God, and looked back for a final glimpse of Sodom, she turned into a pillar of salt (Genesis 19:26). Try guessing which of the pillars you see is really Lot's wife. You'll find this is a wonderful way to keep kids busy during the ride!

Back on Highway 90 you will see, to your left, evaporation pools built by the Dead Sea Works. Every year the level of the Dead Sea falls by about a meter. The Dead Sea Works accounts for only 25 percent of water loss; the

Route No. 10: The Southern Dead Sea to Eilat

rest is due to other projects that collect and store water in the Sea of Galilee and along the Jordan River.

Continue until you reach the intersection where a sign points to Ein Hatzeva, site of a modern-day settlement called Ir Ovot, (literally, "city of our forefathers"). It was named for a place where the Jews rested in the desert (Numbers 21:11). Next to the settlement is a jujube tree well over 900 years old, possibly the oldest in Israel, and certainly the biggest!

Jujube trees bear a tiny, delicious fruit which tastes like crabapples. Their thorns bend inward and it is easy to get to the fruit, but woe to the person who picks it and quickly pulls back his hand! This tree originated in Sudan and is common along Israel's Syrian-African rift.*

The jujube tree is located near a spring that supplied water to the Israelite fortress of Hatzeva and to later way stations here. Known in Arabic as *Hutzuv*, or "flowing spring," the fortress was called Tamar in the Bible and only recently Hebraized as *Hatzeva*. Unfortunately, freshly dug wells have dried up this excellent water source.

During Hatzeva Fortress's long and exciting history, it towered over a vital junction. When the kings of Israel ruled the Negev, Ein Hatzeva was an inn on the way to Eilat, where King Solomon's merchant fleet was moored. The Nabateans* built a caravansary here long afterwards, and later still the site was used by the Romans. When the British controlled Israel, they operated a police station at Hatzeva.

Simha Perlmutter, a Jew who believes in Jesus, came to live in Ir Ovot in 1966 with a few other messianic Jews. He believes that we are now in the last stage before redemption when the final war between God and Gog will be fought (see Ezekiel, chapters 38–39). Because they contend that redemption will come from the hills of Edom, they chose this site nearby.

Next stop is SHEZAF, a fabulous nature reserve near the Hatzeva Field School. Park near the observation point and take the easy climb to the top. To get there, turn right (south) off the road which leads to the moshav.*

After visiting Shezaf, continue on the Arava Highway. You will pass six delightful Jewish National Fund (JNF) picnic spots, where acacia trees shade wooden tables. Soon you will reach Sapir Park.

When the settlers of Mercaz Sapir began building permanent homes, quantities of water from a shallow aquifer* surfaced on the ground. Instead of draining this saline water, the JNF helped them build a jewel of a park.

To visit this little-known gem turn into Mercaz Sapir. Park by the green gate and walk around it to enter. A closed-circuit system keeps the pool filled with water and creates enchanting waterfalls. There are picnic tables in the park, as well as green grass of a special type which thrives on brackish water. Resembling a desert oasis, the pool is shaded by palm trees

205

Route No. 10: The Southern Dead Sea to Eilat

which are reflected in the water. Sit on rock benches to rest, or walk on the dock, almost into the pool.

Now drive in the direction of Eilat. In spring (and throughout most of the summer) the Arava Highway is lined with desert fleabane whose large yellow flowers with mustard-colored centers emit a sharp smell. The strong smell repels insects and keeps bugs and mammals away from the plant; Bedouin hang fleabane—whose Latin and Hebrew names come from the word for "flea"—around their tents to keep goats away.

Fleabane can be used instead of mothballs if you dry the plant in a cloth bag in the shade and put it in your cupboard. It may actually be preferable to mothballs, for it is easier to wash the smell off your clothes. Fleabane tea is good for rheumatism and in general is said to give a sense of well-being.

Just south of Ein Yahav turn right into ancient Moa (see also SPICE TRAIL). This is the first spot in Israel where camel caravans on the Nabatean Spice Trail stopped to rest, and a small citadel constructed in the third century B.C.E. guarded the road. It provided security for camel drivers and their beasts, who camped out next door. Two centuries later a khan was built, featuring a Roman-style bathhouse.

The "roman arches" discovered at Moa make you wonder which came first, the arches, or the Romans? Did the Nabateans develop this innovative style of architecture, or did their customers, the Romans who bought the spices, teach them how to construct arches?

Moa is close to the aquifer and apparently water was more abundant here in ancient times than it is now. The terraced slopes at Moa were watered from a spring. Archaeologists found an olive press on the site, which is peculiar since olives do not grow in today's dry climate.

If you have been to Ramon Crater (see RAMON CRATER) and its Saharonim Inn (called Sha'ar Ramon on some maps), you will realize that the khan at Moa is almost identical. They are both 42 square meters in size, with a central courtyard and surrounding buildings from the Nabatean period. Thousands of remains from fires discovered here indicate that Moa was one of the traders' main resting stations. Travelers may even have remained here for several days, for there are a number of springs in the area and caravans needed to rest before attempting the trek through the Negev.

Moa was a large town with permanent settlers, a khan for travelers and a bathhouse decorated with a fresco. Ritual worship was performed on a hill nearby. While the site was never completed, there are four rooms and three caves cut into the rock.

Under the acacia tree you will see a large pool. It wasn't a cistern, for those are deep and narrow; this is an open pool with two canals. To the right is green vegetation indicating the presence of a spring. The spring

206

Route No. 10: The Southern Dead Sea to Eilat

would have drained into the pool. Climb the path to the top of the hill to see the building which overlooked the town and probably housed Moa's governor. Much of the edifice has been reconstructed with rocks taken from the Roman town below. Ascend the excellent path up the short hill.

Walk around the courtyard and in and out of the rooms. You can even climb stairs to what was a roofed second story, possibly used to observe the surrounding roads (or maybe as a penthouse).

Now leave Moa, and continue on the Arava Highway. Here, and in SPICE TRAIL, we described the Nabatean caravans which traveled across Israel. But in the 1950's and 1960's some Jews tried going in the opposite direction, so they could visit the legendary Petra. Since Israel and Jordan were at war, this was a wholly illegal act which some considered the ultimate test of courage. Indeed, several young Israelis were killed in the attempt. Two memorials to the youths are located by the kiosk with a big sign reading "101," near Menuha Junction.

Proceeding south, you will pass two kibbutzim* associated with the Reform Movement (Progressive Judaism). The first, Yahel, was created by Jews from abroad, primarily from the United States. Neighboring Lotan was founded by Israeli youth. The next kibbutz, Ketura, was established by Jews from abroad who belonged to Young Judea.

Other sites you pass on this route are: AMRAM'S PILLARS, WADI SHEHORET, EIN EVRONA, the HAI BAR BIBLICAL WILDERNESS RESERVE and TIMNA PARK. All of these are described in detail in the EILAT chapter.

Vital Information
You need a flashlight for the flour cave. People who have trouble climbing will find the exit from the cave difficult to manage.

The Dead Sea

While tourists often visit Israel to get a spiritual "high," others enjoy a healthy "low" at the country's extraordinary Dead Sea. Minimal ultraviolet rays combine with the Dead Sea's unparalleled waters to transform the lowest place on earth into a veritable health spa.

Because the Dead Sea is lower than the surrounding area, no water can flow outwards and the Jordan River is trapped the moment it streams inside. Much of the Dead Sea's water has evaporated over the millennia, leaving its minerals behind. Today, the Dead Sea contains the highest concentration of salty water in the world: 32% salt compared with 3% in the Mediterranean! Not an animal, plant or fish can live in the murky waters: this is how it gets its name.

During the Roman conquest of Israel, commander Vespasian decided to test the qualities of the water. Non-swimmers—probably Jewish prisoners —were thrown into the sea with their hands bound behind them, and floated on the surface "as if blown upwards by a strong wind" (Josephus, *The Jewish War*, 4:464). Contemporary tourists, their hands thankfully unbound, relax and read a paper while floating on their backs.

In the past the sea's precious minerals included not only salt, at times worth its weight in gold, but also tar (Genesis 14:10). This was used for caulking boats, such as Noah's ark, and as a component in medicines. The ancient Egyptians employed tar for embalming their dead.

Today, modern factories extract potassium, salt and bromine from the Dead Sea waters, earning an annual 632 million dollars. On the eastern side of the Dead Sea, Jordan's factories do the same as their Israeli counterparts.

Across from the Dead Sea is a dry, desolate area which, according to the Bible, was once covered with lush green. The Bible tells of the infamous cities of Sodom and Gomorrah that flourished along the Dead Sea shore, ultimately destroyed by fire and brimstone (Genesis 19:24).

The final blow to Jewish independence was the conquest of Massada by the Roman legions in 73. Massada, famous for its heroic last stand, remained in ruins for the next two thousand years. But now the Dead Sea is coming to life. Massada today is the largest tourist attraction in Israel. Millions also flock to Qumran where the Dead Sea scrolls were found, hike through the oasis of Ein Gedi in the footsteps of King David, or simply absorb the sun and waters of the sea.

The Dead Sea Works

In 1902 Theodor Herzl, considered the father of modern Zionism, published a book in which he described his vision of Israel 50 years hence. Among his futuristic dreams was a factory that would extract minerals from the Dead Sea and a canal that would link the Mediterranean with the Dead Sea to provide hydroelectric power. The first of these aspirations has been accomplished; the other is at present in its planning stages.

Russian mining engineer Moshe Novomeisky was influenced by Herzl's book in the 1920's and began the first serious research into realizing the Dead Sea's commercial potential. After a long political battle with the British authorities, he was granted permission to establish such an enterprise. The Dead Sea Works opened in 1930. Forced to close during the War of Independence,* in 1948, it reopened in the mid 1950's—modernized, and ready to change the face of the Dead Sea.

The initial process of producing potash involves evaporation of water and, as a result, the southern edge of the Dead Sea completely disappeared. To solve this problem, a 12-kilometer channel has been built to link the otherwise dry south with the rest of the sea. This channel and evaporation pools are clearly visible from the road.

Today the Dead Sea Works is a thriving company employing over 1,600 people. They produce 40% of the world's bromine, potash for agriculture, magnesium chloride and, of course, salt. One interesting new product is a bath salt used for cosmetics.

Wadi Tzafit

Wadi Tzafit

Peace of Mind was a little cloud looking for a place on God's earth following the Creation. After trying all kinds of noisy, dirty, and dangerous sites, Peace of Mind drifted to Wadi Tzafit. If you are looking for peace of mind, you, too, may find it within this stunning and tranquil riverbed.

Southern nature reserves are generally way off the beaten track. This is especially true in the oft-neglected Arava, whose biblical landscape has been practically untouched by man. Peppered with splashes of bright color, the Arava's rocks, hills and wadis* are absolutely breathtaking.

A superbly exciting trail through upper Wadi Tzafit, on the edge of the Arava, includes scary ascents on knife-narrow ledges. Try to make the trip before April, while there is still water in the rocky hollows. The trail takes from five to six hours with stops for swimming and food.

To navigate this trip you need at least two vehicles. You will leave one where you complete the trail and the other where you begin the hike, at Tamar Fortress.

Hikers coming from Beer Sheva pass Dimona, and drive in towards Sodom. Although you will see a sign that reads Wadi Tzafit, do not stop. Continue on to Tamar Fortress, located near kilometer marker 118. A sign on the right reads "Little Machtesh" and "Ma'ale Hatzera." You will know you are close when you see a number of Motorola antennas.

Passengers get out at the sign and drivers go on to the end of the trail to drop off a vehicle. Stay on the Dimona-Sodom Highway, going east. Drive 5.8 kilometers to a sign pointing to "Hamachtesh Hakatan" and "Negev Phosphates." Turn right, and drive to the first orange sign pointing right to Wadi Tzafit. Take the dirt road as far as you can, then park.

Return in the other car to Tamar Fortress, turning right so you can park above the site, and begin your tour of the ruins.

Dating back to the third century C.E., Tamar Fortress was a very large and important Roman citadel. The fortress controlled important trade routes used by the Nabateans and later by the Romans themselves.

Cross the street, then wander through the 36 x 36-meter structure which once housed 120 soldiers. Two of the corner towers are still standing.

Wadi Tzafit contains a chain of water-filled hollows.

Wadi Tzafit

Wadi Tzafit

Rooms were built around a central courtyard, which contained a pool for storing rainwater that fell onto the roofs. No bones have been found in the Roman cemetery at Tamar Fortress, apparently because the soldiers cremated their dead and buried only the ashes.

Now carefully cross the highway and begin following blue trail-markers up the path to the very top of the hill. You can rest from the climb on stone remains from a Roman lookout.

From this spot you have a wonderful view of the whole fortress below. Enjoy the sight of the Moav Mountains (north, on the left side) and Edom Mountains (south, to the right) and between them the tongue of the Dead Sea. To the south is the Hatzera Mountain range, one of four large ranges in the Arava and your destination on this walk.

Take the blue-marked path again, following it down the hill. You will be traveling south most of the way and eventually swerving southwest. Desert or not, there are at least a dozen different species of flower in full bloom in late February, and you should be able to identify violet desert stork's bills. The name is a literal translation of the Hebrew term for the flower, bestowed on it because of its resemblance to a stork's beak. When the weather changes and becomes more humid, the flower twirls around and pushes a seed into the ground. There it is protected from voracious seed-eating ants, and prevented from sprouting too soon after a light rain.

The slope you are descending is to the right of a rich, green riverbed bursting with foliage. As you walk, the mountains in front of you suddenly open up and part of the Hatzera range peeks through. Hug the rocks to get around a particularly narrow ledge; then the path curves with the hill and the riverbed is to your right.

Once you reach the wadi, you will see two crosses painted on a boulder. The vertical blue line points towards Ma'ale Hatzera and the Little Crater (*Hamachtesh Hakatan*), but you go right with the black line to Ein Tzafit. From this point on, and until the end of the trip, you follow black trail-markers. The markers lead to a spring. It was created when water dripped through hard limestone to an impenetrable layer and burst out of the rock. Look for a plant called vartemia, found near the spring. When rubbed, the plant's sharp smell comes off onto your hands.

Backtrack to the junction where you saw the boulder and two crosses and this time go in the other direction, east along the riverbed. You will be staying in the gully until you return to your cars.

Green leaves on tall, bare stalks may be the plant called *cazoah akum* in Hebrew and untranslatable in English. Take a whiff: if it smells of celery, it tastes wonderful in soup. But if you smell carrots, what you have encountered is a close relative, the also untranslatable, poisonous *cazoah t'lat*

212

karni. This is a nature reserve so you can't pick the plants; even if you could, you wouldn't want to try your luck: only an expert botanist can tell for sure.

Eventually, you come up behind a 30-meter-high dry waterfall. Be careful not to fall, especially if you lean over to look at the palm tree far below. The tree apparently grows out of an underground water source.

Pale crag martins will probably fly close to where you are sitting and put on quite a show. Watch their maneuvering: crag martins can dash straight towards a cliff and pull up only a centimeter from the rocks. Another bird commonly seen in the desert is the brown-necked raven. As soon as you are resting comfortably and have pulled out a snack it begins flying over your head—wondering, perhaps, if your leavings will make a good meal.

To continue your walk, follow a very steep incline to the right and go several dozen meters around and above the waterfall. Be very careful here, and don't look back until your footing is steady. Then, see if you can find the tiny spot where you were sitting next to the falls. At least one raven will probably be feeding on your crumbs!

Spectacular rock formations meet your eyes as you begin the long descent to a fabulous sculpture garden on a smooth, rock plain. Two layers of flat white rock form benches where you can rest while your youngsters play on the boulders. Next to one huge rock is a spring whose water spurts out of several cracks in the stone.

Walk through the riverbed on slabs of rock until you reach an unusually large boulder, topped by a man-made pile of stones. Follow the black trail-marker you see to the left of the boulder, and immediately afterwards reach a second dry waterfall. As you walk around it to its left, look down to see a splendid sight: far below you is a chain of water-filled hollows.

Now you descend the slopes towards these pools, left over from winter rain. For a real treat, swim from one pool to the next. But be careful, for the water may be over your head!

Immediately beyond the hollows is a third waterfall, this one 20 meters high and ending in its own recessed pool. Tzafit's waterfalls were formed when water flowing on a gradual slope through a riverbed ate away at soft stone situated below hard limestone rock. Eventually the tougher rock, which no longer had a base on which to rest, dropped away. This explains, as well, the gigantic, scattered boulders you see in the wadi.

Two thousand years ago a waterfall made an enormous impression on Akiva. He was an ignorant shepherd watering his flocks along waterfalls.

A young man named Akiva worked for the richest man in Jerusalem. Although the boss's daughter fell in love with Akiva, she agreed to marry him only on condition that he study Torah (Judaism). Akiva went to school,

Wadi Tzafit

but found studying much too difficult. One day he ran away and sat down near a waterfall. Suddenly, the shepherd noticed how the soft water cut through the hard rock. And, he thought, if he applied himself to the Torah, its words could cut through the stone that was his heart.

Akiva returned to school. And in time he became one of the most important sages in Jewish history, Rabbi Akiva.

A surprise awaits as you continue walking to the right of the waterfall and through the riverbed: one side of the gully shines with layers of colored sand. Wadi Tzafit is one of those very rare rivers that flows through a mountain range instead of around its slopes. As it cut through the rock, it exposed not only the top layers of 80 million-year-old limestone rock that had lain under a sea, but also dry Nubian sands almost 150 million years old.

Stop at a surprisingly large field of bright yellow groundsel. If you are quiet, you might glimpse some rock hyraxes nearby. Rock hyraxes live in groups under one leader, which sends the others scurrying away when it senses danger and remains bravely in front until they are all under cover.

King David wrote that "the high mountains belong to the wild goats; the crags are a refuge for the hyraxes (coneys)" (Psalms 104:18). When son Solomon wrote Proverbs, he found the hyraxes to be "creatures of little power, yet they make their home in the crags" (Proverbs 30:26). Indeed, the hyrax's body is well designed for climbing. It has a special muscle that raises the center of its paw, creating an empty hollow which helps it ascend. It can jump as high as a meter, and on a flat surface run as fast as a human being.

Hyrax mating season begins in spring. Males sit on different rocks and "sing" to mark off their territory. They then begin to fight by lining up back to back, then trying to bite one another while yelling loudly. In the end, one dominant male remains, while the others form a separate group.

With the approach of winter, the males become more friendly to one another. Because they are essentially sociable animals who live together and sleep together for warmth, they exist well underground. In fact, their combined body heat keeps the temperature above 16 degrees centigrade.

After about 45 minutes you come to a passage between two rocks, each with a horizontal black marker. From here a path leads up the side of the riverbed, ascending a little and descending a little until it encounters the dirt road where your car is parked. Stick with this black trail-marker all the way to your vehicle so that you don't accidentally remain in the riverbed.

Vital Information
Recommended for people 10 years and older. Don't forget a change of clothes or bathing suit.

Shezaf Nature Reserve

Even without the dazzling canyons and refreshing pools that turn a Negev hike into an unforgettable desert experience, Shezaf Nature Reserve* is an enchanting stretch of land. It may, in fact, become one of your favorite Negev spots, especially if you revel in isolation, cherish flecks of exquisite foliage that brighten up endless brownish sands and find tranquillity in an infinite hush.

Open to all comers from dawn to dusk, the Shezaf Reserve covers 44,000 dunams. It name comes from the big jujube (*shezaf*) trees that grow in Wadi Shezaf, the wide riverbed which cuts across its sands.

To get there, take the Arava Highway (90). Turn east at Hatzeva Junction and after driving about 600 meters further you will see a sign for Shezaf Nature Reserve. Follow signs to the entrance.

Located 100 meters below sea level, Shezaf Nature Reserve includes a low range of sandstone hills stained red by iron oxides. There is no water source within the reserve and it receives an average of only 50 millimeters of rain each year. The temperature variations are astounding: in summer it can sizzle at 50 degrees centigrade—and in winter fall to zero!

If you have only a short time for Shezaf, you can limit your visit to an interesting viewpoint on a hill. Sunset from the top is superb, and you can watch the mountains changing colors. Once a month, a full moon slowly rises over the distant Jordanian hills in perfect harmony with a red-orange sun setting over the Negev.

Visitors with more time on hand should take two to three hours to enjoy a circular walk. Five kilometers long, it involves strolling through masses of sand, riverbed foliage, gorgeous sandstone formations and, if you are lucky, the sight of slithering dabb-lizards. With their long tails and short fat feet, it is astonishing how fast these creatures can run over the sand. Dabb-lizards are over half a meter long. Their necks are topped by thick heads which would seem more appropriate on turtles. While they look very frightening (indeed, Bedouin are said to greatly fear the dabb-lizard) they are strictly vegetarian.

Drive towards the water tower, visible from almost anywhere in the reserve. The reddish hills you see as you ride along are made of clay mixed with iron-rich sandstone. Keep your eyes on the riverbed as you pass Wadi Shahak, and you may well see herds of gazelles.

215

Shezaf Nature Reserve

If your destination is the viewpoint only, park your car at the top of the hill. If you are taking the circular walk, go left at the bottom of the hill, park and walk up.

The observation point was built in memory of Oren Lior, killed by terrorists in 1989. Pick up a few of the black stones you see on the hill to detect green spots. The stones are leftover from the time, thousands of years ago, when people from Punon—across the Jordanian border—mined copper at Hatzeva. Please replace the stones when you are finished.

Ever since the Syrian-African rift* opened up, Jordan's Edom Mountains have been moving north. Millions of years ago they were located directly across from TIMNA, an area rich in copper, and perhaps that's why Punon contained this important mineral. But they needed wind and trees to refine the copper and brought the raw materials here to this hill, where many trees grow.

The northern and western sides of the observation point are shady, and you can see all the trees below. In winter the area is green and lush. From here you can make out the Yo'adan Hills, Wadi Shahak, Horseshoe Hill (two mountains with a curve between them) and Hatzera Ridge.

On the southeastern side of the observation point your view is quite different. Located above the trail, it tops what looks like a wasteland with a few desert plants. Shezaf was declared a nature reserve because it is the only sandy area in Israel where acacias grow in white sand. The sand is blown here from the Edom Mountains. Now, if you are taking the hike, follow the green signs with white arrows down a short but steep descent to the riverbed. Here you find acacia and jujube trees covered with the colorful strapflower parasite.

Expect to see Arabian babblers, which may come close enough to touch. For over two decades scientists have been studying the birds inhabiting the region in and around Shezaf, and today the babblers are tame enough to let you get quite near. Grayish-brown birds, they are endemic to the Middle East. Because their tails move so much they were given the name *zanvan*—from the word *zanav* or "tail", in Hebrew.

Each group of babblers marks off its own territory, protecting its land primarily by screeching. They may also fight each other to the death, a type of behavior which is very rare in animals.

During flight, the babblers make certain that everyone in their group is accounted for at all times. When a bird gets lost, it gives a distress call and the others go back to find it. Another babbler habit is truly unique. Every morning before sunrise the birds all dance together for up to half an hour.

Babblers do not fight over food—it is first come, first served, regardless of social standing. Normally one babbler, usually the dominant male, stands

216

Shezaf Nature Reserve

guard, while the others look for food. The dominant male and female build a nest which is shared by several other birds and the whole flock helps feed the chicks.

After hatching, the male chicks fight among each other for a week. The outcome determines the social structure for life, and males that lose are often expelled from the group. All females are ousted from the flock at three, to mate with babblers from a different group and prevent inbreeding.

The path is sandy, making it easy to find animal tracks, many of them illustrated on marked-trail maps. Porcupine tracks are the easiest to identify; they resemble baby feet and their droppings look like dry black olives. While you can expect to catch sight of at least a few dorcas gazelles roaming the reserve, it is far less likely that you will spot Shezaf's nocturnal carnivores—wolves and caracals.

Follow the arrows, which direct you around to the left. The path leads into Wadi Shahak, thick with acacia trees. There are two species of acacia in the reserve: umbrella acacia, which has a triangular base and three or more trunks and the twisted acacia, with only one.

Growing on the acacia is the strapflower parasite, with brilliant red flowers. The strapflower, also known as the acacia mistletoe, reproduces with the help of two different birds. It is pollinated by the sunbird, whose beak fits the petals perfectly. And when the flower's sweet fruit and sticky seeds appear in autumn, they are spread by the common bulbul.

While the parasite does harm to the tree, everything in nature has its balance and camels enjoy eating the strapflower. In one part of the Negev, however, the balance has become distorted. It is, of all places, at the HAI BAR BIBLICAL WILDERNESS RESERVE, where there are no camels. As a result, parasites proliferate on the trees.

The riverbed's landscape resembles the African savanna, probably because there is so much sand and there are so many acacia trees and other plants. Look for spider traps—holes in the sand with a white ring around their tops.

At least one dabb-lizard has a den along your trail. Look for tracks that lead to its hideout. Off the path to the right is a huge jujube tree, dying from the strapflower which is entangled in its leaves.

By now you have reached the fabulous red cliffs, where the river cuts through the sandstone. An arrow seems to point back to the channel and then, almost immediately afterwards, another leads a bit to the right into the hills. Everything is dry and sandy, the perfect place to hunt for animal tracks—and the animals that made them. And you may see a little insect called *gamal Shlomo* or "Solomon's camel." It is precisely the color of the rocks, with long, skinny legs. Small though it is, this insect is a cannibal and

217

Shezaf Nature Reserve

eats its own species. While mating, the female often devours the male by biting off its head!

According to legend, the mole once boasted to his wife that he was the fastest and handsomest animal in the world. Just at that moment, King Solomon rode by on his swift camel and heard the mole's boast. He challenged the mole to race him to the top of the Temple. Undaunted, the mole agreed. Solomon's camel raced to the top only to discover the mole waiting at the finish line.

Just as Solomon was about to concede, a bird flew to him and begged him to punish the mole. It seemed the mole had bumped into a flock of birds when he emerged from the ground! And that's how Solomon learned that the mole had cheated by using a tunnel.

Choosing a punishment to fit the crime, Solomon made the mole live the rest of its life underground, where moles have remained to this day. And because he was upset with his camel for losing the race, Solomon changed it into the insect known in Hebrew as *gamal Shlomo*, and in English as the praying mantis.

Among the desert vegetation is saxaul, dispersed by the wind. Saxaul bushes are about two meters high and have no leaves; their branches are built of joints and parts of them lean towards the ground, like the branches of the weeping willow.

Animals in this part of the reserve include a variety of snakes and Israel's largest lizard, the desert monitor. Over a meter long, the desert monitor resembles a large snake. Its mouth is filled with sharp teeth which curve backwards and its long forked tongue helps it sense a victim. Desert monitors, once common in the Negev and coastal plane as far north as Holon are rapidly disappearing. And no wonder: a male desert monitor needs 1.5 square kilometers of space in which to survive!

When you reach the water pump, you will be close to a road. Cross to the other side and continue along the riverbed. About 700 meters from the point at which you crossed, veer left. You will be well to the right (its left) of a water tower and further still to your right, you will see distant reddish peaks. Soon you will reach your car.

Vital Information

Don't drive off the road; tires can cause untold damage to the natural environment. There is a picnic area, with water, under the water tower.

218

Spices

Two millennia ago, Nabatean* traders accumulated fantastic
wealth by trafficking in extremely rare and valuable commodities. Traveling
in camel convoys, they transported their goods—perfume and
incense—from Arabia and the Far East to the port of Gaza. At Gaza, these
were distributed by ship all over the Mediterranean basin. The route they
took is known, today, as the SPICE TRAIL.

The perfume called myrrh, and the incense frankincense, were
produced from trees grown naturally only in northern Somalia and southern
Arabia. For obvious reasons, the secret of their manufacture was heavily
guarded and no one knows for certain which trees were used in their
production.

Scientists believe, however, that cuttings were made in the bark and that
sap dripped out. The sap hardened as it came in contact with oxygen and
formed a substance called "tears," which were collected in autumn. They
were preserved in specially prepared storehouses until May, when the
spices and perfumes were produced. During the Roman era, an extra crop
was manufactured at the beginning of spring.

Frankincense and myrrh were quite unlike the perfumes we use today.
Because of the sterilizing characteristics contained in their source plants,
the ancient spices were utilized primarily for healing. Their additional traits
helped preserve food and repel insects. Several peoples of the ancient
world, Jews among them, employed frankincense as incense during
religious rituals.

Jews were commanded to make a special incense from a variety of
spices solely for use in the Temple. No one was allowed to copy this special
combination of fragrances (Exodus 30:34–37).

Incense was widely used to create a pleasant fragrance after meals by
the people of the Middle East. Many an incense pan has been found during
excavations of private homes in Israel.

Before crucifixion by the Romans, the were offered wine mixed with
frankincense as a painkiller.

In Rome, frankincense was burned at funerals. It is said that Nero burned
an amount of frankincense at his wife's funeral that equaled Arabia's entire
annual production of the spice!

Myrrh was different. A highly flammable substance, it created hardly any
smoke. Together with cinnamon, myrrh was an important component in an
Egyptian perfume and is mentioned several times in the Bible in this

Spices

connection. Myrrh was also mixed with other spices to make the holy oil which anointed the tabernacle (Exodus 30:23). When Ahasuerus held a beauty contest to choose a new queen, all the young girls taking part were treated with myrrh for six months before being presented to the king (Esther 2:12).

Although the Nabateans had a monopoly on the spice trail for several centuries, their luck came to a resounding end during the Roman era. Trade between Romans and Nabateans had been decidedly one-sided, for the Romans bought enormous quantities of spices at high prices and the Nabateans were totally uninterested in Roman products.

The Roman solution to this "unfair" trade was quite simple—they annexed the Nabatean kingdom. As a result the Roman Empire gained full control of the spice trade, and the Nabateans were forced to find alternative and less lucrative sources of income.

Moa was a large city.

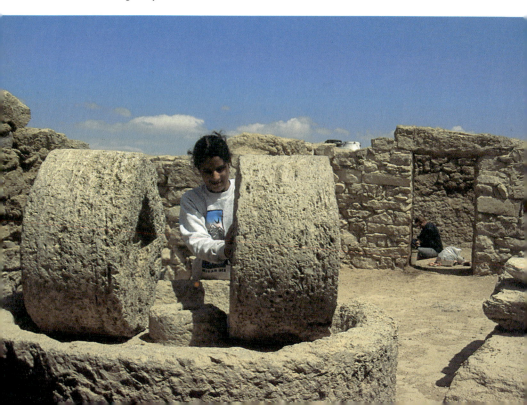

The Spice Trail by Jeep

Five millennia or so ago, people rode donkeys throughout Asia and the Middle East. But donkeys need water daily—and this limited the routes that travelers could traverse.

Transportation was revolutionized when the camel was domesticated, around the 13th century B.C.E. And camels really came into their own during the age of the Nabatean* SPICE TRAIL, from the third century B.C.E. and for the next 600 years. A number of small way stations set up for travelers and their camels along the route eventually blossomed into magnificent Nabatean cities.

It is estimated that spice trail caravans consisted of 1,000 to 2,000 camels. The trip presumably presented them with little difficulty, for camels have long legs that keep the sand's blistering heat far from their bodies while their spread-out feet help prevent them from sinking into the sand. Camels can manage without water for up to 18 days in winter and eight in the summer, and can drink all their fluids at once—as much as 100 liters at one blow! Contrary to what many people think, humps store fat, not water. This fat keeps them satisfied when they are hungry and refreshed when they are thirsty.

The spice trail originated in Somalia, India and Southern Arabia, the latter over 2,000 kilometers from the destined port at Gaza. Although there were 65 stops along the ancient route, only a handful of these are located in modern Israel.

You need camels—or a jeep—to travel the Israeli portion of the spice trail. Either way you sense how it felt to sway up and down hills and through riverbeds. On our own jeep trip along the spice trail, we had to hold on for dear life and practically hung backwards while ascending steep mountains!

There were actually several spice trails. The best known is the original Nabatean route which passed close to Petra on its way west to Gaza, crossing territory where these mysterious early peoples reigned supreme. Almost as famous is a second, used a few centuries later by the Romans and located slightly further north where they controlled the roads.

Jeep trips often begin with a lookout over the Roman spice trail as seen from Scorpion Ascent (see ROUTE NO. 7), for the Romans traveled along a trail almost adjacent to the highway in use today. From the lookout point at Scorpion Ascent you will see a building atop the mountain. This is Meitzad Tzafir, a guard post for the Roman spice trail. Follow the ridge down the mountain with your eyes, and you will see the path running along its

The Spice Trail by Jeep

shoulder where the Roman camels ascended the trail. Down to your left are the remains of two more buildings and further south stands Rogem Tzafir (again, ROUTE NO. 7.)

Although you will learn about the Roman route on your trip, it is likely your jeep will travel the Nabatean spice trail. Thus from Rogem Tzafir you will take the Arava Highway to Moa (see ROUTE NO. 10) just south of Ein Yahav.

Moa is close to the Jordanian border and was the first rest station on Israel's stretch of the Nabatean spice trail. You will enjoy walking through what remains of the way station, including the governor's quarters, high on a hill where he could get some air (it can be pretty stuffy in the Arava). Then you will get back in your jeep and ride through Wadi Omer to a famous spot called Khirbet Katzra.

No one knows for certain exactly where the camels climbed the hills. While it is possible they walked through all of Wadi Omer before scaling the mountains, riverbeds make good targets for highway robbers located above the trail. Besides, the riverbed is strewn with gravel and curves around quite a bit. This would wastefully squander time and energy, for people walked the trail along with their camels and even 2,000 years ago time was money!

That's why it is much more likely that the caravans moved left, onto the plateau which rises above Wadi Katzra. So, like the camels, your jeep will begin to climb.

If you take the spice trail in winter or early spring you will see a wealth of luxurious vegetation from your vantage point above the riverbed. Look for deep green trees, pink bloodwort, yellow fleabane and scented oxeye, a plant whose yellow flower smells of peaches. The view as you ride is stunning, for the plateau is flecked with broken pieces of black flint and below you winds the wadi. In the distance you can distinguish, like the camel-riders and their handlers, the tiny mound which was once the Katzra inn.

Your jeep will move back and forth between riverbed and plateau until you finally reach Khirbet Katzra. Fortified way stations, like this one, guarded the caravans. As you explore the ruins of Katzra you will see some interesting holes in the doorways which held curtains that screened out the light and heat.

Back in your jeep you continue on your journey. Among the flowers you see is the rose of Jericho—a name bestowed upon it by the Crusaders. The rose of Jericho is a wonderful example of how desert plants adapt to extreme climates. The plant's tissues contract when the air is dry and this protects the seeds. When it rains the rose of Jericho swells, opens up, and

The Spice Trail by Jeep

the seeds are dispersed. If rainfall is scanty, it releases only a portion, then closes up again. The rose of Jericho can live through decades of dry periods and return to life after it rains.

Your guide will probably stop for a minute to pour a tiny bit of water on top of the flower so you can watch it slowly open up to look just like a miniature rose. Christian tradition considers this plant as symbolic of the resurrection, and its Greek name means "awakening." The flower is immensely popular with pilgrims.

Another plant that grows on this route is desert henbane, whose spring flowers are a creamy yellow color with a distinctive purple center. The branches are tall and slightly wavy; they are covered with hairy fibers. Like others of the henbane species, this is a deadly plant and can set off a heart attack if eaten.

When you reach Wadi Nikarot, begin looking for the plant called *saharon meshalshel*, which hangs over the wadi. In its native Africa and India the plant—whose English name is unknown—grows on trees. Here in the desert it is seen in rocky crevices and sometimes, as it does here, the plant hangs down from the top of a cliff. The Hebrew word *meshalshel* means "dripping down."

Ein Saharonim and Khan Saharonim, which you will be visit later on, may have been named for the *saharon meshalshel*, which at one time grew nearby. When it flowers, in winter and spring, the plant's petals are small and creamy green. The *saharon meshalshel* is found only in areas which receive less than 100 millimeters of rain a year.

You will now travel west through Wadi Nikarot and perhaps stop for lunch in the shade of an acacia tree. Here you will walk through remains from Nikarot Fortress and a large cistern so well hidden you may not be able to find it without your guide's assistance.

Concealed water was an integral part of the Nabateans' success. Because the exact location of their cisterns was a trade secret, they were the only ones who could convey the spices across the desert and reap the profits.

Our guide told us about a group of Israel Air Force pilots on a survival course who were dropped here one night, about 300 meters from the cistern. Instructed to find it, not one of them succeeded. And, indeed, on our own spice trail trip—in daylight—we were practically on top of the cistern before we discovered it was there.

In ancient times buildings were constructed very close to the water source. Yet Bor Nikarot, or "Nikarot cistern," is relatively far away. Historians looked for the reason, as it wouldn't have been done by choice. And they found an excellent one. Nikarot Fortress was located at the perfect spot for

223

The Spice Trail by Jeep

guarding the passageway through Wadi Nikarot into Ramon Crater. From here sentries could clearly see the riverbed and easily protect the convoys. Unfortunately, the rock by the fortress is both sandy and soft and was unsuitable for construction of a reservoir. The cistern had to be built elsewhere.

Although it is at least six meters deep, the reservoir looks much shallower than that, for it is full of gravel and debris swept here by floods. At the moment the cistern is being excavated by archaeologists but has not yet been restored. It is the only stone-covered Nabatean cistern in Israel which still has its original roof. Considering that it hasn't been cleaned for at least 1600 years, it's in pretty good shape. Arches, and the slabs of rock between them, have remained intact and you can even see the original plaster.

Water ran into the cistern from the rocky ridge above, and if you walk on the slope you will see some of the channels cut into the stone. While the shortest route to the cistern is a straight line, the channels leading to it twist and turn and slow down the rate of flow.

Under the thick weeds are several pools that the Nabateans carved in the solid rock. Gravel and sand sank to the bottom of the pools and stayed out of the reservoir. The system of pools and zig-zagging channels greatly decreased the amount of waste in the cistern's water.

You will also notice overflow outlets on the sides of the cistern and in the corner a larger opening with steps cut into the wall. At the end of autumn, just before the first rain, the ancient Nabateans entered through this opening and cleaned out the reservoir.

During their excavations archaeologists may find coins in the cistern, for at similar Nabatean sites large caches of coins have been discovered. While it is possible they were dropped inside by mistake, they could be forerunners of the contemporary custom in which you throw money into a pool when you make a wish.

Next to the cistern is a broomrape plant, rare for its purple color. This is the first broomrape we had ever seen that wasn't yellow.

The spice trail now moves up into the mountains, but your driver-guide will probably remain in the riverbed among some enchanting rock formations. Some of the stones look like mocha-flavored cake with chocolate frosting dripping from the top. There are spots where the rocks seem to have been severed in a straight line by a knife, and others which look like elephants' feet.

Eventually Wadi Nikarot leads into Ramon Crater. Camels would have joined you here at some point, and then, like you, would have climbed up by way of the Palm Tree Ascent, a natural opening into the crater. Before

224

The Spice Trail by Jeep

you enter you will undoubtedly get out of your jeep to examine colorful rocks in the sand.

Now continue into the crater, and stop at Khan Saharonim. Almost identical to the caravansary in Moa, the two were possibly built, or at least designed, by the same people at the same time. The most exciting find here at Saharonim was a hidden bag of period coins.

It is probable that the convoy leaders slept inside the khan. But the average camel driver slept outside with the camels for there was no way that up to 2,000 camels could fit inside the inn.

This particular way station was deserted when the Nabateans lost their monopoly to the Romans in the second century (see NABATEANS) and the Romans took over the spice trail. Their new and easier route was through AVDAT AND MAMSHIT; the tougher route, which you crossed with your jeep, was abandoned.

Wadi Nikarot runs on an east-west axis. But the riverbed turns south, so Nabateans didn't use the river itself but instead followed a difficult trail up Ma'ale Mahmal. Unlike camels, jeeps can't continue through the crater and climb this ascent. Imagine if a jeep can't do it what the camel riders had to face! So you drive the long way round, through Ma'ale Noah.

On this route are Roman milestones almost a mile apart. While the Nabateans did just fine without milestones, the Romans were afraid that their drivers, who weren't always in eye contact, would get lost. In addition to marking distance, the milestones carried the name of the contemporary Roman ruler.

Watch for graceful dorcas gazelles as you drive along this trail. While dorcas gazelles are now quite common, in the late 1940's, when the Israel Defense Forces first moved into the Negev, the animals were hunted intensively for sport. Once the Society for the Protection of Nature in Israel was established and stepped in, the dorcas gazelle became a protected species. And although their number had dropped from about 50,000 in the early forties to 1,500 in the early 1950's, there are now almost 5,000 gazelles in the Negev.

Your jeep continues on to the Avdat Plateau and finally to the ancient city of AVDAT, a large and elegant Nabatean-Byzantine city. And finally, you will return home or go to your hotel for a hot, relaxing bath. You can wash off the day's dust while reflecting on the trials and tribulations of the Nabatean drivers– and their camels.

Vital Information
To book jeep tours, call the Negev Highlands Tourism Reservations Center, at 177-022-2646 or 07-588319.

Introducing Eilat

Eilat is blessed with a truly unparalleled landscape. Surroun-ded by serene granite mountains which tower over beautiful coral reefs, it is the sole land bridge between Asia and Africa. And it is a paradise for bird-lovers, who can observe millions of birds crossing continents during the changing seasons of the year.

Graves and prehistoric temples dating back to the Neolithic Age indicate that people lived in the Eilat region at least as long as 10,000 years ago. It may be they who invented the stone plow, and who first used wood as a form of worship (veneration of Ashera, goddess of fertility, and related to successful crops). Eilat was well-known in Chalcolithic* times for the high level of metallurgy that developed at the copper mines of TIMNA.

In the days of King Solomon, Eilat was the only port available in the Kingdom of Israel. A joint Israelite-Phoenician fleet sailed from Eilat to develop trade links with Africa and India long before the age of Columbus and Vasco da Gama (I Kings 9:26-29).

During the Hellenistic period the Nabateans* used Eilat's Red Sea port for their lucrative spice trade. The Romans annexed the Nabatean kingdom in 106 C.E. and built a new road from Eilat to Damascus, setting up outposts along the route to protect the precious spices.

Two hundred years later the Romans based their 10th legion in Eilat and forced Christians to work in the copper mines in Jordan. Shortly afterwards, however, under the Byzantines,* Christianity became the state religion. Led by a bishop, a large Christian community developed in Eilat. Until the tenth century a small group of Jews also lived in the town.

Under Moslem rule, which began in the seventh century, Eilat was the meeting point for tens of thousands of pilgrims. Their caravans journeyed from Damascus and Cairo to Mecca and joined up in Eilat.

Besides developing intensive agriculture in the desert (EIN EVRONA), the Moslems dug for copper near AMRAM'S PILLARS. Using their own method of extracting gold dust they were able to take out 20 grams of gold per ton of rock!

In 1115 the Crusaders conquered Eilat. At first they only charged Moslem pilgrims a fee for passing through their lands, but later they became more greedy and decided to attack Mecca. After transporting wood across the desert by camel, they constructed boats at Eilat and set sail for Islam's holiest city. The attack failed and provided a rallying point which united the previously divided Moslem world against the "infidels."

226

Introducing Eilat

Beginning in the late 19th century, steamships brought pilgrims from Egypt directly to Mecca, bypassing Eilat. The opening of the Hejaz Railroad in 1907, which also circumvented Eilat, was a death blow to the city. Once host to tens of thousands of pilgrims, Eilat became a neglected outpost on the fringes of the Turkish Empire.

Eilat witnessed frequent clashes between the Turkish and British Empires during the early 20th century. Eventually they agreed that the border between them would begin at Taba, some 10 kilometers south of Eilat. During the British Mandate the new rulers left Eilat in its sorry state, using the now almost uninhabited town as a small police station (UM RASHRASH).

The dramatic liberation of Eilat by the Israel Defense Forces in March of 1949 essentially marked the end of the War of Independence.* Cease-fire agreements that Israel signed with Jordan and Egypt placed Eilat and all of the Negev within the boundaries of the new Jewish state.

Since then the city has taken on new life. Modern Eilat was founded in 1950 and today the city is internationally famous as a popular resort. Visitors enjoy riverbed hikes, mountain climbs, birds and coral reefs. Many, especially from Scandinavian countries, come just to soak up the sun. Others flock to Eilat for special events such as the city's annual summer jazz concert. Now that Israel is at peace with Egypt and Jordan—and someday, perhaps, with Saudi Arabia as well—Eilat will undoubtedly continue to grow by leaps and bounds.

The Underwater Observatory
CORAL WORLD

Remarkable for its unusual anatomy and flashy colors, the magnificent lion fish is a dangerous creature. While it seems to be languid and unaware, and far too lovely to be of any concern to its fellow fish, the lion fish pounces murderously on sea creatures too complacent to see it coming. Also known as zebra fish, sun fish and fire fish, the lion fish has transparent flapping fins and threatens with venomous prickles. It fears nothing, neither fish larger than itself nor humans diving in the sea.

You can watch the lion fish and other dangerous creatures from a safe distance at Eilat's Coral World. Once inside, pick up the electronic guide (a tape-recorded tour available in many languages) and fish chart (both are included in the entrance fee for tourists) and start with the aquarium and marine museum. Every one of the 25 small aquaria is a piece of art; a beautiful blend of color, coral and fish. Each aquarium represents a separate area of the coral reef and contains life forms associated with particular corals at different depths. Some fish possess a stunning beauty, others are so bizarre that they have faces only a mother could love.

Learn about a species that can change its sex. All of the fish are born female and when a male dies, the dominant female is transformed into a male. If several females think they are dominant, all of them will begin to alter their gender. Only one will complete the change; the others remain part male and part female.

Some fish protect their heads by sporting a false eye near their tails. If attacked, one of them may lose part of its tail, but keep its head. Others blend in so well with the coral that you have to look hard to find them. Most of the fish are dark on top and silver-bottomed, for camouflage.

Look for the blowfish. When it senses danger it swallows water, tripling its size. The blowfish's large mass and thorny skin deter potential predators.

Many fish help one another. One, which cleans other fishes' teeth, is aptly named the dentist fish and is never attacked. Another species of fish is protected simply because it resembles the useful and well liked dentist.

Step into Coral World's darkroom to be greeted with eerie bright spots moving in all directions, fish found deep below the sea that produce their own light. A strategically placed mirror gives you the impression of being totally surrounded by flashes of iridescent light.

Having seen the fish individually, continue to the coral reef tank to see how they interact. The tank holds 350,000 liters of sea water and live coral.

The Underwater Observatory

Now its time to overcome fear and meet up with "Jaws" face to face. In the adjacent shark pool, these powerful fish swim literally under your nose. Contrary to popular belief, sharks eat fish, not people. Nevertheless, they are ferocious looking creatures with six to eight layers of teeth.

After stopping at the friendlier turtle pool, proceed to the underwater observatory. This is a large building located six meters below the level of the sea, and set in the middle of a rich coral reef. Use your chart to identify the fish as they swim by.

Vital Information

Open daily 8:30-17:00. Entrance fee.
Tel.: 07–376666; fax: 373193.

Each aquarium is a piece of art; a beautiful blend of color, coral and fish. Photograph by Phyllis Shalem.

Coral Beach Nature Reserve

Coral Beach Nature Reserve

What does it take to create an exotic coral reef with astound-ing and unusual fish? The first requirement is a tropical sea in which the temperature is a least 18 degrees centigrade; the second is clear, deep water, through which the sun's rays can penetrate. Fortunately for a nation which contains far more desert than tropical plants, Eilat was blessed with exactly the right conditions for a stunning coral reef.

A coral reef provides food and refuge and is an excellent habitat for many life forms. Some fish can break the coral and eat it. Others hide from predators in the reef, whose coral shades are excellent protection for brilliantly colored fish.

Israel's portion of the Red Sea's 4,500 kilometer coral reef is the most northerly in the world. Stretching from the Gulf of Eilat to the Egyptian border at Taba, it parallels the Eilat shoreline.

All of the reef is a nature reserve* and most of it can be perused at no cost and at your leisure. But the part richest in marine life is located within the Coral Beach Nature Reserve, which is operated by the Nature Reserves Authority. Visitors to Coral Beach Nature Reserve will have a wonderful time weaving near and around a plethora of fascinating underwater creatures. You will be amazed at their ability to maneuver; some species swim sideways and even backwards as they make a fast getaway.

Look for sea urchins, which resemble prickly black balls. During the day they peek through holes in the reef. At night they materialize in large groups to search out food.

You do not need to be a great swimmer or diver to see the fish up close; non-swimmers can simply rent a life jacket and float. If you do any swimming at all, rent a mask and snorkel—it shouldn't take more than a few minutes to learn how to use them. Once inside the water you will be surrounded by fish of every imaginable color. The fish seem quite used to being a tourist attraction and approach without hesitation.

Vital Information
Daily 9:00–17:00. On holiday eves the reserve closes at 13:00. Entrance fee. Tel.: 07–376829.

Dolphin Reef

Nature lovers may wonder whether the dolphins at Eilat's Dolphin Reef, located three kilometers south of the city, enjoy their part in a thriving commercial venture. Part of your answer becomes clear when you visit the reef, for you see how freely the dolphins come and go. Besides, the dolphins are not forced to perform in order to get a yummy, fishy meal.

Snorkeling with the dolphins is an unforgettable experience, for they swim through your legs and are happy to be touched as long as you stay away from the blow-holes on top of their heads. It is tremendously exciting to wait for a dolphin to leap up from the depths; sensational when it comes close enough for a stroke.

Scuba diving is even more surreal, for you simply lose all track of time and pray your dive will never come to an end. The dolphins are friendly, playful, gentle and independent. And the encounter is something to remember.

No one seems to know why dolphins like humans so much, but they truly enjoy constant contact with people. Among the world's most intelligent creatures, the dolphin is the only wild animal in the world which has established an unconditional bond with humans.

Although not pressured to perform, the dolphins seem to find it fun to entertain. Visitors can watch them from the pier, or sit on a raft only inches away from where they are playing. In fact, the dolphins often put their heads down right next to thrilled observers and wait for a pat.

The group of bottle-nosed dolphins, including four born at the reef, live in an enclosed area of the sea comprising 10,000 square meters and reaching a depth of 18 meters. Because this compound is part of the Red Sea, they are afforded the most natural environment possible. In addition to feeding before training sessions, the dolphins catch fish independently and thus continually hone their natural instincts.

Truly gentle and nonviolent animals, dolphins have no natural enemies (except man). Even among themselves they are wholly nonaggressive; males and females travel as a group and seem to experience no jealousy at all. Dolphins have quite active sex lives, enjoying all kinds of varied positions, and have sex with whomever they want whenever they are in the mood.

Female dolphins are pregnant for 12 months (and "breastfeed" for a whole year following the birth). Other female dolphins act as midwives during the delivery. The baby emerges tail first, and is lifted to the surface

Dolphin Reef

where it begins to breathe. When the dolphins go out to hunt for fish, they leave babies with a dolphin nanny.

On occasion, dolphins from the open sea approach the reef. They carry on what appears to be conversations with the reef's inhabitants—perhaps inviting them to join their own group—and leave. Yet the reef's dolphins remain. And even though reef dolphins are often free to venture into the open sea, they always return to their home on the shores of Eilat.

Vital Information

A very hefty entrance fee to the reef includes use of a private beach, chairs, nature movies and observations of dolphin training sessions. Picnic baskets are not allowed on the beach, which is clean and peaceful. Wheelchairs can get all the way from the parking lot to the pier near the dolphin training area.

Snorkeling, scuba diving and joining the dolphin trainer on the raft cost extra. You must reserve these activities in advance.
Tel.: 07-375935 or 371846; fax: 373824.

For some inexplicable reason, dolphins really like human beings.

International Bird Center

Eilat's unique position as the only land bridge between Asia and Africa makes it one of the world's most important migratory routes. Most birds prefer to fly over land than sea, and every year millions of birds from as far away as Siberia and Scandinavia pass over this region. Some fly more than 10,000 kilometers a year.

The biannual migration north and south takes place in stages. Birds eat along the way, often almost doubling their weight in stored fat, then take off for the next place to find a good meal. For birds coming north, Eilat is the first resting place after crossing the Sahara Desert. Its desert oases, fish ponds and trees all encouraged the birds to discover Eilat long before the development of modern tourism.

Because the birds come from such varied climates, Eilat's migration season is exceptionally long. Some migrants go home early, while others return later in the season. Fall and spring are the main migratory seasons, but birds can be seen crossing continents every month of the year, except in May and June.

In recent years Israel's air force and commercial airlines have become increasingly sensitive to these migrations, and organize their flight plans and training exercises accordingly. They know that the impact of one bird can destroy an aircraft—and its pilot. In one instance a bird smashed into the windshield of a plane and knocked the pilot unconscious. Fortunately the bird also hit the ejection button, propelling the pilot out of the plane and saving his life.

The prophet Jeremiah talks about avian migration when he laments the Israelites' disobedience to God's laws. "Even the stork in the sky knows her appointed seasons, and the dove, the swift and the thrush observe the time of their migration. But my people do not know the requirements of the Lord," he says (Jeremiah 8:7).

A walk north along the salt ponds gives you the opportunity of viewing migrators who land in Israel to rest or stay the winter. Take your stroll alone (with good binoculars) or join a tour guided by the International Bird Watcher Center. Start off by rambling along the Red Sea coast towards the Jordanian border. A wooden sign on your right describes the region's most typical fowl and shows you that you are on the right track. Just a bit further to the left is a brown structure and, behind it, a bird bulletin board and a path. Take this path due north, preferably an hour or so before sunset—a

233

International Bird Center

particularly beautiful time because you are situated between the Edom Mountains on the east and the Eilat Mountains to the west.

Large numbers of birds feed along a stream of sewage which runs into the Red Sea to the right of the path. Others enjoy the fishponds and salt water pools to the left. Little stints are among the most frequent visitors here and stay throughout the winter. Among the many birds you see are flamingos, which like salt water, are very sociable and travel in flocks. You may not spot their heads, as they stick them underwater to catch shrimp for their dinners.

Redshanks, which have long red legs, hail from Europe. When worried, the redshank begins flying around sounding an alarm, a melodic sound often heard near fishponds in winter. Like most shore birds they can swim only a little and their feathers, which have no protective oil, get soggy when wet. This can make it drown, or catch a fatal cold.

Wagtails have yellow chests and tails which are longer than their wings. Their name probably comes from the way they move their tails as they walk. Wagtails mainly eat insects plucked from the ground.

Don't confuse the ring plovers you see with spur-winged plovers, which are larger and have black heads. The spur-winged variety will bravely defend its territory both while hatching its eggs and after the chicks are born. They use the spur in their wings to ward off other birds.

Caspian terns are grey with red bills, and you may see gulls whose yellow bills have black bands on their tips. More common is the grey heron which feeds on algae and insects and spends most of its day just standing still.

Just past the palm trees to your right is a little (and precarious) bridge for crossing the stream. Wander through the palm grove to observe even more of your feathered friends. In spring you can also visit a ringing station, where staff from the center ring the birds so that they can keep tabs on their flight.

The first salt pools to receive water pumped in from the Red Sea are slightly north of Eilat. Consequently, an unusually large quantity of birds—especially flamingos and ducks—congregate at these ponds.

 To get there, follow the Arava Highway north to kilometer marker 20, turn right, and follow the road as far as you can to the east.

Vital Information
There is a fee for the guided tour. It is advisable to phone the center to find out when the tours take place. Tel.: 07–374276; fax: 370890.

234

Um Rashrash

HISTORIC POLICE STATION IN EILAT

Israel's War of Independence* concluded dramatically at a former British police station in Eilat. In February of 1949, near the end of the war, Egypt relinquished all claims to the Negev. But Jordan insisted that the Negev was hers—mainly because Jordanian solders were stationed along the Arava. Therefore, before concluding comprehensive cease-fire negotiations, Israel decided to establish a land link with Eilat. The name of the operation was *Uvda*, Hebrew for "fact."

Two different Israeli units set off in what turned out to be a race to Eilat. The Negev Brigade began by descending from Beer Sheva to Uvda Valley, then moved into the southern part of the Arava. Unable to scale the hilly terrain, they crossed the Egyptian border into Sinai, circled around and returned north to Eilat. The Egyptian army did not intervene.

Soldiers of the Golani Brigade were sent down the Arava's Scorpion Ascent (see ROUTE No. 7). They traveled its treacherous serpentine curves in the dead of night, without a single light to guide them. As they continued through the Arava they occasionally ran into Jordanian soldiers, but circumvented the enemy's troops. Jordanian forces subsequently withdrew.

From both directions and within two hours of one another, the Israeli brigades reached the deserted town of Eilat (the Jordanians had left shortly before Israeli troops arrived). The Palmach's* Negev Brigade was anxious to get the credit for Eilat's liberation and raised the Israeli flag in the police station. This became the famous "ink flag," improvised on the spot with white sheet and a bottle of ink.

A month later a cease-fire agreement was signed with Jordan, recognizing Israel's sovereignty over the entire Negev. Although the United Nations had awarded the Negev to the Jewish State, it took many months of bitter fighting and Operation Uvda to make it part of Israel.

A few years ago the police station witnessed another struggle, when city fathers decided to tear it down to make way for new construction. Eilat residents who wanted to preserve this historic landmark surrounded the building and stopped the bulldozers with their bodies!

You will find Um Rashrash next to the Red Rock Hotel, near the center of town. Signs are in Hebrew.

Evrona Spring (*Be'erot Sharsheret*)

Ein Evrona is a place that seems to defy nature: the inhospitable, barren terrain seems an unlikely place for a farm. Yet Ein Evrona contains exciting remains from precisely that—a large farm dating back to the eighth century!

To get there, drive north from Eilat on Highway 90 (the Arava Highway). After about 15 minutes you will reach kilometer-marker 20. A sign points left to WADI SHEHORET and AMRAM'S PILLARS. You, however, turn right off Highway 90 onto a dirt road and drive about 100 meters, then turn left and continue another 1.3 kilometers. Now go right, and continue until you reach a prominent wooden structure with signs explaining that you are at an ancient farm. The farm was on the route of the haj, (the journey made by Moslem pilgrims to Mecca, see WADI GISHRON) and provided food for the thousands who passed by.

What makes this trip such fun is the chance to crawl through a tunnel that once provided enough water to cultivate over 1,500 dunams of land. Long ago farmers carved out tunnels to reach fresh underground water, then transported it to the fields. Every 10 meters a vertical shaft was dug for air to circulate. To reach one such tunnel, follow wooden arrows to the left where yellow railings mark its entrance.

You can descend a six-meter shaft by ladder, crawl about 20 meters through the tunnel and surface through another shaft. Flashlights help but are not essential. If you are concerned, let the kids go first: they will quickly find the way.

Back on the surface, reverse direction and return to Highway 90. Continue driving north (by turning right) and turn right at the orange sign (Dom Palms) onto a dirt road. After driving about 1.4 kilometers more you will be struck by the uniqueness of the site—palm trees that look like giant slingshots.

This is the northernmost place in the world where the dom palm is found. In Sudan, where dom palms originated, they grow in a tropical environment. The fact that these trees moved this far north from Africa and

Evrona Spring (Be'erot Sharsheret)

adapted well to the environment is an indication that long ago the weather here was very different than it is today.

The fruit of the dom palm is the size of an egg, and protected by a hard cover. A bit of the fruit can ease constipation; too much tends to aggravate the problem. Dom palm trees are different from other palm trees because they have several trunks. The fruit is tasty and its fibers can be woven into baskets and ropes.

A Jewish legend describes a female palm tree that would not give fruit. All efforts to graft a male branch onto this tree were unsuccessful. It turned out that she was in love with a particular palm from Jericho and produced fruit only after a branch from that precise tree was grafted onto her trunk.

The trees here thrived for thousands of years. Recently, however, wells have been dug to provide water for households in Eilat. As a result, the water sources for the dom palms dried up and but for the intervention of the Nature Reserves Authority,* they would have died. Black hoses indicate that the dom palms are now regularly irrigated.

 From here you can return on the dirt path back to Highway 90.

Some people call Amram's Pillars Israel's Petra.

Amram's Pillars

Few natural attractions in Israel are as stunning as a strange-looking phenomenon a few kilometers north of Eilat. Popularly referred to as Amram's Pillars, the site boasts a rock structure which resembles a pagan temple. Indeed, at nearby TIMNA there is a large pagan temple at the foot of a similar natural formation.

To visit the site, head west off Highway 90 (the Arava Highway) at kilometer 20, where there is an orange sign for Amram's Pillars and Wadi Shehoret.

On your right soon after the turn you will see a daemia plant, a climber with heart-shaped, greyish leaves and a velvety texture. The leaves contain a poisonous substance which repels most insects. The black and yellow grasshopper is the only insect which finds nourishment in the daemia. Indeed, the plant's liquid helps create the grasshopper's venom! Look for the daemia's brownish-yellow-to-white flowers from February to April.

A few dozen meters further, also on your right, you will see one of the region's rare leafless silk vine plants. Although from a distance the plant may look dry and dead, from March to May it contains tiny, deep red blossoms surrounded by a halo of white strands.

Other winter flowers include the light purple thorny zilla and furry-leaved yellow fleabane. The fleabane blooms until June, its size dependent on the amount of rainfall during the year. Containing a sweetness unusual for a desert herb, fleabane is delicious in tea. Bedouin claim this tea relieves stomach pain.

When you reach a fork in the road, green trail-markers lead to Wadi Shehoret and blue ones to Amram's Pillars. Don't be confused by other roads; just bear right and keep following the blue markers. The drive on the dirt road is about five kilometers.

Considering their location so close to the Sinai Desert, Amram's Pillars could logically have been named for Moses' father Amram. In fact, their name derives from the riverbed in which they stand: *Amrani* in Arabic, with the Hebrew name simply resembling the Arabic.

As you drive, you will see magmatic rocks of shimmering black, dusty green and burnt-red hues, mingling deliciously with cream-colored

Amram's Pillars

dolomite and yellowish limestone. The view is especially stunning when a raven-colored hill suddenly juts out of a lighter mountain.

Park next to the green nature reserve sign, and the remains of a shelter. After an easy 10-minute walk along a black-marked trail you catch a preview of the pillars which are to come: look for exposed red and white marbled sandstone mixed with limestone and dark magma.

Suddenly you reach five towering pillars, well over a dozen meters high—a stupendous sight which some call Israel's Petra. These columns, however, were not made by man: they were carved out of sandstone by water which trickled through cracks in the rock.

It is a Jewish custom to say a special prayer on seeing an extraordinary natural site. The prayer praises God for "doing works of creation" and when you see Amram's pillars, you will probably add, "Amen."

The Amram riverbed contains numerous tunnels and vertical shafts where miners hacked out copper at the same time that Timna was being mined (6,000 years ago). Hunt for the openings—you can even crawl inside! But be careful when climbing on the rocks as sandstone crumbles under your feet. On the way back to the car, look on your left side for green minerals along the wall, signs of copper deposits.

You will find your drive back to the road even more beautiful on the return trip. Watch for a delightful sandstone mushroom, resembling the exciting phenomenon at Timna. At one spot the white sandstone is colored with red blotches, looking for all the world as if a painter dropped his bucket.

Vital Information
You don't have to clamber up to the pillars to enjoy this amazing sight; the short walk is suitable for practically everyone.
This is a nature reserve: don't touch the foliage.

Wadi Shehoret

Wadi Shehoret

Only a few kilometers away from the glittering lights of Eilat rise mountains of incredible beauty. Riverbeds and canyons within these mountains offer colorful hiking trails with spectacular vistas. Wild animals are a frequent sight within the enchanting hills.

Wadi Shehoret is a delightful, circular family walk through a stunning canyon. A relatively easy two to three hour outing, the trip involves short ascents up a few dry waterfalls.

 To reach Wadi Shehoret, locate kilometer marker 20, about eight kilometers north of Eilat. An orange Nature Reserves Authority sign points to Wadi Shehoret and AMRAM PILLARS. Turn onto a blue-marked dirt road and drive another two kilometers, towards the Eilat Mountains Nature Reserve. Turn left at the first intersection, a green-marked dirt road which you follow for four kilometers to the gorge's entrance.

Little brown desert birds called sand partridges may be walking in the sand near the road. They get their Hebrew name *koreh* ("call") because they tend to cry out, over and over. The sand partridge is a vegetarian which picks seeds and little flowers out of the sand.

The astonishingly long and uniform wall on your left as you get really close to the canyon consists of alluvial* deposits tens of thousands of years old, a sign that at one time the mountains here were completely covered by water. During that period and following formation of the Syrian-African rift,* the area acquired a pronounced tilt. Rain which fell on the mountains began flowing swiftly towards the depression that would eventually become the Dead Sea. As it rushed through the riverbed it left deposits which later solidified (called conglomerate). In addition to this surprising conglomerate wall there are still patches of alluvial deposit atop some of the granite mountains.

Although the beginning of the walk is not marked, you will be following a green-marked trail through the gorge. Park at the Nature Reserve sign, where the road ends and you see, ahead of you, a narrow entrance to the canyon. On your left is a large caper which seems to defy gravity, for it is suspended in the cliff. Birds devour the caper's attractive red fruit and the seeds, which pass through their digestive system, occasionally fall into the tiny cracks on the sides of the mountains. Look closely at a caper leaf. Its

Just outside of Eilat rise mountains of incredible beauty.

240

Wadi Shehoret

Wadi Shehoret

plastic-like cover keeps moisture inside and helps the caper survive in the desert.

Inside the canyon you will be surrounded on all sides by towering granite cliffs. Three different varieties of caper (Egyptian, fig, and thorny caper) add bright green splashes of color to the landscape; they live in crevices within the rocks and both their fruit and their leaves provide sustenance for the region's animals.

Dozens of ibex roam the nature reserve and you will probably see at least a few, even if you come at midday instead of more advisedly in early morning or late afternoon. Look for them on top of the mountains and along the slopes.

A reddish-white rock wall—a dry waterfall—will block your way. Pick the easiest place to ascend and pull each other up.

All kinds of vibrant hues run through the rocks. The variations in color depend on whether the magma crystallized below or above the earth's surface, and the temperature of the air at the time it occurred. Enjoy tall cliffs surrounding the canyon, some up to 100 meters higher than ground level. In the distance you can see the most impressive of them all, 200 meters above where you are standing.

You will probably come to foxthorn (thornbush) plants whose leaves have been eaten by animals. Among these diners are hyraxes which live here in the rocks and you may get a glimpse of them if you are really quiet. The foxthorn sports light purple flowers during the rainy season, and red fruit in spring and summer. Birds relish this small red fruit and disperse its seeds with their droppings. Look for droppings below an acacia tree and try to find toenail marks on the bark—more evidence that the hyraxes were hungry. The bottom leaves were most likely devoured by ibex.

Blackstarts—grey birds with black tails—are often found in riverbeds and especially those, like Wadi Shehoret, with a number of acacia trees. A very friendly species of bird, blackstarts may follow you along the trail.

Many a dike runs through the granite mountains. Dikes begin as molten rock flowing swiftly through vertical cracks in existing rock and widening the crevices. When the material hardens it either remains in the crack, creating a different color and texture within the original stone, or it crumbles and leaves an empty space. If you haven't spotted one earlier, look for a very obvious dike right before you come to the end of the gorge.

Outside the canyon you will find a rare rock wall where white limestone touches granite. Although limestone is the youngest sedimentary material and is generally found at the highest horizontal layer, in Wadi Shehoret it stands vertically next to magmatic rock. Here there is also a pocket of

242

Wadi Shehoret

sandstone mixed with clay; oxidation of various minerals within the rocks created the differing shades of color you see.

If you look very carefully you might notice that some of the circular "rocks" on the ground are really the fossilized remains of oysters and sea urchins. These fossils indicate a radically different climate here in the past, for the sea creatures live only in shallow water. Apparently the end of the wadi* where you entered the canyon was blocked in the past and water remained in the riverbed, a perfect environment for oysters.

In the middle of the open space where you should now be standing look for red and green colored crosses on a rock. Turn right, following the red marker northeast.

At the beginning of the path is a plant with white or yellow flowers that resembles a small bush. Known as Syrian rue, this plant thrives in soil rich in nitrates and is normally found near animal pens and garbage dumps. The source of nitrates in this particular spot is hikers who pause to relieve themselves. Within the leaves of the Syrian rue is a poison which animals try to avoid. As a result, although vegetarian creatures have ravaged other plants, the Syrian rue remains whole.

As you follow the trail along a light-colored limestone slope, look directly across you to the right to see a starkly contrasting granite mountain. This is a rare opportunity to walk on a geological fault line. Notice the different colors on both sides of the path: black on the east contrasts sharply with the lighter colored stones on the west.

When you reach the top of the cliff, turn around and gaze at the view behind you—a natural sight virtually untouched by the hand of man. Note how strong natural forces have forced limestone rocks to tip over onto their sides. You can make a slight detour off the path for an even more fantastic view. Turn to the right, then climb to the top of the mountain—about a five minute walk. Then return to the path.

Now head right along the cliff (you will see a red trail-marker). To your left (northeast) are fabulous black ridges; further north, feast your eyes on layer after layer of different colored rocks.

The trail leads you southeast directly into a reddish-brown hill, stunning against a background of black cliffs, the pinkish Edom Mountains, and to the south, the greenish-blue color of the Gulf of Eilat. Below you in the distance is the road which connects the highway and the canyon. Descend in that direction (east), through crevices and over rocks.

At the bottom is a red-marked path which you take down to the riverbed. Soon it will connect with a black-marked trail heading to the right (south) to the ravine entrance where your chariot awaits.

243

Wadi Shehoret

A huge complex of reddish rock should now appear on your right. Leave the trail to circle around it; this is red sandstone mixed with clay and if you pour water on the powdery ground you can create your own make-up.

Past the red sandstone is a granite hill with some fantastic formations, not to be missed before you return to the black-marked path and walk to the canyon (due south). If you do not see the black markers, just keep heading south, with the Edom Mountains to your left. When you run smack into the conglomerate you will know that you are just above the parking lot.

Hiking in Timna

Timna Park

Famous for its stunning cliffs, enchanting canyons and vibrantly colored stone, Timna is also an exciting historical site. Ancient miners pried copper out of the rocks at Timna for several thousand years, leaving behind riveting historical landmarks.

 You can view this spectacular collection of geological and historical sites at Timna Park, located 25 kilometers north of Eilat along Highway 90.

It would take days to explore all of Timna's archeological finds and dazzling scenery. This chapter describes the major sites—all accessible by car. It concludes with suggestions for a thrilling half-day hike off the beaten track, and a one-hour circular walk.

Begin with the movie, available in many languages at the entrance to the park. The production explains the formation of Timna's geological phenomena and describes how copper was mined in ancient times. Before your hike/s you may want to visit several major attractions: Solomon's Pillars, the Temple of Hathor, the "mushroom," a wall inscription called "the Chariots," workshops and a second Chalcolithic* temple. All are clearly marked both on the road and on the pamphlet you receive at the entrance.

Solomon's Pillars

It was nature, not King Solomon, that fashioned incredible 50-meter-high pillars from Timna's sandstone. Water streaming down a crack in the mountain "polished" the walls and created an awesome site, similar to AMRAM'S PILLARS. And when you stand in front of the pillars you feel very, very small.

In the words of the Bible, "I lift my eyes to the mountains, where will my help come from?" Spiritual thoughts like these may have motivated many cultures and religions over the millennia into worshipping at the base of these very rock pillars.

The Temple of Hathor

Over 11,000 archaeological finds were made in this temple—not surprising, since it was in use for about 1,000 years. Built in the 14th century B.C.E., this place of worship was dedicated to Hathor, the Egyptian goddess

Timna Park

of music, love, dance, cats, cows and miners! A central platform was used for offerings, and niches in the wall probably held idols.

Jews never worshipped in this particular pagan temple, but they did venerate a snake cast in copper which was called "copper" (*nehushtan*), perhaps their way of deifying metal. During a plague in the desert, when the people spoke against God and Moses, "the Lord sent venomous snakes among them; they bit the people and many Israelites died" (Numbers 21:5–6). God commanded Moses to make a bronze snake. And He said "put it up on a pole; anyone who is bitten can look at it and live" (Numbers 21:8).

Moses' brass snake was preserved in the Temple in Jerusalem. Many other copper snakes from the biblical period have been uncovered in holy sites throughout Israel. The snake in the Temple was destroyed during the religious reforms of King Hezekiah (II Chronicles 18:4, see TEL BEER SHEVA).

Carved into the rock on the sheer wall above the temple is a picture of Pharaoh making an offering to Hathor. In similar Egyptian inscriptions the Pharaoh is depicted smaller than the god, but here they are the same size. Perhaps Pharaoh had to humble himself before the gods in Egypt, but when far away from home he could allow himself to appear more powerful.

Those who want a closer look at the inscription can walk up the stairs behind the temple for a 20-minute circular route. A small pipe along the way points directly at the rock carving.

The "Mushroom," Workshops and Second Chalcolithic Temple

The mushroom is a prominent natural site made of eroded sandstone. Near the mushroom are the remains of miners' workrooms and another temple, both from the Chalcolithic period. Restoration of these remains has been minimal.

First to the workshops, which today are not very impressive. Seven millennia ago, however, they represented a significant technological revolution: this was the first time in history that man separated metal from rock and fashioned it into tools! Timna's copper mines are the oldest mines in the world. Somehow the ancients understood the value of the green-colored rocks and developed the tools necessary for mining and smelting.

Miners dug vertical shafts up to 30 meters deep, using rock and, later, metal hammers. Then the shafts went horizontal, following the ore deposits under the ground. Over 9,000 such shafts have been uncovered here.

The copper-rich rock extracted was placed in a smelting furnace dug into the ground. The process required a strong supply of air, and the bellows had not yet been invented. So they chose this spot, which is fairly open to the wind. Iron oxides were added to the ore and heated to over

246

Timna Park

1,200 degrees centigrade. To give you an idea of the enormous effort involved in producing copper here are some statistics: 50 kilograms of copper ore, 100 kilograms iron oxide and 150 kilograms of coal were required for the production of a mere 1.5 kilograms of pure copper!

Some 3,000 years after ancient man began smelting copper, he discovered how to produce iron. Perhaps this was an accidental by-product of the iron oxides heated together with the copper, for iron melts at 1500 degrees.

Next to the workshop is the Chalcolithic temple. Look for five offering tables, a basin for liquid offerings and five standing stones. Worship of stones was very common thousands of years ago, for the stones symbolized the gods. In the Bible, the Jews were specifically commanded to destroy such pagan holy stones (Deuteronomy 12:3).

Animal and fruit remains discovered here were probably offerings to the gods. Since the site is Chalcolithic, there are no written records and we can only make educated guesses about the ancient faith.

The temple's sides were of stone, and its tent-like covering was not preserved. Its structure is similar to the Chalcolithic temple in Uvda Valley (see the LEOPARD TEMPLE).

The Chariots

Follow the blue arrows for about three minutes to reach a stairway. Walk up the stairs and enter a small crevice. Facing the wall is a picture of Egyptian chariots in which one soldier directs the horses and a second stands with a bow. Comparable to the modern tank, the chariot was Egypt's main weapon.

One of the chariots on the wall is manned by a third soldier, something which helps us understand a verse in the Bible. When Pharaoh chased the Jews with 600 chariots they lost heart immediately. In Hebrew (Exodus 14:7) it is written that Pharaoh added "shileshim" to every chariot. This word is often translated as "officers," but the correct understanding is "a third:" he loaded up the chariots to maximum military capability. The third warrior would dismount, fight man to man and then jump back on.

Look for the picture of an oryx with its long horns. Unfortunately, this lovely animal no longer roams the Negev; the last ones were slaughtered in honor of Lawrence of Arabia. A few were recently reintroduced to the Israeli desert at the HAI BAR BIBLICAL WILDERNESS RESERVE.

Short Circular Walk

Now for an easy, 45 minute circular walk. Drive to THE ARCHES, a superb natural phenomena hewn out of the rock by mountain floods. Park your

Timna Park

car, then follow the blue arrows up and down some small hills to the cave (just past the sign that says "trail continues here"). After exploring the cave, walk back to the sign "trail continues here" and you will reach an excavated mining shaft, covered by an iron net. The protective cover makes it difficult to see into the tunnel. If you continue to the right, uphill, you will quickly reach a second, uncovered shaft, which offers a better view. The vertical niches were used by the workers climbing up and down. Now return to the covered shaft and follow the blue arrows down the hill. On the hill to your right, you will see many circular patterns in the ground. These are the tops of mining shafts, now filled with dirt. It is unclear if they were intentionally covered to preserve the underground treasures for the future, or if this is the work of nature.

When you reach the bottom of the hill, cross the riverbed, and continue along the trail (up a little hill), following the sign that reads "ancient dugouts." Soon you will reach a series of entrances to horizontal mining shafts. Enjoy exploring here; the tunnels are short so you will not get lost and there is no need for flashlights. While you cool off in the comfortable tunnels, you can appreciate the sweat and toil required to cut through these rocks some 6,000 years ago. The workers burrowed there way through lying flat on their stomachs!

From here the trail continues straight to the parking lot, about five minutes away.

Half Day Hike

If you have two cars, you can try this half-day hike. Leave one car at the end of the trail, at the Mushroom, and take the other to the Arches.

Enjoy the arches and cave (see above). When you exit the cave, retrace your steps a few meters. Right before you reach the iron-covered shaft, move up and to the right. You will see a little hill and a smooth stone path running between the rocks. This takes you straight down to a wide riverbed which you may want to slide down on your bottom. You will be facing a sandy staircase built into the rock. Ignore it, and turn left with the wadi.

Watch the cliffs as you walk between them, for bright green copper layers will sparkle in the sun and some mining galleries are open to the riverbed path. The sight of stunning, copper-rich rocks was apparently impressive in biblical times as well: "For the Lord your God is bringing you into a good land...a land where the rocks are iron and you can dig copper out of the hills" (Deuteronomy 8:9).

The Egyptian Empire took pains to guard this precious raw material. Copper was so important that it was worshipped by the people: not unlike a modern reverence for gold and diamonds, perhaps!

248

Timna Park

Note, especially, a pair of tunnels which are from two different eras: miners in the older, higher one used a stone hammer, while those in the lower one mined with metal chisels. At the time the tunnels were covered with sandstone, and miners dug down from the top of the cliffs not far from where you are standing. The shafts were exposed during the last few thousand years, when flood waters washed away the rock and created the riverbed.

Soon you will run smack into one of Timna's blue-and-white markers (not the standard blue trail-markers on marked-trail maps), one of many which you begin to follow. A little further note a blue-white angle; here, veer to the left.

The cliffs along the path are amazingly colorful, the result of their minerals' exposure to air. Study the fossils strewn along the path. Look for sea creatures left from when oceans covered the area, as well as fossilized bark and a few seedlings, frozen for all time.

When the path ends in a T-junction, turn right towards a blue-marked angle, then go right again. Within minutes the rocks turn a glorious pinkish-red hue, for you have reached the entrance to "pink canyon."

As you walk through the canyon, hug the left wall and follow the blue-white marked path left. You will be trekking through some strange and wonderfully surrealistic rocks on both sides until you come to a plateau. Follow a bright blue marker, to the right.

On your right are a series of Chalcolithic mining tunnels. Follow the markers straight ahead (don't turn right). After the path curves sharply, you should see a hill with a bright blue marker at its crest. Climb up to the top, where you will get a great view of the Timna cliffs.

Follow the path down to a narrow wadi, then back up the hill. If you mistakenly turn right instead of continuing straight ahead, a marker should block your way. Once you are on the hill again, you will see another marker in the distance, as a guide.

The path takes you over little stones and leads down to a lovely white canyon on the left. Look for slits in the rock as you walk through. These are exposed portions of mining shafts built millennia ago.

Continue up and around the mountain. While there are a number of paths to take (all going to the same place) try the one furthest to the right. The trail leads to a huge plain where you may see groups of ibex. Stay close to the mountains to your right.

Below your feet the ground suddenly turns into fine sand sprinkled with pieces of dark metal. Walk up a sand hill, then take an exhilarating run all the way down to the bottom!

Timna Park

On your right is a dead end that contains some astonishing sights: a unique, richly colored rock, a black one ribboned with red that looks exactly like a prime rib, an enormous "boot," and a gigantic rock formation which will become another "arch" in a few thousand years or so.

Now return to the path that led left. Keeping close to the cliffs, follow the trail into a gully, then to a sensational white gorge. If it contains water you may have to climb along its sides.

Once out of the gorge, you may find the regular path swept away by floods (although the trail-markers probably hung on!) If necessary, take a parallel path, under an impressive block of overhanging red stone: oxidized iron. In a large gap between the red cliffs note Timna Mount. It juts out of the valley, a dark protrusion against the pale Edom Mountains you see in the distance.

When you reach a T-marker—horizontally black and vertically blue—you will have joined a black-marked trail leading down from Mount Berech on your right. Continue straight ahead, now following black markers. Watch for two markers on some small rocks which lead to a sandy red path to the left. This is a shortcut to the park's main road.

Turn left and walk along the road, on its left side. When you reach a sign which says "keep to the road," leave it for open ground on the left and walk straight towards a needle-topped hill—the Mushroom is right behind it, and so is your car.

(Should you miss the markers leading to the shortcut, simply continue on the riverbed path until you get to the road, then follow the signs to the Mushroom).

Vital Information

Every day from 7:30 to nightfall. Entrance fee.
Tel.: 07–356215, 372542.
You need a car to reach the many sites within the park.
Toilets are located at the main entrance and by the pool.
On hot days begin the early in the morning or after noon. Toddlers will have to be carried through the rough spots of the longer hike.
If you have only one car you can leave it at the Arches parking lot. When you finish, at the Mushroom, you have another three to four kilometer hike from the Mushroom back to your vehicle.
The HaAretz museum in Tel Aviv has an entire wing devoted to Timna's historical mines.

250

Yotvata Hai Bar

BIBLICAL WILDERNESS RESERVE

Established in 1968 to return once-extinct biblical animals to their natural Israeli habitats, the Yotvata Hai Bar has since developed and expanded. Hundreds of animals now populate the exciting animal reserve, and special features include a predatory center and an unusual darkroom.

Yotvata Hai Bar is run by the Nature Reserves Authority, and guides accompany you on a comfortable minibus tour of the compound. As you ride through the Hai Bar's 12,000 dunams and observe dozens of oryx, addax, wild ass and ostriches, the guide explains the purpose of the Hai Bar and enthralls passengers with stories of animal habits.

You will learn that four groups of Asiatic wild ass (onager), which vanished from the Israeli scene centuries ago, have been "reintroduced" into the Negev. The Bible places the wild ass specifically in this region: "Who let the wild donkey go free? Who untied his ropes? I gave him the wasteland as his home, the salt flats as his habitat" (Job 39:5–6).

As this animal was never domesticated, its Hebrew name is *pereh*, or "wild." Asiatic wild asses live in two separate herds, one male and one female. The dominant male marks off its territory and only then does it mate. After two years or so, the ruling male gets worn out and a younger male takes over.

Dorcas gazelles lived in the area at the time that the Hai Bar was first set up, and a number were enclosed within its borders. You will enjoy watching their swift progress through the savanna-like landscape, and may smile at the antics of their offspring.

Two groups of mammals—the scimitar-horned oryx and the beautiful white addax—were brought to the Hai Bar in the 1970's for eventual reintroduction into the Arava. Now, however, it seems they may never have crossed the Nile from Egypt to the Holy Land. It is unwise to change the natural order of things by releasing foreign animals into the environment, and the horned oryx and white addax are being kept in the compound. Perhaps one day Israel's neighbors will be interested in preserving these species, which are endemic to their region.

Arabian oryx disappeared from Israel only a decade or so ago, and are currently being prepared for a return. Born with ground colors for camouflage, a young oryx instinctively lies down and blends with the landscape in times of danger. As an adult it turns white, which is why one of its Hebrew names is *re'em lavan* (*lavan* is "white" in Hebrew).

Yotvata Hai Bar

Arabian oryx are known for their long, straight, black antlers which tip slightly backwards. This animal is used in the Bible as a symbol of power. Seen from the side, the Arabian oryx appears to have only one horn. The oryx may be the basis for the unicorn symbol adopted by the British royal family!

In some cultures Arabian oryx meat is considered a delicacy and there are Bedouin who believe it can make a person invincible. Perhaps that's why this animal has been hunted throughout the Arab world.

If you visit the Hai Bar in spring, the ostriches may be mating. During the season the ostrich—the world's largest bird—sports a bright red neck. In the mating dance the males puff up their necks and roar, then get down on their knees and swing their feathers from side to side. Females do their own dance on bended knees, opening and closing their mouths.

The brown-and-black speckled ostriches you see are toddlers. Only at a year-and-a-half will their sex become apparent; at that time males turn black and females grey. After the female ostrich has laid one of its tremendous eggs—the largest in the world, weighing a kilogram and a half—ostrich parents split their time on the nest. The female's colors provide good camouflage during the day, when she hatches the eggs, and the male takes its turn at night.

Looking somewhat like an unfinished zebra, the Somali wild ass has black stripes down its legs. Without doubt the progenitor of the domesticated donkey, the Somali wild ass is, today, very rare. Those in the Hai Bar are from Ethiopia; the first babies born here did not survive but the youngest, Hope, is doing well.

While it's fun to ride past small groups of wild animals roaming around the compound or dozing in the shade, you will find the Predatory Center equally exciting. Originally set up to safeguard species of Negev predators in danger of extinction, today it is a sort of minizoo and features a tunnel from which you can comfortably gaze at the animals. Explanations from the guide, who accompanies you to the center, add an extra dimension to the tour.

Israel's biggest predator is the striped hyena. Other predators in the center included an aging leopardess and a caracal, the world's second largest cat. Its fringed ears are used for communication (caracal means "pretty ear" in Turkish).

Leopards eat all kinds of small animals, generally caught in an ambush. A solitary hunter, the leopard catches a porcupine by circling around it and grabbing at its unprotected head.

Quite rare in the Eilat region, the sand cat is wonderfully adapted to its environment, for it has hairy feet, camouflaged colors and the sense to lie

252

Yotvata Hai Bar

flat on the ground when attacked. It also has a terrific trick for scaring enemies: it spits at them and puffs up. Ancestors to your household tabbies, sand cats were considered gods by the Egyptians because they gobbled up the rodents which damaged farmers' crops.

If you are enamored of snakes and rodents, you will have great fun with the center's large collection. You can also view some rare, large birds, including griffon vultures, Egyptian vultures and lappet-faced vultures.

Darkroom animals are housed in cubicles constructed to seem as natural as possible. Guides claim the animals are not bothered by visitors, even though they can see you looking at them through the darkened window. All of the animals in the darkroom were born and bred in captivity.

Vital Information

Entrance to the Hai Bar is off the Arava Highway (Highway 90) opposite Kibbutz Samar.

Open every day 8:30–15:00. Entrance fee.

Bus tours of the open park leave from the entrance every hour on the hour 9:00–14:00 on Sunday, Tuesday, Thursday and Saturday.

Tel.: 07–373057, 376018.

It is best to come early in the morning at feeding time, when the animals are most active.

Mount Yoash

For a stunning view of Israel's south and the neighboring Arab countries, take a 10-minute drive out of Eilat to the observation points on Mount Yoash.

 To get there, drive west from the main hotel intersection in the direction of Yoseftal Hospital (Yotam Road). Almost nine kilometers past the hospital you will see an orange Nature Reserves Authority sign pointing left to Mount Yoash and Wadi Gishron. Turn in and drive on, passing a little parking lot near the bottom, then continue up the dirt road to the mountain's lookout points.

The ruins you pass during your ascent are all that's left of a khan (caravansary) from the Mameluke period, when this road was apparently part of the pilgrim road to Mecca (described in WADI GISHRON). Quarrying here after the Six Day War* toppled all but a few of the two-meter-high walls and an arched stone entrance.

At the top of the mountain are a number of observation balconies equipped with illustrations that help you get your bearings. Mount Yoash is one of those unusual spots from which you can gaze at four countries at once: Israel, Egypt, Jordan and Saudi Arabia.

Look for the Netafim Border Checkpoint, to the northwest, and to the south, adjacent to the mountain, the dirt path leading to the cliffs of Wadi Gishron. East of Mount Yoash and on both sides of the highway is the dark, massive range of Mount Shlomo. Your view in this direction is marred by electric lines that were put up during the years when Sinai was part of Israel. At the time tourists passed up the Eilat Mountains in favor of points further south, and it never occurred to engineers that one day this nature reserve would be so well-traveled.

Israel's border with Jordan to the northeast lies along the salty plains of the Arava between Mount Shlomo and the Edom Mountains. Low structures beneath the Edom Mountains are part of Akaba Airport. Since Eilat Airport is small and cannot be expanded, Israel hopes one day to use the nearby Jordanian airport for large aircraft.

Mount Yoash was the last obstacle faced by the Israel Defense Forces in 1948, as they moved towards Eilat during the Independence War.* Shortly before the Israelis attacked they heard a Jordanian military communication

Mount Yoash

that the Jordanian army had abandoned its position on Mount Yoash, opening the way to Eilat.

From here you can look down at the site where the peace agreement between Israel and Jordan was signed in 1995, on the Israeli side of the border northwest of Akaba. U.S. President Bill Clinton expressed the hope that peace would enable the Arava to flourish according to the promise in Isaiah: "The desert and the parched land will be glad; the wilderness will rejoice and blossom" (35:1).

Vital Information
The ascent to Mount Yoash is part of the WADI GISHRON–WADI YOASH hike.

The Gishron Outlook is directly above the spectacular dark cliffs.

Wadi Gishron and Wadi Yoash

*Two splendid outings:
An easy walk for families—rainbow sands in Wadi Yoash, and
A more difficult hike—fantastic rock formations and ancient art in
Wadi Gishron*

Despite Eilat's growing tourist trade and an enormous change in character, it is comforting to know that the magnificent mountains just outside the city have retained their natural beauty. Characterized by jagged outlines and rich, deep colors, Eilat's granite mountains were formed when molten magma seeped through the earth's crust, cooled and crystallized. The Eilat region is the only area in Israel where igneous rock (solidified molten magma) has been exposed to view.

Two spectacular hikes begin at exactly the same point, with an ascent to MOUNT YOASH. They then both follow the blue-marked trail at the bottom of the mountain.

At a junction of blue- and black-marked trails, more energetic hikers continue for about four hours on the blue trail through Wadi Gishron. There are points at which you must detour on a black-marked trail to avoid crossing the Egyptian border; at this writing new signs are being prepared. The shorter and easier walk (two hours) follows a black-marked trail through enchanting Wadi Yoash.

Wadi Gishron

Of all the splendid canyons and riverbeds found in the Eilat Mountains Nature Reserve immediately west of the city, the deepest and perhaps most spectacular is Wadi Gishron. Nature buffs with an adventurous streak will enjoy a four-hour walk that begins at Mount Yoash, takes you along sandstone, leads you below the magmatic cliffs of Upper Wadi Gishron, and ends at Mount Yehoshafat.

While you don't have to be in peak physical condition to walk through Wadi Gishron's magnificent riverbed, you must be able to climb up and down rocks and rocky paths and squeeze through one rather narrow spot. Take this excursion in fall, winter or spring, preferably on Friday or Saturday, when the trails are not jam-packed with high school pupils. You need two cars for this hike.

 Begin by driving west out of Eilat in the direction of the Yoseftal Hospital (Yotam Road).

Wadi Gishron and Wadi Yoash

To your right is a recently restored portion of *Darb el Haj* ("Road of the Celebrants"), an ancient pathway followed by traders and travelers for several thousand years. After Mecca was declared Islam's holiest site, this became the main route for pilgrims coming from Egypt. In the ninth century the road was improved by Egyptian rulers.

Pilgrims from North Africa and Spain gathered annually in Cairo for organized trips to Mecca in caravans of up to 40,000 travelers. Moving 40 kilometers a day, it took them 37 days to complete the march. The caravans ceased in the 19th century after steamships began sailing between Egypt and Saudi Arabia.

Continue until you reach kilometer marker 5. The trail through Wadi Gishron ends below Mount Yehoshafat about 400 meters directly to the left. Leave one vehicle here, on the left side of the road.

From the hospital, it is exactly nine kilometers to a big orange Nature Reserves Authority (NRA) sign leading to Mount Yoash and Wadi Gishron. Turn left and drive in, passing a little parking lot near the bottom, then follow the dirt road to the observation point on the mountain.

Wadi Yoash

A charming riverbed almost buried within the vast emptiness of the Eilat Mountains, Wadi Yoash is easy to follow and practically anyone can stroll above and within its channel. A hike through Wadi Yoash includes two hours of fabulous cliff walls and stunning views as well as a rather surrealistic journey through a gigantic sandbox—special fun for any kiddies on the trip. There are a few rocky patches on the trail, but if you are unsure of yourself take along a sturdy companion to help you maneuver these minor rough spots as well as the short descent at the end. While it is convenient to have two cars for this trip, in a pinch you can walk along the road about two kilometers back to a single vehicle.

Begin by driving west out of Eilat in the direction of Yoseftal Hospital (Yotam Road). One of the best parts of the tour, the ride takes you past soaring granite and sandstone mountains in a mind-boggling array of colors.

Look for oil pipes on the right side of the road, part of an oil line from Eilat to Ashdod on the Mediterranean coast. First built it 1957, it was expanded 10 years later when the Suez Canal was closed after the Six Day

Wadi Gishron and Wadi Yoash

War.* It is much cheaper to transport oil from the Persian Gulf overland through Israel than by ship around Africa.

Jewish philanthropist Baron de Rothschild agreed to finance the project in return for seven years of royalties. And, indeed, for about seven years vast quantities of Iranian oil passed through these pipes—up 60 million tons a year—and Rothschild made a fortune. After seven years, when the Israeli government was eagerly looking forward to taking control of the pipeline, Ayatollah Khomeini seized control of Iran and the oil stopped flowing.

Politics and economic realities do not, however, always go hand in hand. Iran still wants to sell its oil and it is cheaper to do so through Israel. Iranian oil, though in lesser quantities, now passes through Israel under the auspices of fictitious companies.

From the hospital it is exactly 6.8 kilometers to a strange mountain with knife-like peaks. Between kilometer markers 6 and 7 is a large orange sign that reads Wadi Yoash and it is here that you will end your hike. Drive around the curve and park one car to the right. Continue in your second vehicle about two kilometers until you reach a big orange NRA sign that points left to Har ("Mount") Yoash and Wadi Gishron. Drive in, passing a little parking lot near the bottom, then continue up the dirt road to the observation point on the mountain.

Both hikes begin here...

At 734 meters above sea level, Mount Yoash offers a spectacular look at sights you will see in bits and pieces during your walk below. Among them are Mount Shlomo, Wadi Gishron, volcanic Mount Yehoshafat, Taba and Sinai. As you gaze towards the Red Sea, the water glimmers invitingly in the background and the sharp outlines of the mountains begin to blur against this shimmering backdrop. This stupendous viewpoint is described in its own special chapter, called MOUNT YOASH.

After enjoying the view, all hikers drive down to the lot and park their car, then walk a few meters to the bottom of the mountain and look for an electric pole. Two different trail-markers have been painted onto the pole not far from where you turned left off the highway. The orange and blue mark indicates that you are about to walk part of the Israel Trail.* A blue line sandwiched in between white ones signals the path which begins here and leads to Wadi Yoash and Wadi Gishron.

As you walk, look above and to your left at Mount Yoash. In this area of the Eilat Mountains you find three major rock layers. They begin with very

Wadi Gishron and Wadi Yoash

hard granite. Above the granite is a layer of sandstone which has been eroded by the elements. On top you discern hard limestone, which once completely covered the towering mountain.

In fact, all kinds of geological phenomena are visible in the region, the result of folding and other movements related to the Syrian-African rift.* Strong natural forces have even tipped some of the limestone rocks onto their sides, so that instead of lying in the more typical horizontal layers they have been pushed into 90 degree angles.

Soon after you begin your hike, splendid marbled sandstone peeks out of the lime. Made of eroded magma exposed over time by the elements, they are called "halva" (an Israeli snack of streaked sesame and sugar) by some hikers; others think they resemble thick, American steaks.

Limestone often contains marine and plant fossils. Examine the rocks and see if you find any fossils—but remember that they are protected by nature preservation laws and must be replaced.

Some interesting eroded sandstone on the path bears a marked resemblance to sea limestone, which you see on the shores of the Mediterranean. The similarity is not surprising, for sea limestone is composed largely of sand. Almost symmetrical black blocks on a hill are reminiscent of the Carpentry Shop in RAMON CRATER and, in fact, there are many similarities between them. This, too, is baked sandstone covered with a black patina, which has broken into cubes.

Continue following the two different trail-markers. Eilat's mountains are so close to the Syrian-African rift area that the tilt which resulted was unusually strong and caused flowing rivers to forge gorgeous canyons in the soft sandstone. In places where the sandstone was especially compressed into a solid mass, the elements have created enchanting shapes and clefts in the rock.

The path above the splendid canyons of Wadi Yoash now winds around a curve next to a hunk of dark red stone. Try calling out at just this spot: it will cause tremendous echoes to reverberate in the riverbed below. Above you to the right, over some granite slopes, you will see an Egyptian border marker.

Climb down some natural rock steps to reach an intersection. Take careful note of the junction for, after a short detour, those on the shorter walk through Wadi Yoash return to this junction and then descend into the riverbed by way of the black trail-markers. Hikers through Wadi Gishron simply continue following the blue trail-markers.

But for now, everyone walks along the blue-marked and Israel Trails to a superb observation point atop the stunning crags of Wadi Gishron. Take the branch of the path which leads to the right, up the hill and to the edge of

259

Wadi Gishron and Wadi Yoash

the cliff. To your left in the distance is the granite splendor of Mount Shlomo, 705 meters above sea level, and the upper channel of Wadi Gishron.

If you look carefully at the granite mountains below and straight ahead, you may be able to make out vertical stripes—dikes*—of a different color. Dikes begin as molten rock flowing swiftly through a vertical crack in existing rock and widening it out. When the material hardens, it sometimes crumbles and leaves an empty space. But on other occasions, as it does here, the material remains within the crevice and creates rock of a different color and texture inside the original stone.

Straight ahead in the distance is Sinai, with Taba at 11:00. On the right below the cliff is the dry Gishron Waterfall.

In fall and early spring you will see any number of raptors. Mount Yoash is a major migratory route for the millions of birds which fly over Eilat twice every year (see BIRDS). Raptors—mainly buzzards, eagles and kites—sleep on the Eilat mountain cliffs. Early in the morning they catch a rising warm air current for an easy ride north. These currents form only over land, making this the major bird flight path for crossing from Asia to Africa.

If you brought binoculars, see if you can identify a Bonelli's eagle (*ayit nitzi* or "hawky eagle"), a bird graced with the strength of an eagle and the agility of a hawk. It is reddish, with black tips on its wings. But never use binoculars while walking on a mountain top or near a cliff. They distort the scenery and could cause you to take a wrong step.

Even after a winter drought there will be at least some foliage in the riverbed below, and many animals can survive under those conditions. Although in early spring it is too cold to behold great numbers of living creatures, by April you should be able to spot lizards and snakes (or their tracks), and perhaps ibex and hyraxes. Hyraxes do well in the desert for they need no fluids other than those provided by wilderness vegetation. Rock gerbils and sand rats, as well as other creatures that feed off desert plants, may be too well hidden to detect.

At this point the two trails separate. A description of the easier hike through WADI YOASH follows.

Wadi Yoash

You may find the scene here so delightfully tranquil that you are loath to get up and move on to Wadi Yoash, below you to your left. When you summon the energy, however, return to the junction you crossed on your way to this lookout point. As you walk towards it, look down to the right to see the bright sands of Wadi Yoash. Watch your step when following the black marker into the riverbed.

260

Wadi Gishron and Wadi Yoash

After a rocky descent into the gully, you suddenly find yourself walking on soft, thick sand. Here kids will have a blast playing in what is essentially a giant sandbox, while you admire beautifully colored rocks or look for animal tracks. A natural phenomenon called *tafuni* in Arabic is especially evident here in the riverbed. *Tafuni* are circular holes in the sandstone walls, formed by a whirlpool motion. Humidity is higher on cracks in the stone, so sand located on a crack crumbles more easily. The wind picks up the crumbled sand and twirls it round and round on the face of the stone, eventually creating a mini-crater.

After a lovely and colorful walk, return to limestone. You will be on the other side of the sharply jutting rock where you parked your first car. Note the interesting limestone layers which, instead of lying horizontal, have been pushed into an upright position by the pressures of the rift. The black marker will take you up a stony path for a few meters and then along the slope and back to your vehicle.

If you are continuing your hike through Wadi Gishron

From this point, called Gishron Outlook, you are directly above the fabulous dark cliffs which surround the Gishron riverbed. The Israel-Egypt border agreed upon by the two countries during the 1979 peace talks cuts through its smashing canyons in two different places. Today parts of the riverbed are out of bounds, for they are close to the Egyptian border or actually cross into Egypt. Stay strictly on the marked trail. Warning signs are sometimes washed out during winter floods.

At one point and to your right as you descend into the riverbed you pass a 20-meter-high dry waterfall, the only place in the riverbed where rappelling is permitted. Continue on the wide marked path which eventually swerves left and you will begin to savor a fabulous array of layered sandstone in shades of blue, green, red and yellow. When you reach a black tongue that juts out over the riverbed below, turn around and look behind you. Gorgeous rock formations resemble a large red cake with dripping white frosting.

Besides watching your feet as you descend into the riverbed you should be constantly looking up and around you. Each twist and turn of the trail offers a different and exciting view, landscapes that wring an "ooh" and "aah" from the most hardened of travelers. Granite cliffs begin to tower above you on both sides.

261

Wadi Gishron and Wadi Yoash

An angled marker—and the Israel Trail marker—lead you to the left. Follow the trail carefully here, for a right turn will take you into Egypt. Trail-markers are black on this detour, although planned future signs will contain both blue markers and black. The descent becomes more difficult at this point and you may need help clambering down some of the bigger rocks.

Eventually you reach an acacia tree. According to numerous passages in Exodus, acacia wood was used to build the Lord's tabernacle. Jewish legend holds that Jacob, who could predict the future, planted acacia trees on the way down to Egypt. He knew that the Jews would use them hundreds of years later when they returned home.

Past the tree the trail leads up and then down a small hill to a breathtaking view. Now the riverbed widens and the walls become lower. A lot of sandstone has been exposed in this segment of Wadi Gishron and the sight of bright green acacia trees offers a dramatic contrast to all the red rock.

If you hike in autumn you will see only scarce vegetation at the beginning of the trail. But as you get deeper into the wadi there are thorny capers on the ground and in crevices in the rock walls. They become larger and healthier looking the further you move along the riverbed: as the ground levels, flood waters move more slowly through the channel and are

Red sandstone rocks at Wadi Yoash.

Wadi Gishron and Wadi Yoash

more easily absorbed by the soil.

One of the few plants flowering in autumn is called *ba'ashan agol alim* in Hebrew (probably "round-leaved cleome," in English). This roundish, huddled over plant has sticky leaves and deep roots which help it survive hot, desert climates. Round-leaved cleome gets the first part of its Hebrew name from its outrageous smell: *boash* is the Hebrew word for skunk! Their "fragrance" is apparently the secret of their survival, as the plant is shunned by animals. Fortunately, bees are attracted to the plant and are happy to pollinate it.

At a major swerve in the wadi, you run right into a gigantic horizontal slab where you can sit down and rest in the shade of red sandstone cliffs. Long-ago travelers stopped here as well, for if you look hard among the latter-day graffiti you will make out ancient drawings of ibex, camels and hunters.

Back on the trail you reach an enormous wall of conglomerate, several dozen meters high. Conglomerate consists of alluvial* deposits tens of thousands of years old, from the time when the mountains here were completely covered by water.

About 300 to 400 meters from the drawings, you come to a junction complete with signposts leading in all different directions. Before you continue on the trail, however, backtrack a few dozen meters and see if you can find a second group of pictures on the rock walls (to your right, if you are retracing your steps). Located in a less obvious and therefore graffiti-less spot, they include a boat with several masts, camels and an ibex.

Once at the junction you leave Wadi Gishron and take the green-marked trail into Tzafra Pass, named for a corpulent young lady who couldn't squeeze through. This makes it a bit of a misnomer—it should be called Tzafra Didn't Pass! To get there, follow the green trail-markers to the left; you may need help maneuvering up the rocks and into the canyon. Although the passage is narrow, you can squeeze through on the right side. The stunning pass leads to an overwhelmingly beautiful sandstone canyon and eventually up Ma'ale Yehoshafat. The trail goes up to the right into the hill about ten minutes after the Tzafra Pass.

While the final ascent on hiking trips can be less than exciting, this time the climb is different. At the top you reach a large NRA sign, where you continue following the green trail-markers (take the trail below you on your left, which hugs the hill). Suddenly the landscape changes color and you find yourself among a superb combination of red and green stones and delightful rock formations. Here and there are patches of bitter gourd, also known as desert watermelon. A plant with deep roots, the desert

263

Wadi Gishron and Wadi Yoash

watermelon has bitter yellow fruit the size of oranges. It may have been the fruit mentioned in the Bible, tossed into a stew by mistake during a famine.

Elisha sent one of his men into the fields to gather herbs. "One of them went out into the fields to gather herbs and found a wild vine. He filled the fold of his cloak with some of its gourds, returned, and cut them up into the pot of stew, though no one knew what they were. The stew was poured out for the men, but as they began to eat it, they cried out, 'O man of God, there is death in the pot!' And they could not eat it. Elisha said, 'Get some flour.' He put it into the pot and said, 'Serve it to the people to eat.' And there was nothing harmful in the pot." (II Kings 4:39-41). According to biblical interpretations, it wasn't the flour which made the stew edible. It was a way for the Lord to provide food for people who were faithful to His commandments.

Ancient Greek texts describe the bitter gourd as a medicinal plant effective against a wide variety of illnesses, and modern research has verified its medical properties. During the late 19th century trade in desert watermelons was big business in Israel: a Jewish merchant living in Gaza sent 22,000 kilograms of the fruit abroad for 1,000 British pounds sterling!

You may come across ibex during your walk through the riverbed. These graceful animals were almost wiped out when Bedouin, trying to keep them away from desert springs, indulged in massive hunting. Today they can be seen traveling in herds all over the desert. Identify the males by their long, curved horns.

Large black beetles are common in the desert and you may see them crawling around near your feet. Although they once sported wings, with time the wings hardened and united to form a sort of helmet on their backs. The space between the beetles' bodies and the shell on top insulates them from the heat.

When you get to the top of Ma'ale Yehoshafat, rest, enjoy the view, then you have another slight climb to reach your car.

Vital Information
If you have only one car for Wadi Yoash, you can walk back to it at the end of your hike (about two kilometers).

Droplet Spring (*Ein Netafim*)

Ein Netafim is very aptly named. Although it is the only constantly flowing source of water in the Eilat region, the tiny spring offers but one cubic meter of water a day.

To reach Ein Netafim start at Eilat's main hotel intersection and turn towards Yoseftal Hospital. Drive for exactly 9.5 kilometers, past black, red and yellow mountains outlined against a brilliantly blue sky. The view will be even more striking on your return journey.

Watch out for ibex running across the road, (on our trips we usually see at least half a dozen)! Turn to the right, towards Ein Netafim, continue about 50 meters and park your car. Follow the gutted, flooded out dirt road by foot two kilometers to the cliff above Ein Netafim.

You will be descending through a landscape very reminiscent of the colored hills in craters near Mitzpe Ramon. At the bottom looking over the cliff you will see two trail-markers: green, pointing left into the riverbed; and black and red starting at the base of a small hill to the right.

If you are in very good shape, take the shorter and more exciting green-marked trail, lowering yourselves through narrow crevices in the rock: you will need a hiking companion so that you can assist one another. You will return along the black-and-red-marked trail, where you pull yourself up rungs. Hikers who are alone take the black-and-red trail there and back (much easier, but you do need to ascend and descend a few rungs).

The spring is surrounded by bright green, strikingly beautiful maidenhair fern. Because the fern's leaves are covered with oil, they never get wet even though they grow along waterfalls. For this reason, the Romans named the plant for the goddess of love, and called it Venus's hair. Venus sprang from the foam of the sea without getting wet.

Maidenhair ferns have been used to treat many ailments, from Greek times to the present. By far the most remarkable is the idea that the fern's roots can successfully cure baldness. The ancients apparently believed that the shape of a plant is significant in curing a similarly-shaped part of the body.

The water flowing in Ein Netafim is rain that has trickled down to a layer of impermeable clay and then flowed along it horizontally. Water bursts out of the ground at Ein Netafim.

Droplet Spring (Ein Netafim)

If you are very patient, you sit above the spring and watch for the ibex which come there to drink. Because the ibex's body is so sturdy and its legs relatively short, it is easy for it to live on the cliffs. Ibex need water daily and therefore can be found nearby most of the year. They venture away from the water sources only in winter and spring, when juicy plants grow in rock hollows.

A male ibex can weigh as much as 60 kilograms and is easily distinguished from the female by the greater length of its horns. Used in battles of strength against other males, the ibex's horns help determine its status in the herd. Ibexes have one dominant male to each herd, and only he mates with the ladies.

While sight is the most highly developed of its senses, the ibex also possesses keen senses of hearing and smell. It moves around cliff edges at night, hopefully far away from the leopard which is its worst natural enemy.

Ibex were picked to symbolize the Nature Reserves Authority, perhaps because, in the Bible, they denote beauty. "A loving doe, a graceful ibex—may her breasts satisfy you always, may you ever be captivated by her love" (Proverbs 5:19).

The sweet call of Tristram's grackles is frequently heard above the rocks in winter. Song birds identified by English clergyman Henry Baker Tristram in the 19th century, they are mainly found in desert cliffs along the Syrian-African rift.* Tristram's grackle has a very low metabolism and saves water by reducing its body heat. As a result it can live in both hot and cold regions.

Almost all of its feathers are black, yet the grackle's wings are rimmed with orange. According to legend, it wasn't always this way: there was a time when the grackle boasted every color of the rainbow.

Then one day, when King Solomon needed some fancy feathers to impress the Queen of Sheba, he asked all the fowl in his kingdom to contribute to his gift. Although every other species brought its finest plume and laid it at Solomon's feet, the arrogant multicolored grackle refused to donate even one of its feathers.

In his rage Solomon picked up the object nearest at hand—an inkwell—and threw it at the grackle. Only the bird's wings retained their original orange color.

Caper plants thrive at Ein Netafim. Notice their round, greenish-blue leaves and delicate white flowers with feathery pinkish edges. Each separate flower blooms only one day a year. But since not all bloom on the same day, during the season (March to August), the caper is constantly in bloom.

Droplet Spring (Ein Netafim)

Rabbi Gamliel, head of the rabbinical court at the end of the first century, used the caper to make a point. He told his students that in the world to come trees would give a different kind of fruit every day. When his pupils seemed incredulous, he showed them the caper as an example of the fruit of the future.

Red Canyon

Nothing can describe Eilat's glorious Red Canyon better than its popular name. Forged through a deep, rich, red sandstone rock, the superb little gorge is at its most exquisite when sunlight touches the canyon walls. Best of all, a circular stroll through this enchanting natural marvel can be completed in less than two hours.

To reach the Red Canyon from Eilat, drive west out of the city in the direction of Yoseftal Hospital, and continue on that road towards Uvda Airport. Pass the turnoff for Ein Netafim and drive for another 10 minutes or so until you spy a sign leading to the Red Canyon. Take the dirt road to a parking lot.

Begin your short trek on a path marked in green. At first the riverbed runs through silt, bordered by steep walls of conglomerate left from when tremendous rivers flowed through the region. Over time these alluvial* deposits hardened and later rivers that streamed through cut into the conglomerate to form the channel.

Sand partridges may accompany you part of the way. Well camouflaged by their color, sand partridges manage well on very little water. They don't care if it is saline or fresh and drink only if they eat dry seeds. When mother sand partridges sense danger, they call out and the babies instinctively lie still, their desert-colored bodies hiding them well. Pretending she has a broken wing and cannot fly, the mother bird draws attention away from her chicks. Then, once her young are safe, she suddenly flies away from her enemy, probably laughing because some animals fall for the same trick time after time.

Sand partridges are mentioned twice in the Bible. In the first passage, David calls out to Saul that he (David) is insignificant, and that the king is wasting his time by looking for him, "for the king of Israel went out to look for a flea, as a sand partridge chases in the hills" (I Samuel 26:20). Later, Jeremiah predicts that "as the partridge sits on its eggs and does not hatch them, so he that attained riches wrongfully shall leave them in the middle of his days" (Jeremiah 7:11).

After a short walk you reach Wadi Shani's main riverbed. Within the wadi* are saltbush and white broom, both of which bear delicate white flowers in winter and early spring. The author of Psalm 120 describes the white broom's characteristically long-burning embers: "Save me, O Lord,

Red Canyon

from lying lips and from deceitful tongues. What will he do to you, and what more besides, O deceitful tongue? He will punish you with a warrior's sharp arrows, with burning coals of the broom tree" (Psalms 120:2–4). One interpretation is that just as the embers of this tree smolder for a long time, so do the effects of treacherous words.

Desert plants suffer from heat, lack of water and brackish ground, for there is little rain to wash salt out of the soil. Saltbush (silvery orache) adapts itself by excreting excess salt onto its leaves. A greenish-grey plant about a meter and a half high, saltbush gets its color from the tiny hairs on its leaf which protect it from strong rays. Bedouin add the leaves to season their flour before baking pita and, in theory, you could eat the leaves right off the bush or cook them at home in omelets and vegetarian meatballs. But this is a nature reserve* and you must leave the plants as they are!

Soon the riverbed begins a steep descent to the canyon, a red sandstone gorge less than 300 meters long and only two to four meters wide. By the end of the canyon you have dropped several dozen meters. Some of the canyon's sandstone rock is truly ancient—several hundred million years old, covered with later conglomerate. Huge limestone boulders, swept here during floods, have lodged in the gorge and created steps.

As you pick your way carefully along, look up at the sides of the gorge. You will see gorgeous rock formations in stunning colors as well as conglomerate cliffs on top of the sandstone, adding extra height to the sides of the canyon. Dozens of meters above the canyon floor is a rock which seems to be teetering on a precipice of conglomerate. Take a good look now: it seems to be ready to fall! Enjoy the bell shapes created by erosion of the rock over time.

Of course, the most exciting part of this little canyon walk is a sight of the stone's fabulous colors. Oxidized minerals create an incredible shade of red stone which dominates all other rocks and changes according to where you stand and the time of day.

Immediately upon leaving the narrow part of the canyon, you'll find a trail that climbs up the southern wall (on the right) and returns to the parking lot. Be careful! It runs right along the edge. Don't get too close or the crumbly rocks on top may fall on the head of someone below. If you prefer, you can go back the same way you came.

Vital Information
Eminently suitable for a family hike.

Jeep Trip through Uvda Valley

Portions of Israel's south are so raw and wild that only a truly experienced hiker can reach them by foot. Everyone else must opt for a guided tour atop a camel, or take a trip in the ever-popular jeep. One particularly splendid jeep route leads to the peak of Mount Shaharut, traverses through a valley at the top of the mountain (Uvda Valley) and takes you to remains of a temple where Nabateans* once worshipped their gods.

The climb up Mount Shaharut is fraught with fantastic desert views. Piles of limestone in hundreds of different shapes, from curlicues to flattish tops to designs only the hand of nature could create, are all spread out before you. Jordan's granite Edom Mountains glow with a deep red sheen in the afternoon sun, and minerals in the limestone and sandstone that stretches from Jordan to Israel turn the rocks a hundred different hues.

At the top of Shaharut, about 600 meters up, your guide may suggest you sit on the cliff and look out over the Arava Valley. Patches of green in the distance are the Jewish settlements of Yotvata, Ketura and Samar. Billions of years ago, Jordan's mountains and those in Eilat were part of one huge mountain ridge. The Syrian-African rift* changed all that, forcing them apart and opening the valley below.

Ever since the split, the granite mountains in Jordan have moved steadily northwards—one to two centimeters a year for the last several billion. Thus the Edom Mountains you see were once located in Sinai. And those originally across from you, now face Ein Yahav (north of Yotvata) about 170 kilometers to the north.

Below you on the rocks a caper plant clings to the top of the cliff. According to legend, a king once lived here in the mountains with his beautiful daughter. One day, when the princess was swimming in a mountain pool, she caught a leech in her throat. Her father searched far and wide for someone to remove it, even offering the hand of his daughter as a reward, but no would-be suitor managed to succeed. Finally the caper plant said it would try to save the princess; the king, after a bit of hemming and hawing, agreed. The caper then thrust one of its branches into the princess's mouth and pulled out the leech. But the princess didn't want to marry a caper plant. She fled deep into the mountains with the caper running after her. And that's why you find caper plants climbing mountain slopes and cliffs.

Jeep Trip through Uvda Valley

If you examine the caper closely you will see why it is so well suited to the job of pulling out leeches. The caper's thorn is bent and can be thrust into a throat without doing any damage, then it can pull out a leech. Arab shepherds often use the caper to remove leeches swallowed by their sheep.

Acacia trees along the trail up the mountain originated in the Sudan and progressed along the Syrian-African rift. They are perfectly adapted to the Sudanese climate and also function well in the Negev. Acacia trees have deep roots which penetrate to the ground water. The leaves are very small and as a result water evaporation is minimal. At least one of the acacia trees you see may be two plants in one—the acacia and a parasite wrapped around it called strapflower, or acacia mistletoe. The strapflower's meaty leaves have a tough covering which enables them to retain lots of water. Strikingly bright red flowers and a sticky fruit attract birds, which carry pollen to other trees and continue the parasitic process. With time the mistletoe sucks the life out of the acacia. The tree dies, but then, with true poetic justice, so does the parasite.

Your jeep will probably bump its way along *Ca'ar Shaharut*, a huge flat terrain, way up in the mountain heights. Up here in Uvda Valley you pass rows of archaeological sites, evidence of rich Nabatean life in ancient times (see LEOPARD TEMPLE).

Once into Wadi Kasui you reach the greatest surprise of all: gigantic mounds of clean soft sand, a stunning sight in the desert. The sand dunes have long, long ripples from top to bottom, wave-like lines formed by the wind and sun. Children and adults can run up one side and down the other over dune after dune, especially inviting when you find that once the sand runs down the hill it climbs back up again. This beautiful and amazing phenomenon is an optical illusion.

Later you will drive through countryside which resembles an African savanna. Your trip includes a roller-coaster-like ride up and down the sands. And when you reach the other side of the mountain, in the afternoon, rock formations that looked brownish from above seem to have turned black. It is the angle of the sun's rays which so drastically changes the scenery.

Vital Information

A number of jeep companies run tours in the Eilat area. For information call the Eilat Tourist Information Office at 07-372111.

The Ancient Leopard Temple

Although Uvda Valley north of Eilat is one of the driest places in the country, archaeologists excavating the region have uncovered remains of over 150 sites dating back 6,000 years. At that time several thousand people prospered as farmers in this barren valley. One of the most impressive artifacts they left behind was the "leopard temple."

To reach the temple and related sites start at Shizafon Junction. Go south on Highway 12 and turn left at the first intersection towards Shaharut. After driving another 7.4 kilometers look left to see white signs put up by the Antiquities Authority (if you reach a second orange sign leading to Shaharut, then turn around and go back half a kilometer).

The first white sign marks the temple, unique because it was used continuously from 6000 to 2000 B.C.E. Since no written records have been uncovered, we can only guess the architecture's symbolic meaning.

Within a large open courtyard with a closed-off area for the holy of holies are tall stones which probably represented gods. Four large stones seem to "protect" the smaller ones they encircle. You will see altars both above and below ground.

Behind the temple are stones whose outlines resemble male and female leopards. The large stones were found on the site, while the small ones were added by archaeologists to complete the original design. Very similar temples from the same period have been uncovered at TIMNA and at Ein Gedi near the Dead Sea.

When you finish exploring, return to the car and drive several hundred meters further to see how people who worshipped in this temple lived. The round, ancient house next to the next white sign resembled a tent whose central pillar held up the skins (look for a stone in the middle of the ruins).

Contrast the discolored rocks which were exposed to the elements with the uniform shades of those shielded by dirt for the millennia that the house was covered. Next to the circular "house" is an animal pen. On one rock in the enclosure you will see a picture of an ibex with long antlers.

Why did people choose to live and farm in this bleak valley? The answer lies in its unique geographical conditions for, incredibly, it contains both water and fertile soil. Uvda Valley is a natural drainage area of 400 square

The Ancient Leopard Temple

kilometers. Its soil is an airy mixture of mud and sand, and excellent for agriculture.

The culture exposed in the valley points to one of the most significant changes in mankind. In this valley migrant hunters were slowly transformed into semi-nomadic farmers, and this is where archaeologists found the world's oldest stone plough!

Back on the road going south to Eilat, you will pass Uvda Airport. Normally a tranquil airport unfamiliar to most, Uvda was the focus of international attention in 1995, when an Iranian steward hijacked a plane and brought it to Israel for a night.

History of Man in the Negev

The phrase "man's history in the desert" sounds like a contradiction in terms, for we tend to think of deserts as barren wastelands with only a sprinkling of nomads. Yet over the millennia, especially when strong central governments had an economic and/or military interest in the Negev, Israel's desert came to life with prosperous cities and waving fields of green.

When the ruling kingdoms collapsed, desert sands covered all that they had built until a new people resolved to settle the Negev again. The Negev has thus repeatedly witnessed cycles of settlement and destruction.

In prehistoric times there was intensive and ongoing occupation of the area. Flint tools indicate that groups of roving hunters searched for game in this region from the late Paleolithic Age through the Mesolithic (45,000 to 5000 B.C.E.). During the Neolithic period (5000 to 4000 B.C.E.), however, settlement moved to the loess plains, which hosted what were possibly the first Negev farmers. Perhaps this change was linked to the climate, for the Negev was less arid at that time than it is today.

Man's "jump" to the Chalcolithic* period (4000 to 3150 B.C.E.) is quite remarkable. New technology enabled people to mine and process copper at TIMNA and near Beer Sheva many underground villages were uncovered. Each one specialized in a different aspect of metallurgy or pottery and left the earliest remains of ore-smelting in Israel. Many cult objects from this period and a temple decorated with leopards were recently discovered in Uvda Valley (see the ANCIENT LEOPARD TEMPLE).

After this advanced civilization vanished, there was a break in Negev habitation which lasted over 1,000 years. Settlement resumed for a brief period during the middle Bronze Age (2200 to 2000 B.C.E.), primarily in the Negev highlands where archaeologists have found ruins from over 150 villages. Most striking are hundreds of stone burial mounds called tumuli.*

Another thousand years passed before people again came to live in the Negev—this time in the Iron Age (c. 1200 B.C.E.). During this hiatus in settlement, however, dramatic events took place in the wilderness which were to shape the Jewish people. Abraham moved from Mesopotamia and lived the life of a nomad in Israel, digging wells and planting trees near BEER SHEVA (Genesis 21:33). When the Jews left Egypt they received the Torah at Mount Sinai.

The Jews returned to Israel around the year 1200 B.C.E. Two hundred years later King David and King Solomon built a network of citadels and

History of Man in the Negev

forts as part of a comprehensive state-initiated program. Some 40 agricultural communities sprang up along a military chain.

Solomon built a navy in Eilat and opened trade routes in Arabia with his new business partner, the Queen of Sheba (I Kings 9:26–10:15). Renewed interest in the Negev was probably connected with a revival of the TIMNA copper mines, a surge in trade and the need for safe roads along the trade routes. This network was destroyed or abandoned probably in the wake of Pharaoh Shishak's campaign in Judah in 924 B.C.E. Later Judean kings rebuilt the Negev fortresses.

After the Babylonians conquered Judah, settlement in the Negev again ceased for some 300 years. But when it resumed, it did so on a grand scale. A new people, the Nabateans,* appeared from across the Jordan. Skilled in raising camels and traversing the desert, they were able to maintain a monopoly on the SPICE TRAIL along which they transported precious spices from Arabia to the Mediterranean. They became immensely rich and built cities along their trade routes. With some brief intervals described in detail in the chapter on NABATEANS, they effectively controlled the Negev for some three hundred years.

For all their skills, the Nabateans were no match for Rome. The Romans developed an alternative sea route for spices, which tremendously weakened the economy of the Nabateans. Later, in 106 C.E., Rome annexed all of the Nabatean lands and organized them as a Roman province.

Under Byzantine* rule (fourth to seventh centuries), the Nabatean cities prospered again, for the Negev became strategically important as the border of the empire. Old trade routes were revived and the Nabateans developed agriculture, as well. Extensive water systems were built to gather and store water. During this period, the Nabateans converted to Christianity and erected lavish churches. Many monks and hermits chose to live in the desert as a means of attaining greater spirituality. Pilgrims on their way to Saint Catherine's monastery at the foot of Mount Sinai passed through the Negev.

The prosperity of the Byzantine era came to an end with the Moslem conquest of 636. No longer on the border within the vast Islamic empire, the Negev lost its military significance. Trade routes were altered and by the ninth century the once prosperous Nabatean cities lay in ruins. BEDOUIN Arabs became the masters of the desert, but they did not master the desert. Nabatean farms were neglected, and for almost 1,300 years the Negev lay barren.

Only in the late 19th century did the Ottoman Turkish authorities begin to exert nominal control over the Negev. With Britain controlling Egypt, the Negev once again became an important divide between two rival empires.

275

History of Man in the Negev

In 1906, after many disputes, Britain and the Ottoman Turks agreed on a border. But peace was not to last for long.

During World War I (1914 to 1918) Turkey and Germany battled the British and their allies in the desert. Britain's heavy reliance on her fleet made the Suez Canal of crucial importance to the Allied war effort. In 1915 the Turks succeeded in crossing the Sinai desert undetected by the British. They approached the canal at night when the Australian guards were sleeping. Screaming a battle cry, Bedouin scouts who led the Turks woke the Australians, and enabled the Allies to repel the attack.

The British were now resolved to protect the canal by conquering all of Sinai and Israel. Turkey was determined to launch another attack and began building a railroad to bring vital military supplies and water across the desert. The tracks were never laid further than Nitzana, however, and in 1917 the British conquered the Negev.

During the British Mandate (1920 to 1948) there was very little development in the Negev. The British built a few police stations, but didn't establish a single new settlement. The first dirt roads in the Negev highlands were paved to facilitate the search for oil, but no oil was ever found.

For the Jews, the Negev was a vast unknown land until the 1940's; in fact they were not even allowed to spend the night south of Beer Sheva! In 1902 the British suggested to Theodor Herzl that the Jews create a homeland near El Arish. (El Arish was then part of Egypt, under British control.) A Jewish committee visited the site and rejected the proposal when they saw how little water there was in the area.

The first modern Jewish settlement in the northern Negev was Ruhama, founded in 1901. It was an agricultural success, but was destroyed during World War I. Several subsequent attempts to break into the desert failed for lack of water and/or military opposition from the Arabs.

In 1938 a British commission proposed dividing Palestine into three parts: a tiny bit in the north and central part of the country would be Jewish, Jerusalem would become an international city, and everything else including the entire Negev would be in Arab hands. A year later Britain's infamous White Paper severely limited Jewish immigration into Palestine and forbade acquisition of land in the south.

Leaders of the Jewish community in Palestine were dismayed. They began working on a plan that would place the Negev inside a future Jewish state, despite the British decree which absolutely forbade Jews to settle in the south.

The first phase was activated in 1943, when three small groups were dispatched into the Negev. While touted as agricultural researchers, they were actually trying to gain a foothold on the land in outposts called

276

History of Man in the Negev

mitzpim. Following these outposts were 11 settlements established on Yom Kippur night in 1946, and seven more in 1947. At this time the Jews laid a water pipe to the Negev.

Successful settlements and the water pipe played a crucial role in determining the borders of Israel. The U.N. awarded all of the Negev to the Jewish state, for the Negev settlements had convinced U.N. commissions that only Jewish pioneers could make the desert green.

However, political agreements are one thing; military reality is another! The Egyptian army invaded immediately after Israel declared independence. Israel's scant, widely-spaced Negev settlements were terribly vulnerable and Israel did not control the few existing roads. On many occasions the water pipeline was damaged.

Each kibbutz was besieged and had to face the Egyptian army alone. Several fell to the enemy. When the first cease-fire went into effect on June 11, 1948, the Egyptian army was deep inside Israeli territory, only 32 kilometers from Tel Aviv.

During the course of the following months, Israeli forces drove the Egyptians out of the Negev and established a land bridge to Eilat. Both Egypt and Jordan signed cease-fire agreements with Israel and recognized Jewish rule in the Negev.

In recent years the cease-fire agreements have turned into full-fledged peace agreements between Israel, Egypt and Jordan. The borders are now open between all three countries and there are many mutual economic enterprises underway. By the end of 1995 there will be a joint Israeli-Jordanian-Egyptian electric grid located near Eilat.

The Negev's History: Key Events

The Negev's History: Key Events

Mesolithic and Neolithic Age 12,000–4,000 B.C.E.
Roving hunters search for food on the hilltops and mountain regions.

Towards the end of the period, early man begins worshipping in temples and farming.

Chalcolithic* Age 4000–3150 B.C.E.
Ancient Chalcolithic peoples mine copper at Timna for the first time.

Bronze Age 3150–1200 B.C.E.
Remains of hundreds of seasonal settlements and tumuli* in the early part of this period indicate that large parts of the Negev were settled. However, the intense colonization of the Negev stopped for almost 1,000 years from around 2100 to the Iron Age.

Israelite Period (Iron Age) 1200–586 B.C.E.
c. 1200–1000: period of the Judges; Samuel's sons are judges in Beer Sheva.

c. 1000: King David controls the Negev.

c. 970: King Solomon builds fleet in Eilat.

925: Shishak king of Egypt destroys many Negev cities. Subsequently the later kings of Judah build a network of 45 fortresses throughout the Negev.

586: The Babylonians destroy the First Temple in Jerusalem.

Babylonian and Persian Period 587–332 B.C.E.
During this period the Second Temple is built in Jerusalem. Caravans cross the Negev deserts; however there was apparently no Negev settlement.

Hellenistic Period 333–63 B.C.E.
332: Alexander the Great conquers Israel. Nabatean cities develop along the SPICE TRAIL.

176: Judah the Maccabee initiates a revolt against the Greeks.

100: The Negev is conquered by Alexander Yannai, a Maccabean king. Many Nabatean* cities are destroyed.

The Negev's History: Key Events

Roman Period 67 B.C.E.–324 C.E.
The Nabateans rebuild their cities and develop Negev agriculture.
c. 0–30: Life of Jesus.
70: The Second Temple is destroyed.
106: Rome annexes the Negev and builds many fortresses and roads.

Byzantine* Period 342–640
Nabateans and other Arab tribes convert to Christianity. The Nabatean cities prosper.

Early Moslem Period 640–1099
636: Moslems conquer the Negev. Subsequently the Nabatean cities are abandoned and there is a drastic decline in Negev population which continues for some 1,200 years. In contrast, Eilat develops as an important site along the pilgrim route to Mecca.

Crusader Period 1099–1291
Crusaders battle Moslems. There are no new Negev settlements.

Mameluke Period 1291–1516
Caravans of pilgrim en route to Mecca pass through Eilat.

Turkish Rule 1517–1917
1900: Modern Beer Sheva is established.
1906: The Negev becomes the border between England (which rules Egypt) and Turkey.
1914–1918: World War I; England conquers the Negev.

British Rule (Mandate) 1918–1948
1943: Jews set up the first three Negev outposts.
Yom Kippur night, 1946: Eleven Jewish settlements are established.

Israel 1948–present
1947–1949: War of Independence:
May 15 1948: Israel becomes a state.
5.1948: Egypt invades Israel and captures Yad Mordecai.
12.1948: In Operation Horev, Israeli advances through the Negev.

The Negev's History: Key Events

3.1949: After Operation Uvda, Eilat is in Israeli hands.

1949–1996: Intense development of the Negev. Increased agriculture, industry and tourism.

1979: Historic peace agreement signed with Egypt at Camp David. Israel evacuated Sinai.

1994: Dramatic agreement signed with Palestinians.

1995: Momentous peace agreement with Jordan.

History of the Nabateans

Scientists today are in awe of the Nabateans. Not only were the Nabateans able to collect water and grow crops in the barren desert well before the Common Era, but they managed to accumulate enormous wealth and to construct lavish cities in the Negev.

Yet no one knows where the Nabateans came from and why they disappeared. They left no written records at all; what is known about them is derived from non-Nabatean historical sources, a few inscriptions and archaeological remains.

Even their origins are unclear. Some contend that the Nabateans are the descendants of Nebaioth, Ishmael's firstborn son (Genesis 25:13). It is plain, however, that the Nabateans were a Semitic people related to the Arabs.

Greatly influenced by Hellenistic culture in the fourth century B.C.E., the Nabateans began to build cities in the Hellenistic style. They even found a way to combine their religion with the Greek gods of the Hellenists.

During this period the Nabateans built their first four cities in the Negev along the path that crossed the desert to the Mediterranean: AVDAT, SHIVTA, Halutza and Nitzana. By the end of the second century B.C.E., they had metamorphosed from groups of nomads focused on inter-tribal fighting into an organized kingdom.

For some 200 years their relationship with the Hebrews was excellent. Both had a common enemy—the Hellenistic empire based in Syria (the Seleucids)—and the Nabateans even gave shelter to the Maccabees (I Maccabees 5:25, 9:35). After an alliance lasting 70 years, however, both the Israelite and Nabatean Kingdoms sought to expand their territory and war broke out between these former allies.

Israelite King Alexander Yannai conquered Gaza, the main Nabatean trade port, in the year 100 B.C.E. But if Yannai expected to benefit from the spice route, he certainly miscalculated, for the Nabateans developed new routes which excluded the Negev. Nabatean cities across the Negev were subsequently abandoned.

Years later Hartat IV, a new Nabatean king, (9 B.C.E. to 40 C.E.) reconquered the Negev. He rebuilt the Nabatean cities and many small fortresses along the roads. Since Hartat ruled during the peak of the Nabatean spice trade, his main buyers were Romans.

The Nabateans used their wealth to build elaborate homes. At this time they also developed a unique and very delicate style of pottery. While most of the world's cultures produced a pottery that was refined over the

History of the Nabateans

centuries, the Nabateans did exactly the opposite: after not creating any pottery at all for centuries, they suddenly began to manufacture a very delicate and beautiful product. When their economic situation later worsened, so did the standard of their pottery.

AVDAT NATIONAL PARK contains remains of a Nabatean pottery workshop. The main artifact is the large circular oven. While the site is not very impressive (unless you happen to be fond of old Nabatean pottery workshops) it is extremely significant from a historical point of view. Here is another example of the Nabateans' incredible versatility: nomads who excelled as potters!

Similar workshops were found in the Nabatean city of SHIVTA. The pottery is very delicate, only 1½ millimeters thick, but strong and of a unique color design. Durable colors were derived from rocks mixed with sesame oil and then baked. The products were not for local use. They were sold— apparently to the Romans.

During the first century C.E., the Romans built new boats that could withstand the winds of the Red Sea and finally broke the Nabatean monopoly on the SPICE TRAIL. Having lost their main source of income, the Nabateans were greatly weakened and, again, their Negev cities fell into desolation. Eventually, the Nabatean kingdom was resurrected by a new king, this time Rabelle II. In many inscriptions he is called "the savior of his people." At this time the versatile Nabateans began to develop desert agriculture, utilizing the techniques for catching and storing water which had served them so well along the spice trail.

Rabelle's rule, which began in the year 70, was brought to an abrupt end when Rome annexed all the Nabatean lands in 105 and created a new Roman province. The Romans neglected the security needs of the central and southern Negev and new non-Nabatean tribes poured into the area from Saudi Arabia. The Nabatean capital of Avdat was destroyed in the early part of the second century.

Only in the middle of the third century did the Romans begin to fortify the Negev, building new roads and fortresses. With increased security, the Nabateans began to prosper anew. Many received a steady income as Roman soldiers and others engaged in agriculture or raised race horses.

During the Byzantine* period the Nabateans embraced Christianity. The former Semitic and later Greek gods and temples were replaced by large churches. Many Nabateans became church leaders; Nabateans began writing in Greek and involved themselves in all aspects of public life and Byzantine administration. They had transformed themselves from an idol-worshipping people who spoke Aramaic to Christians who wrote in Greek.

282

History of the Nabateans

The prosperity of the Nabateans during the Byzantine Empire ended when the Moslems conquered the Negev in 636. Most of their towns were destroyed, and those that survived were abandoned within the next century.

Where are the Nabateans today? No one knows for sure. Perhaps they again converted—this time to Islam—but no such event is recorded in history. They simply disappeared, leaving behind only the remains of their cities.

The Bedouin

Once upon a time there was a respected sheikh named Abu Sussa (owner, or father, of a mare). He wasn't especially important or famous, but he possessed the most beautiful horse in the world. People made pilgrimages to Abu Sussa's tent, just to look at the animal and fill their souls with delight.

Although overwhelmed by repeated offers for the mare, Abu Sussa refused to part with his treasure. He wouldn't even sell it to the sultan, who wanted the mare in order to possess the most beautiful horse on earth.

Finally the sultan sent two messengers to Abu Sussa, to convince him to sell. But the desert is hard to traverse and it was winter. Floods impeded their progress, and they worried that if they failed in their mission the sultan would chop off their heads. Nevertheless, as the storm grew worse, they decided to give up and just look for a tent in which to shelter. They knew that according to Bedouin custom any tent-owner would offer hospitality.

From a distance, they saw an encampment. They walked in, to find the sheikh smoking a nargila. Another man immediately began grinding coffee in a mortar-shaped vessel called an *azam*, making music that told anyone within hearing that the sheikh had a guest.

The wife of this sheikh was stranded with the herd across the river and wasn't around to offer dinner. Instead, the sheikh himself prepared and served a delicious meal.

In the morning, the sun sparkled on the desert sands, and the men continued on their way. They walked into the fields and asked where they could find Abu Sussa.

"You just came from Abu Sussa's encampment," they were told. So they returned to the tent.

The sheikh was surprised to see them, asking if they had left something behind. No, they said, they were from the sultan, come to persuade Abu Sussa to sell his horse.

"I would sell it, if I could," said Abu Sussa.

"We'll pay anything you ask," they insisted. "The sultan is really angry, you'd better agree."

"I can't," replied Abu Sussa. "You came here last night. My herd was stuck on the other side of the river and I didn't have any goat or sheep to slaughter for dinner, so I killed my horse and gave it to you!"

From the 10th century until the establishment of the State of Israel, Bedouin were the only residents of the Negev. Their nomadic lifestyle was

The Bedouin

based primarily on tending animals, and some agriculture. When they roamed around looking for a good winter spot, the Bedouin left all their effects behind. No one touched their possessions.

Long ago, the typical Bedouin family ate supper in the waning light of dusk near the fire. They used candles made of woolen threads dipped in fat left from an animal slaughter; more recently they have swiched to kerosene lamps.

In the near darkness of the tent they would eat, talk and play together. Then they would roll out a huge communal pillow and place mattresses on the floor. Any candles or lights were extinguished, leaving the interior in complete darkness except for a faint glow from the ashes.

If it was cold they would cuddle under heavy, wool-filled quilts. Mother slept next to her youngest child and everyone else lay in a row according to age. A man might have more than one wife, each in a separate tent: he slept next to Mom. When the children were asleep, either parent signaled the other and together they crept outside for some romance under the stars.

Bedouin ended their working days early because they often rose before dawn. They were reluctant to gallivant about anyway in late evening, since everyone knew that spirits and devils roamed at night and the Bedouin didn't want to attract their attention. Loud noise and fighting were absolutely forbidden, in case this angered the demons in the earth.

Bedouin tents traditionally run lengthwise from north to south with the entrance facing east, the direction of the sun, and the back towards the west. This may be connected with superstitions about light and dark: to many Bedouin, sunrise symbolizes life, and sunset sleep, or death.

Any tent used to host visitors was divided into a small section for guests and men folk and a much larger area for women and children. The translation of *shig*, "guest area," means both reception tent and storytelling site.

The women's portion had a less inviting title. Called *machram* from the word for forbidden, it was strictly off limits to strangers. In fact, so strong was the custom of avoiding the *machram* that non-family passing by a tent avoided even looking in its direction, walking with bowed heads to accord the inhabitants a measure of privacy.

Traditionally, tents were covered with wide strips made of black goat hairs. Preparing each band took over a year and the entire covering nearly a decade: by changing strips one by one as they wore thin, the top was constantly kept in tip-top shape. Bedouin goats were shorn only once every 12 months, after a year of perspiration created a layer of fat on their coats which would make the tent impervious to rain.

The Bedouin

Although in the past most winter tents were made of just such strips, passage of the Black Goat Law in the 1950's severely limited the number of black goats in each herd. When it became difficult to find enough black goat hair to cover their tents, the Bedouin, wise in the ways of survival, searched for a suitable substitute much as they had scouted out grazing and water in the past. Modern tents are generally covered with cheap and easily accessible jute sacking and plastic.

Goats were also the source of many and varied dairy products. Each night during milking season, their milk was placed next to the ashes in the tent and by morning it was pasteurized. It was then churned in goatskin to separate the buttermilk from the fat. Goat droppings were important as a source of fuel.

Today, this traditional picture has all but disappeared. The process began at the end of the 19th century, when the Turks began asserting their control over the Bedouin—who facilitated the process by clashing among themselves.

At present the Bedouin are undergoing a period of rapid transition, from traditional nomadic life to house dwelling, from tending sheep to holding jobs and dealing with the economic realities of the modern world. Bedouin are Moslem and speak Arabic. Negev Bedouin are Israeli citizens but are not drafted into the army; nevertheless many of them volunteer and serve as trackers whose desert skills help defend the country. Today, most of the Negev is a military training ground and out of bounds to the Bedouin. Israel is urging the Bedouin to move from tents to permanent houses and, indeed, there is now one Bedouin city (Rahat) and there are six smaller Bedouin towns. The first, Tel Sheva, was built in the mid 1960's, when the government decided to concentrate the Negev Bedouin in seven towns. It was constructed according to a plan which was wholly unsuitable for large Bedouin families accustomed to wide open spaces and was abandoned by its residents after a few weeks.

Only after the far more successful Rahat was established in 1972 did Bedouin begin returning to Tel Sheva. The government had finally understood that Bedouin needed to plan their own homes in neighborhoods made up exclusively of extended families.

Remnants of Bedouin life in the desert can almost always be found inside the towns. Many homes are built on "stilts" to make room for Bedouin flocks beneath the building. Fancy houses commonly have adjacent tents in their yards so that tea and coffee can be prepared in the customary way. Besides, family elders often prefer to sleep outdoors.

Bedouin never cooked inside their tents because of the fumes and the smoke. And even today, despite their modern kitchens, many Bedouin

The Bedouin

prepare meals in tin shacks next to the house. They do, however, make endless pots of coffee in the tent. As a result there is a constant smoky haze inside, especially in cold weather when the flaps are closed.

Many homes have separate entrances for women and for guests, just as did the old tents. Most telling of all are the living rooms: while they have telephones, television sets and VCR's there is often not a chair or couch to be seen. Parents, children, cousins and other relatives chat and watch TV from the floor!

Traditional and modern, the mixture is fascinating to explore. Rahat has seven grade schools and two high schools, where boys and girls attend classes together. Yet to outsiders, Bedouin women still seem rather shut away, and often won't sit together with Bedouin men. Still, many attend teachers' seminars or even university. And, say the Bedouin men we queried, within the family women have just as much say as their husbands!

Bedouin weddings can last as long as a month; guests hear about the wedding by word of mouth and come from all over the country. Times have changed and girls are no longer wed at a very young age. Instead, like their Israeli counterparts, they must be at least 17 to marry.

There are close to 100,000 Bedouin in the Negev today. Their history and culture are vividly portrayed in two Negev museums: JOE ALON and RAHAT.

Modern Challenges in the Negev

Following a dormant period of some 1,300 years, the Negev is witnessing an interval of rapid development. But is development "good" for the Negev—or does it spell disaster for its 800,000 residents and for the tourists who have begun flocking to the south?

Tourism, even the most benign, exercises wear and tear on the Negev's precious nature reserves. For example, providing water to Eilat hotels depletes underground water sources and causes sewage problems. Mining, too, causes irreversible damage, yet there are many who benefit from mining and want to develop the Negev economically.

After the evacuation of the Sinai Desert in 1982, Israel's army and air force relocated to the Negev. While this made sound military sense, it left only 20 percent of the Negev in civilian hands. And it has had quite a negative ecological effect on the 80 percent of desert used by the armed forces for training.

The DEAD SEA WORKS is a very lucrative operation providing employment for over a thousand people. Yet the once abundant waters of the Dead Sea are quickly disappearing. Human intervention is destroying the very basis of the enterprise.

The clash between economic progress and nature preservation came to a head in the 1990's, when the Voice of America asked to build a large broadcasting station in the Arava. Although this would have produced jobs and demonstrated support for Israel's American allies, nature lovers worried about the effect of strong electromagnetic waves on migrating birds. The legal battles between the groups ended abruptly when the VOA abandoned the project.

Should the Negev be declared one vast nature reserve, and thus preserve its unique flora, fauna and geological formations? Perhaps the armed forces should be restricted to a smaller portion of the Negev. Is it possible to create jobs in the desert while preserving nature?

In October 1995 an industrial park was dedicated north of Beer Sheva. The developer chose that particular site because of its proximity to the NEGEV BRIGADE MEMORIAL. A fitting response to the courage of the pioneers who defended the Negev and made it bloom, the park is meant to balance industry and ecology in the desert.

The Jewish National Fund (JNF) (*Keren Kayemet*)

No book on Israel's south would be complete without special mention of the JNF. Indeed, practically every chapter in *Israel's Southern Landscapes*

Modern Challenges in the Negev

describes at least one of their multifaceted projects. These range from limans to parks, scenic routes and striking memorials and they include wonderful overlooks and numerous Negev settlements.

 As you drive through the south today, it is almost impossible to imagine the Negev wilderness before the age of the JNF.

All over the country, but particularly in the Negev, the JNF develops agricultural land. It has also begun setting up a network of reservoirs and dams which conserve Israel's sparse water resources. The JNF's Yatir Forest (ROUTE NO. 6) and Lahav Forest (ROUTE NO. 5) boast numerous historical sites and recreational areas; fishermen cast their rods with pleasure at GOLDA MEIR PARK and in LAKE YERUHAM.

The JNF has created such a successful model for rolling back the desert that developing countries are now drawing on its experience. Its newest project, Action Plan Negev, promises to revolutionize Israel's agricultural map. What makes this latest initiative possible is a humongous quantity of saline water discovered in the south. Paradoxically, this brackish liquid enhances agricultural growth and, with its help, Negev farmers are producing fruits and vegetables even more delectable than their northern counterparts. Water resources, further depleted as a result of the peace agreement with Jordan in 1995, are going to be increased. Orchards which are disappearing from the center of the country are already springing up in the Negev—thanks to the JNF.

Index of Sites

Index of Sites

Air Force Museum, 89
Amram's Pillars, 238
Andartat Haplada, 60
Anim, 69
Anzac Memorial, 23
Arad, 75
Arad Visitors' Center, 75
Arod Observation Point, 166
Avdat National Park, 136
Avnun Observation Point, 101, 168, 171

Be'er Mashabim, 46
Be'eri, 20
Be'erot Sharsheret, 236
Be'erot Yitzhak, 18
Bedouin Heritage Center, Rahat, 93
Beer Sheva, 81
Beit Yad Labanim, 88
Ben Gurion's Burial Ground, 125
Ben Gurion's House, 123
Besor, 28
Big Crater, 168
Bio Ramon, 185
Bir Asluj, 46
Bor Hemet, 156

Coral Beach Nature Reserve, 230
Coral World, 228

Dangur, 59
Darb el Haj, 257
Dead Sea, 208
Dead Sea Works, 209
Dimona, 117
Dolphin Reef, 231
Dom Palms, 236

Eilat, 226
Ein Avdat, 127
Ein Evrona, 236
Ein Hatzeva, 205
Ein Netafim, 265
Ein Saharonim, 223
Ein Tzin, 112
Ein Yorkeam, 109
Eshkol National Park, 51

Flour Cave, 204

Golda Meir Park, 45

Hai Ramon, 185
Havarim Cistern, 121
Hemet Well, 156
Hurvat Halukim, 100
Hurvat Krayot, 72
Hurvat Rimon, 64
Hurvat Yatir, 69

International Bird Center, 233
Ir Ovot, 205

Joe Alon Center, 63

Khan Saharonim, 225
Khirbet Katzra, 222

Lahav Forest, 63
Leopard Temple, 272
Little Crater, 105
Lotz Cisterns, 161

Magen, 41
Mamshit, 143
Maon Synagogue, 40

290

Index of Sites

Mitzpe Arod, 166
Mitzpe Gevulot, 43
Mitzpe Ramon, 183
Mitzpe Ramon Visitors' Center, 184
Mitzpe Revivim, 35
Mitzpe Zohar, 73
Mitzpor Har Avnun, 101, 168, 171
Moa, 206
Mount Amasa, 71
Mount Sodom, 204
Mount Tzin, 107
Mount Yoash, 254
Museum From Holocaust to Revival, 14

Nahbir, 21
Negev Brigade Memorial, 95
Nikarot Fortress, 223
Nir Am, 16
Nirim, 59

Pura Nature Reserve, 62

Rahat, 93
Ramalia Cisterns, 121
Ramon Crater, 188, 194
Red Canyon, 268
Rehovot-in-the-Negev, 57
Rogem Tzafir, 106

Sapir Park, 205
Scorpion Ascent, 105
Sde Boker Field School, 133
Shepherdess Park, 119
Shezaf Nature Reserve, 215
Shivta National Park, 157
Solar Energy Center, 126
Steel Monument, 60
Sternbergia Nature Reserve, 101
Sulfur mine, Be'eri, 23

Tel Arad, 77
Tel Beer Sheva, 96
Tel Jamma, 25
Tel Nitzana, 151
Timna, 245

Um Rashrash, 235
Underwater Observatory, 228
Uvda Valley, 270

Wadi Gishron, 256
Wadi Hatira, 171
Wadi Hava, 177
Wadi Shehoret, 240
Wadi Tzafit, 210
Wadi Yemin, 171
Wadi Yoash, 256

Yad Mordecai, 12
Yatir Forest, 67
Yeruham, 114
Yiftah Memorial, 92
Yotvata Hai Bar, 251

Zohar Observation Point, 73

291

Hike Index

Hike Index

This hike index allows you to easily choose a route that is suitable for you and your companions. All of these hikes are described in the book. Family walks are relatively easy, and geared for young children and their parents. They are about one to three hours long.

Off the beaten track refers to longer and/or more difficult walks.

Before hiking, read the section called HIKING IN THE NEGEV.

All the hikes are family walks unless marked "off-the-beaten-track."

NORTHERN NEGEV

Ein Yorkeam   Ein Tzin

NEGEV HIGHLANDS

Ramalia

Big Crater walk

Ein Avdat: short walk very easy; longer one entails some climbing on steps
and ladders

Borot Lotz

Walk in Ramon Crater

Wadi Yemin: off the beaten track

Wadi Hava: off the beaten track

ARAVA

Flour Cave: short climb at end of walk

Shezaf nature reserve

Wadi Tzafit: off the beaten track

EILAT

Timna: two hikes, the half day hike is off the beaten track.

Wadi Yoash

Ein Netafim: some climbing

Red Canyon: a few descents with handrails

Amram's pillars

Wadi Shehoret

Wadi Gishron: off the beaten track

292

Important Phone Numbers

ALL NUMBERS ARE IN AREA CODE 07 UNLESS NOTED.

First Aid: 101 no area code necessary
Police: 100 no area code necessary

Telephone information: 144 no area code necessary
Overseas operator: 188 no area code necessary

Tourist Information Offices
Beer Sheva: 236001; fax: 236002
Eilat: 372111; twenty-four hour information: 374741
Reservations in the Negev Highlands
(lodging, restaurants, or tours): 177- 022-2646 or 588319

(Egged) Inter-City Bus Information
Tel Aviv: 03–537–5555
Eilat: 375161
Beer Sheva: 278558
Jerusalem: 02–304555

Society for the Preservation of Nature (SPNI)
General information on nature sites (*Modi'in Teva*): 03–638–8696
Information on organized English-language tours: 03–639–0644

Nature Reserves Authority
Main office: 02–500–5444

Hospitals
Ashkelon (Barzilai Hospital): 745555
Beer Sheva (Saroka Hospital): 400111
Eilat (Yoseftal Hospital): 358011

Youth Hostels and Field Schools

There was a time when people associated youth hostels with bedbugs and other unpleasant phenomena. Fortunately times have changed, and so have youth hostels all over the world.

 Hostels which belong to the non-profit Israel Youth Hostels Association are constantly being improved and you will find them comfortable and relatively inexpensive. Rooms with adjacent bathrooms are available, upon request, in all of ANA's hostels. Ask if the price includes breakfast: it usually does.

Arad
Although Arad's youth hostel is located in the city's center city and near Arad's fabulous new shopping mall, the hostel is, nevertheless, a pastoral kind of place. Recently refurbished rooms are scattered within little houses and gardens. Up to six people can stay in each room.
Tea and coffee, and cable television, are available.
Tel.: 07-957150, fax 955078.

Eilat
From the terrace of the new wing at Eilat's youth hostel, guests have a super view of the Red Sea and the Edom Mountains. Families can stay in one of two sections of the hostel: an older wing where rooms are spacious and have wooden bunk beds, double sinks and lots of light; or the new section, featuring modern bathroom facilities and the kind of metal bunks whose bottoms can be pushed together to form double beds. All of the rooms have air conditioning and attached bathrooms. In the older section the rooms are bigger and towels cost extra.
Located only a minute from the beach, Eilat's big hotels and the promenade, the hostel's facilities include an attractive lobby and a television room. Laundromats are available, and there are small refrigerators for rent.
Tel.: 07-370088, fax 375835.

Mitzpe Ramon
The charming and attractive youth hostel in Mitzpe Ramon is as modern as they come. Rooms include sunken showers, unusually comfortable mattresses and good reading lights. Smaller rooms have single beds as opposed to bunks.

Youth Hostels and Field Schools

The lobby is cheerful, there is a television room and even a discotheque and kiosk. Meals are unusually tasty. Mitzpe Ramon's promenade, crater, Visitors' Center and Hai Ramon are less than a minute away. Also nearby is Mount Gamal—a hill shaped like a camel, with an observation point on top.
Tel.: 07–588443, fax 588074.

For group reservations for hostels and/or tours call regional offices: Beer Sheva: 07–282492; Tel Aviv: 03–5444487; Haifa: 04–9882848.

 There are four SPNI field study centers in the Negev. All provide overnight accommodations, meals for groups on guided tours, and information about hikes in the area.

Sde Boker Field Study Center (See SDE BOKER)

Adjacent to the park where David Ben Gurion was buried is the SPNI's third oldest field study center. It is located within a desert landscape, on the cliffs over the Tzin riverbed. The original rooms are grouped around a central courtyard and each surrounds an even bigger central plaza. Stone arches blend into the desert scenery.

The field study center's new wing is the most luxurious of all SPNI accommodations. Completed in 1994, this portion of the hostel contains suites whose decorative upholstery, blankets, sheets and pastel curtains meld into an overall color scheme. Instead of one large room lined with bunks, the good-sized suites have two rooms. Beds are comfortable, modern bathroom facilities are attractively tiled and each unit has its own small kitchenette.

Sde Boker Field Study Center specializes in all aspects of desert life: survival, desert ecology, navigation, Bedouin and Nabatean* history, and the mountains, craters, canyons and rivers of the region.

Har Hanegev Field Study Center

You can't see Har Hanegev Field Study Center from Ramon Crater even though its buildings are located along the northern rim. This is in keeping with a policy of preserving nature, a philosophy which also extends to the landscaping at Har Hanegev. Thus the housing units are all rocky-looking sand-colored squarish shapes, and the grounds combine desert shrubs and rocks with a bit of grass, a few flowers and some trees.

Built in 1982, Har Hanegev was established when Israel left the Sinai and evacuated the field study center there. Although staff, equipment and desert know-how were relocated to Har Hanegev, today the school has a personality all its own.

Youth Hostels and Field Schools

There are 26 rooms here, each able to house up to six people. What is most elaborate is the food: among the best at any field study center in the country.

Hatzeva Field Study Center

So many of Israel's starkly beautiful wastelands are out of bounds to civilians or have been ravaged by developers that it isn't easy to lose yourself in the wilds. One of the few regions left where you can still walk for days through barren lands is the Arava, site of Hatzeva Field Study Center.

Unlike most other field study centers, constructed to suit the landscape and generally very comfortable, Hatzeva was originally a pre-settlement army base. Thus the rooms, although they are large and air-conditioned with screens and bathrooms, are very basic. Still, there are advantages to being out in the wilds. Nature lovers are right next door to some of the most fabulous landscapes and hiking in the country.

Eilat Field Study Center

Located seven kilometers south of Eilat, just across from CORAL BEACH NATURE RESERVE, Eilat Field Study Center specializes in snorkeling trips and desert tours. All 37 rooms include bathrooms and are air-conditioned. For a small fee you can pitch a tent in the front yard; Eilat Field Study Center is one of the few places in the Negev where you can camp out so close to civilization.

Dictionaries

PLANTS

English	Transliteration	Hebrew
aaronsohnia	aharonsohnia faktorovsky	אהרונסוניה פקטורובסקי
Aaron's rod	lufit metzuya	לופית מצויה
acacia	shita	שיטה
acacia mistletoe (strapflower)	harnug hashitim	הרנוג השיטים
agave	agava	אגבה
alkanet	alkana	אלקנה
androcymbium	betzaltzia	בצלציה
anemone	kalanit	כלנית
Arabian fritillary	gvi'onit aravit	גביעונית ערבית
asphodel	irit	עירית
asphodeline (Jacob's rod)	iriyoni tzahov	עריוני צהוב
Atlantic pistachio	ela atlantit	אלה אטלנטית
banksia	banksia	בנקסיה
barley	se'ora	שעורה
bean caper	zugan hasiah	זוגן הסיח
bee-orchid	dvoranit	דבורנית
bitter gourd (desert watermelon)	avatiah pakua	אבטיח פקועה
bladder-senna	karakash	קרקש
blepharis	risan ne'echal	ריסן נאכל
bloodwort	hum'a	חומעה
butterfly orchid	sahlav parparani	סחלב פרפרני
broomrape (cistanche)	yachnuk	יחנוק
buttercup (crowfoot)	nurit	נורית
caper	tzalaf	צלף
cattail	soof	סוף
daemia	demia levida	דמיה לבידה
Damascene picris	merrarit dameska'it	מררית דמשקאית
desert diplotaxis	tura'im midbari'im	טוריים מדבריים
desert fleabane	par'ushit galonit	פרעושית גלונית
desert henbane	shikaron hamidbar	שיכרון המדבר
desert watermelon	(see bitter gourd)	
dom palm	dekel dom	דקל דום
dwarf oxeye	kochav nanasi	כוכב ננסי
dwarf pheasant's eye	dmumit meshunenet	דמומית משוננת

297

Dictionaries

Egyptian caper	*tzalaf mitzri*	צלף מצרי
eucalyptus	*ekaliptus*	אקליפטוס
Euphrates poplar	*tzaftzafat haprat*	צפצפת הפרת
fig caper	*tzalaf s'husi*	צלף סחוסי
fine muscari	*kadan na'eh*	כדן נאה
foxthorn (thornbush)	*atad*	אטד
frosty sea lavender	*ad'ad me'ubak*	עדעד מאובק
gacea	*zehavit hashluhot*	זהבית השלוחות
gilliflower	*mantur*	מנתור
groundsel	*savion*	סביון
haelava toadflax	*pishtanit sasgonit*	פשתנית ססגונית
hairy leatherwood	*mitnan sa'ir*	מתנן שעיר
herbaceous periwinkle	*vinka esbonit*	וינקה עשבונית
iris	*irus*	אירוס
Jericho rose	*shoshanat yericho*	שושנת יריחו
jojoba	*hohova*	חוחובה
Judean wormwood	*la'anat yehuda*	לענת יהודה
leafless silk vine	*halbiv rotmi*	חלביב רותמי
maidenhair fern	*sa'arot shulamit*	שערות שולמית
marigold	*tzipornay hehatul*	ציפורני החתול
milk vetch	*keded yafeh*	קדד יפה
moricandia	*moricandia mavrika*	מוריקנדיה מבריקה
Negev iris	*irus hanegev*	אירוס הנגב
nitraria	*yamluh pagum*	ימלוח פגום
olive	*zayit*	זית
orchid	*sahlav*	סחלב
oyster plant	*hardufnin*	הרדופנין
palm	*dekel*	דקל
pine	*oren*	אורן
poppy	*pereg*	פרג
reed	*kaneh*	קנה
rose of Jericho	(see Jericho rose)	
round-leaved cleome	*ba'ashan agol alim*	באשן עגול־עלים
rush	*samar*	סמר
saltbush (silvery orache)	*maluah kepeah*	מלוח קפח
saltwort	*malhit ashuna*	מלחית אשונה
saxaul	*prakrak parsi*	פרקרק פרסי
scented oxeye	*kochav reihani*	כוכב ריחני
single-seed wormwood	*la'ana had-zar'it*	לענה חד־זרעית
spiny burnet	*sira kotzanit*	סירה קוצנית
sternbergia	*helmonit gedola*	חלמונית גדולה
stork's bill	*makor hahasida*	מקור־החסידה

298

Dictionaries

strapflower	(see acacia mistletoe)	
sunrose	*shimshon hashalhupiyot*	שמשון השלפוחיות
sycamore fig	*ficus bat shikma*	פיקוס בת שקמה
Syrian rue	*shever lavan*	שבר לבן
tamarisk	*eshel*	אשל
tipuana tipu	*michnaf naeh*	מכנף נאה
thorny caper	*tzalaf kotzani*	צלף קוצני
tulip	*tziv'oni*	צבעוני
vartemia	*ketela harifa*	כתלה חריפה
viper's bugloss	*achnai*	עכנאי
Washingtonian palm	*vashingtonia*	ושינגטוניה
white broom	*rotem hamidbar*	רותם המדבר
white wormwood	*la'anat hamidbar*	לענת המדבר
wild rhubarb	*ribas hamidbar*	ריבס המדבר
wrinkle-leaved sage	*marva tzemira*	מרווה צמירה
Yeruham iris	*irus yeruham*	אירוס ירוחם
zilla	*silon kotzani*	סילון קוצני

ALL KINDS OF ANIMALS

addax	*dishon*	דישון
agama	*hardon*	חרדון
Arabian oryx	*re'em lavan, re'em aravi*	ראם ערבי
bagworm	*sas nartik*	סס נרתיק
beetle	*hipusheet*	חיפושית
black and yellow grasshopper	*kushan arsi*	כושן ארסי
black beetle	*shah'orit*	שחאורית
desert cobra	*peten shahor*	פתן שחור
camel	*gamal*	גמל
caracal	*karakal*	קרקל
dabb-lizard	*hardon tzav*	חרדון–צב
desert monitor	*koah*	כוח
dolphin	*dolphin*	דולפין
Ein Gedi mole viper	*saraf ein gedi*	שרף עין גדי
elephant beetle	*hedkonit*	חדקונית
fat sand rat	*psamon*	פסמון
gazelle	*tzvi*	צבי
hyena	*tzavo'a*	צבוע
hyrax (coney)	*shafan sela*	שפן סלע
Nubian ibex	*ya'el*	יעל
leopard	*namer*	נמר
lizard	*lita'a*	לטאה

299

Dictionaries

marbled polecat	*samur*	סמור
porcupine	*dorban*	דורבן
Revivim gecko	*yeshimonit revivim*	ישימונית רביבים
scimitar-horned oryx	*re'em hanevel*	ראם הנבל
snake	*nahash*	נחש
spiny mouse	*kotzan matzui*	קוצן מצוי
turtle	*tzav*	צב
wolf	*ze'ev*	זאב

BIRDS

Arabian babbler	*zanvan*	זנבן
bearded vulture	*peres*	פרס
blackstart	*sh'hor zanav*	שחור–זנב
brown-necked raven	*orev hum oref*	עורב חום–עורף
buzzard	*akav horef*	עקב חורף
Caspian tern	*sh'hafit kaspit*	שחפית כספית
chukar	*hogla*	חגלה
Egyptian vulture	*raham*	רחם
falcon	*baz matzui*	בז מצוי
flamingo	*flamingo matzui*	פלמינגו מצוי
grey heron	*anefa afora*	אנפה אפורה
griffon vulture	*nesher*	נשר
gull	*shahaf*	שחף
harrier	*zaron*	זרון
lappet-faced vulture	*ozniyat hanegev*	עזנית הנגב
little owl	*oah*	אוח
mourning wheatear	*sal'it livnat kanaf*	סלעית לבנת כנף
pale crag martin	*snunit midbar*	סנונית מדבר
Palestine sunbird	*tzufit*	צופית
redshank	*bitzanit livnat kanaf*	ביצנית לבנת–כנף
redstart	*hahlilit etzim*	חכלילית עצים
ring-plover	*hofmei tzavaron*	חופמי צוארון
rock dove	*yonat sela'im*	יונת סלעים
sand partridge	*koreh*	קורא
shrike	*hankan*	חנקן
spur-winged plover	*siksak*	סיקסק
stint	*hofit*	חופית
swallow	*snunit*	סנונית
Tristram's grackle	*tristramit*	טריסטרמית
wagtail	*nahlieli*	נחליאלי

Glossary

alluvial. Sediment deposited by streams. Often good farm land.

aquifer. Impermeable rock layer which contains underground water.

baptistery. A font used to baptize babies and converts to Christianity.

Camp David Agreement. Peace agreement between Egypt and Israel in 1979. In return for diplomatic relations with Egypt, Israel returned all of Sinai.

Byzantine Empire. Eastern Roman empire founded by Constantine in 330. Christianity became the official state religion during the fourth century. The Byzantines ruled the Negev until the Moslem conquest in 636.

Chalcolithic. Term for the time period 4000 to 3150 B.C.E. Considered prehistoric because there are no written documents from this time, but its people were technologically advanced. This period marks the transition from the Stone Age to the use of metal; Chalcolithic in Greek means "copper and stone." In the Chalcolithic period people began to mine copper at TIMNA.

crater (*machtesh*). A specific geological formation first defined in Israel, in which a deep depression is surrounded by steep walls and drained by one riverbed. Israel's craters began as mountains and were hollowed out by water. Three Negev craters are accessible to visitors: the Big Crater, the Little Crater and Ramon Crater (the largest in the world). Altogether there are seven *machteshim*; five in the Negev and two in Sinai.

firing zone. A military training area. Do not worry, bullets will not go flying across the road. The signs along the highways are a warning not to leave the road. Firing zones are in use from Sunday through Thursday.

Israel Trail. A marked trail 750 kilometers long that crosses the entire country from north to south. The path is designed for families with children.

kibbutz. Communal settlement. The kibbutz movement was founded at the beginning of the 20th century by idealistic pioneers who strove to create an egalitarian, utopian society. Children slept together in separate units; kibbutz members ate in a communal hall. Today the movement is undergoing radical ideological changes. The plural of kibbutz is kibbutzim; members are called kibbutzniks.

layered spring. A spring whose origins are in an underground level which absorbs as much rain water as it can, then becomes impermeable. When it bursts through the ground, it creates a layered spring.

loess. Wind-deposited silt, usually accompanied by some clay and fine sand. A large part of the Negev consists of loess soil, sometimes several

Glossary

meters deep. Because of its favorable water-retaining capacity, loess is highly fertile when water is available. After the initial absorption of water, loess "puffs up" and prevents additional water from penetrating into the ground.

machtesh. See crater

Mishna. The most important book in Judaism after the Torah, edited about 200 C.E. by Rabbi Yehuda Hanasi. The Talmud* is based on the Mishna.

moshav. An offshoot of the kibbutz,* created in Israel in the early 20th century. Children and parents lived together and, originally, industry and agricultural enterprises were jointly owned. The community did not strive for economic equality, as did the kibbutz. Like the kibbutz, the moshav, too, is in a transitional period. The plural of moshav is moshavim; members are called moshavniks.

Moslem Brotherhood. A religious extremist group which strives to make the Moslem law the law of the state. Founded in 1929 in Egypt, the group was outlawed in 1948 after members assassinated the Egyptian prime minister. Units of the Moslem Brotherhood fought in the Negev in the War of Independence.* Members of this group assassinated President Sadat in 1981 and today they are a major force opposing the rule of President Mubarak.

Nabatean. A Semitic people who thrived in the Negev between the third century B.C.E. and the seventh century C.E. They accumulated great wealth by transporting spices across the desert and built six cites in the Negev. In the fourth century, they converted to Christianity and engaged primarily in agriculture. They disappeared as a national entity shortly after the Moslem conquest in the seventh century. See chapter on NABATEANS.

national park. A notable historic or natural site maintained by Israel's National Parks Authority.

nature reserve. An area of unusual natural merit whose flora and fauna are protected from extinction. Nature reserves are maintained by the Nature Reserves Authority. Rangers patrol the reserves to make sure no one harms their natural phenomena.

Palmach. When Palestine was in danger of attack during World War II, the English trained local Jewish commandos to fight the Germans. These soldiers, known as the Palmach (Hebrew for "shock troops") were Israel's elite forces in the War of Independence* and participated in many Negev campaigns. A member of the Palmach is a palmachnik.

riverbed. A channel through which water flows, or flowed.

Glossary

sandstone. Sedimentary rocks, formed primarily from quartz cemented together with iron oxide or silica. Iron oxide gives the colorful look to the sandstone near Eilat.

Sinai Campaign (October 29 to November 5, 1956). Between 1949 and 1956 Egypt supported terrorists who crossed into Israel and caused some 1,300 Israeli casualties. In 1956 Egypt concluded a massive new arms deal with Russia and nationalized the Suez Canal. England and France wanted to maintain their interests along the canal and joined with Israel in an attack on Egypt. During the fighting Israel took all of the Sinai Peninsula. In return for free sea passage through the Straits of Tiran, Israel later withdrew from Sinai and United Nations forces were stationed in Sinai, instead. Removal of these U.N. forces in 1967 sparked the Six Day War.*

Six Day War (June 5 to 10, 1967). In May 1967, Egypt expelled the U.N. peacekeeping force from Sinai and blockaded Eilat. Jordan and Syria formed a joint military command and prepared to destroy the State of Israel. Three weeks later Israel launched a preemptive attack on Egypt. Subsequently Jordan and Syria attacked Israel. In the course of the Six Day War, Israel took the Sinai Desert from Egypt, the West Bank from Jordan and the Golan Heights from Syria.

Syrian-African rift. A vast fault line extending some 6,500 kilometers from Syria to Africa. In the Negev the rift shaped the Dead Sea and the Arava, creating the lowest sites on earth.

Talmud. The compiled works of rabbis in Israel and Babylon (Iraq) at the end of the fifth century. The Talmud includes two works: the Mishna* and the Gemara, the latter a commentary on the Mishna. The ideas and laws expressed in the Talmud were accepted by Jewish communities throughout the world for many centuries, providing the tools for Jewish survival in the Diaspora.

tel (tell). An archaeological site. A tel is often a hill which has several layers of remains from different time periods.

tumulus (plural tumuli). A mound of stones marking an ancient grave.

wadi. Arabic for riverbed, ravine or gully, dry most of the year and flooded in winter. Wadi is *nahal* in Hebrew.

War of Independence (November 29, 1947, to June 1949). Fighting between the Jews and the Arabs in Israel intensified when the U.N. decided to create a Jewish state in November, 1947. The day that Israel became independent, May 15, 1948, the new country was invaded by Egypt, Jordan and Syria. Negev battles proceeded in three distinct stages. In the beginning, Egypt advanced along the coast towards Tel Aviv. Later

303

Glossary

the Egyptians were stopped. During the final months of the war Israel drove the Egyptians out of the Negev and advanced to Eilat.

ZIN CENTER at BEN-GURION MIDRASHA

At "Zin" Center at Sde-Boker Coleege you can find a wide variety of services and products you need while staying at Ramat Negev and the Nahal Zin area.

.1 THE "ZIN" RESTAURANT kosher
Open from 8.00 to 23.00.
Air-conditioned, seats one-hundred.
You can enjoy a variety of foods and delicacies, bar-b-q, Israeli breakfast, self-service or served lunches, hot dinners.

.2 THE "ZIN" COFFEE SHOP
Open from 8.00 to 23.00.
Enjoy a variety of home-baked "Bon-Jour" pastries which include: cakes, French bread, country-bread, light breakfast, toast, coffee, soft drinks, and ice-cream.

.3 THE "ZIN" SUPERMARKET kosher
Open from 8.00 to 23.00.
In a 400 sq.m. air-conditioned supermarket you will find a variety of groceries, meat, vegetables, camping equipment, office and photography supplies. There are more than 5000 products in the "Zin" Supermarket.
Quick and efficient service.

.4 TAKE-AWAY SERVICE kosher
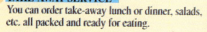
You can order take-away lunch or dinner, salads, etc. all packed and ready for eating.

.5 At the "ZIN" Center you will find a **POST OFFICE.**
Open 9.00-11.00, 13.00-14.00.

.6 Next to "ZIN" Center are the **SDE-BOKER FIELD SCHOOL** offices, giving you information and services regarding trips and tours in the HAR HANEGEV area.

.7 At the "ZIN" Center there is an **AMPHITHEATRE** that seats 400.

.8 Clean premises, bathrooms are on the premises.

.9 GUIDED TOURS in the COLLEGE can be arranged and include :
- Solar energy center.
- Sound&light show -The fulfillment Visiov of Ben-Gurion.
- International Museum for desert sculpture.

for furthur information :
ITZIK UNGER TEL. : 07-565800, 07-555998
050-286276 FAX. 07-565811

See Israel at your own pace...
with the best English language guides

Books by the authors of *Your Guide to Eilat and the Negev*

- *ISRAEL'S SOUTHERN LANDSCAPES: YOUR GUIDE TO EILAT AND THE* .... US$ 20.00 *NEGEV* by Aviva Bar-Am and Yisrael Shalem.
  Postage & handling charge per book: air mail—$7.50; surface mail—$4.00

- *GUIDE TO THE GOLAN HEIGHTS* by Aviva Bar-Am and Yisrael Shalem.. $ 15.50
  Postage & handling charge per book: air mail—$5.00; surface mail—$2.50

- *SAFED — SIX SELF-GUIDED TOURS IN AND AROUND THE MYSTICAL CITY* ... $ 7.00
  by Yisrael and Phyllis Shalem
  Postage & handling charge per book: air mail—$2.50; surface mail—$1.30

- *THE COMPLETE GUIDE TO TIBERIAS AND THE SEA OF GALILEE*.................... $ 7.00
  by Yisrael and Phyllis Shalem
  Postage & handling charge per book: air mail—$2.50; surface mail—$1.30

To order these outstanding guides, send payment (plus postage & handling charges for each book ordered) to Shalem, Sprinzak 329/27, 13351 Safed, Israel. For surface mail allow about 6 weeks for delivery.

Please send me ___ copies of *SAFED —SIX SELF GUIDED TOURS*...
Please send me ___ copies of *THE COMPLETE GUIDE TO TIBERIAS*...
Please send me ___ copies of *GUIDE TO THE GOLAN HEIGHTS*.
Please send me ___ copies of *LANDSCAPES...GUIDE TO EILAT AND THE NEGEV*.
___ I have included payment for surface mail postage and handling.
___ I have included payment for air mail postage and handling.
___ Please contact me when your next book is published.

Name: _____

Address: _____

City_____Country_____Postal Code _____

I have enclosed a check made out to Yisrael Shalem for $US_____

Prices subject to change without notice.

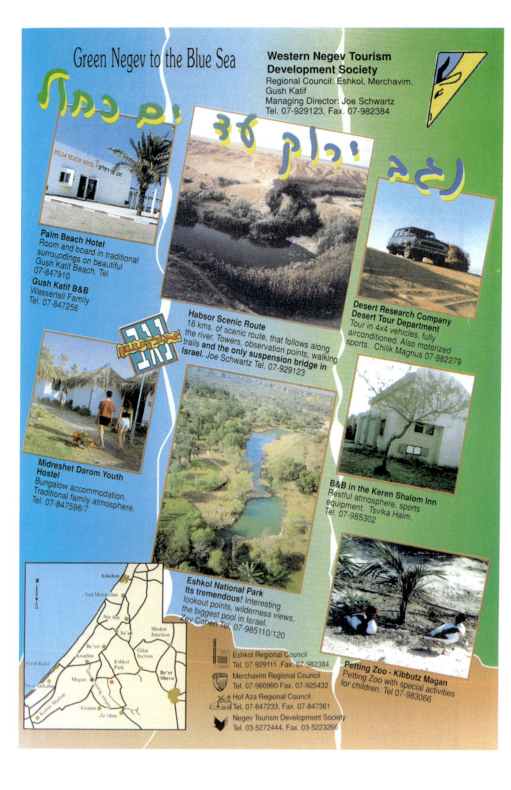

Are you planning a trip to the Negev?

Choose "Mashabim" - Country-style inn at Kibbutz Mashabei Sadeh, the gateway to the the south!

Escape to the wide open spaces, remove yourself from everything and come share the tranquility of the desert. At Mashabim, in the heart of the Negev, you will wake up with the peacocks to the sounds of the animal farm. Overlooking the desert from the green oasis of Kibbutz Mashabei Sadeh.

The facilities available in this friendly and relaxed atmosphere are:
- 39 airconditioned guest rooms with 2-4 beds per room.
- Meals served in the kibbutz dining room.
- All the attractions of the Negev are no more than 40 minutes drive from the kibbutz.
- Free consultations with experts on choosing suitable hiking trails while you are our guest.
- Sports equipment and swimming pool open, in season.
- Meeting rooms for conferences and seminars.
- Clubhouse with snack bar and television.
- Playroom for children.
- Petting zoo.

Call 07-565134/6 and ask for our new brochure.
Room in the country style inn

Swimming pool

View of the kibbutz grounds and dining room

Mashabim
Dsert Vacation

"Mashabim: Country-style inn at Kibbutz Mashabei Sadeh on the Beer-Sheva - Mitzpe Ramon road.
Reservations: Tel. 07-565134/6, Fax. 07-565145, Tourism Director: Beeper 03-5206666 Number 25892

Points of Interest in Beer Sheva

THE NEGEV MUSEUM. holds rotating exhibitions from its collection of early and contemporary Israeli art, and displays exhibits covering various aspects of the Negev's history and archaeology. Sun.-Thurs. 10:00-17:00 Fri. & Sat. 10:00-13:00. Entrance fee free admission on Saturdays. Tel/fax 07-280256, 280257. Govenor's House Ha'atzmaut Street.

ABRAHAM'S WELL. The intersections of K.K.L. St. and Derech Hevron is the spot ascribed by tradition to the biblical Abraham's Well. Free admission Sun.-Thurs. 8:30-14:00; Fri. & holiday eves 8:00-13:00. Tel. 07-234613.

THE BEDOUIN MARKET. Formally opened in 1905 this was the weekly market where the Bedouins sold camels, horses, sheep, goats, wool, leather and grain, and purchased from merchants coffee, sugar, weapons, cloth, jewelry, etc.

The market takes place Thursdays, except for holidays and holiday eves, when it takes place on the preceding Monday. On Eilat Road, near Hebron Intersection.

Promenade/Central Plaza, Old City.

המועצה המקומית מצפה רמון
THE LOCAL COUNCIL OF MITZPE RAMON

Mitzpe Ramon, Desert Vacationland

RESERVATIONS CENTER. To book hotels, tours, restaurant reservations, etc. call 177-022-2646 (toll free number), 588319, or 588290; fax 588298. All phone numbers are in area code 07.

HOTELS
RAMON INN. 1 En Akev St. Tel. 588822, fax 588151.
YOUTH HOSTEL, MITZPE RAMON. Tel. 588443, fax 588074.
HAR HANEGEV FIELD SCHOOL. Tel. 588616, fax 588385

RESTAURANTS
HANNAH'S RESTAURANT. Next to the gas station. Tel. 588158, fax 587047.
GAVISH, desert catering service. Tel. 588054, fax 588883.
TZUKIT RESTAURANT. Tel. 588079, 586163.
HACHAVIT PUB. Tel. 588226.

Sculpture Garden overlooking Ramon Crater

TOURS:
SUCCAH IN THE DESERT — A VACATION FOR THE SOUL. Tel. 586280, fax 586464.
DESERT SHADE. Tel. 03-575-6885, fax 613-0161.
ACTION TOURS. Tel. 588443, fax 588074.
ART IN NATURE, Mitzpe Ramon Colony for the Arts. Tel. 587411, fax 587414.
HADDAS JEEP TOURS. 08-436882, fax 08-436898.

SITES
VISITORS' CENTER, Be'erot Campsite. Tel. 588620, 588691.
BIO RAMON. Tel. 588755.
ALPACA FARM. Tel. 588047, fax 586104.
DESERT ARCHERY PARK. Tel. 587247.

Succah in the Desert, a very special holiday site in Mitzpe Ramon.

The **llama and alpaca farm** at Mitzpe Ramon. Alpaca rides for children.

Ramon Inn. A Luxurious Adventure.

The Ramon Inn offers you an adventurous vacation in the heart of an untamed desert. This is your base for cliff gliding excursions, camel rides, or an exciting jeep safari into the Ramon Crater. You can visit the alpaca farm, or hike around the area acquainting yourself with the desert flora and fauna. At the end of your day you return to your hotel where you can relax in your luxury 1.5 - 3 room suites equipped with everything you need. You are invited to savor our dining experience and enjoy the finest ethnic dishes. Ramon Inn offers you a great holiday vacation at any time of year. In the summer, enjoy an ideal climate with low humidity, refreshing yourself in the many cool water spots in the area and delight in the cool, caressing desert breezes. An added attraction in winter is that you can curl up and relax in front of the hotel's fireplace.
Come and discover a real desert experience at the Ramon Inn.

Tamir Cohen (Jacobson)

ISROTEL
RAMON INN

For bookings and information on the region, please contact Ramon Inn 07-588822, Central Resevations: 03-5178989, Toll-free: 177-022-3636, or your travel agent

ISROTEL. JUST YOUR STYLE

For us the desert is pure nature

BEIT HAMBURG, THE BEN-GURION UNIVERSITY CAMPUS GUEST HOUSE

SDE BOKER FIELD SCHOOL

The recently opened luxurious guest house opposite the "land of springs," Beit Hamburg serves visitors yearning for the desert and its tranquillity.

Situated on Tzin Ravine in the Tzin Desert, Beit Hamburg offers an outstanding view of the vast Negev landscape just a few steps from your room. A promenade along the ravine's cliffs, presently under construction, passes directly below the guest rooms.

The 60-bed facility has rooms for couples and for families equipped with showers, toilets, air conditioning and elegant furnishings; and a comfortable lounge with television, lecture halls and audio-visual equipment. A unique collection of desert artifacts on display adjacent to the guest house adds an enriching dimension to your visit.

The Field School and Information Center staff will be happy to help you plan excursions throughout the Negev.

So come and enjoy the desert air and the magnificent view.

For reservations phone 177-022-3181 (toll free), 07-565828, or 565902; fax 565721.

In the heart of the Negev, Sde Boker Field School's staff of experienced and skilled guides offer 96 different tours throughout the central Negev. The programs' varied contents, developed through years of experience, include courses in ecology, biology, Land of Israel Studies, geology and geography.

The 300-bed hostel is located by a desert promenade on the Tzin cliff. A large, modern dining room holds 300. Exceptionally comfortable students' rooms with shower, toilet, and air conditioning accommodate 4-6 guests. The pleasant teachers' accommodations have 2-3 beds per room. The facility offers lecture halls with audio-visual equipment. Educational displays include a snake room, archaeological exhibit and Bedouin guest room.

Available hiking and touring backup services include jeeps and communications equipment. On weekends and holidays the field school organizes special activities for groups, families and individuals.

For reservations call 07-565016, fax 565721.

The Ben-Gurion Experience: Vision and Fulfillment

A MULTI-DIMENSIONAL AUDIO-VISUAL EXPERIENCE

32 projectors present the dramatic story of the establishment of the State of Israel, which is the story of Ben-Gurion's life. This exciting, 45-minute audio-visual presentation is in a unique hall equipped with swivel chairs and seven screens.

The show is screened at Midreshet Sde Boker, near the home and by the burial site of David Ben Gurion, and is surrounded by the spectacular desert landscape of Nahal Zin.

For group reservations phone 07-565717, fax 558352.

The Ben Gurion National Solar Energy Center

You are cordially invited to the National Solar Energy Center to see how solar energy is harnessed to produce electricity as a clean, inexhaustible power source.

The one hour visit includes

- An audio-visual program (available in English, Hebrew, German, French and Spanish).
- A site tour with explanations.

A visit to the center is suitable for all ages. Open Sun.-Thurs. 8:00-15:00. It is recommended to phone in advance to arrange a tour. Visits on Fridays, Saturdays and holidays must be reserved in advance. Phone: 07-555057 or 555059. Entrance fee, five shekels.

We will be happy to have you as our guests, and make your visit to the Negev a more enjoyable experience.

Tourist Information Center, Eilat

All the information you need for a total holiday experience:

* Hotels * Special Attractions * Entertainment * Shopping Centers
* Border Check Posts * Hostels and B&Bs * Car Rentals * Tours
* Public Transportation * ...and much more.

And for convenient push-button information there are Computerized Information Stations throughout the city.

Opening Hours:
Sun-Thurs, 8:00 am - 9:00 pm
Fri, 8:00 am - 2:00 pm
Sat and Holidays, 10:00 am - 2:00 pm

Tourist Information Center
Intersection, Arava Road and Yotam Road, Tel: 07-372111

THE JEWISH NATIONAL FUND

The JEWISH NATIONAL FUND -Keren Kayemeth LeIsrael has been involved in the Negev from the very beginnings of modern settlement in the region, in the 1930s. Ever since, JNF has been actively involved in the advancement of this southern region and in combating desertification.

Today, JNF has embarked upon a major development project "Action Plan Negev"- which over the next few years will help develop water reservoirs and dams, orchards, olive plantations and vineyards, fish ponds, extensive hothouses and large-scale land reclamation in the Negev and the Arava - all these aimed at reinvigorating Negev agriculture and propelling it into the 21st century while offering residents options for a better living.

JNF's development work around the country includes: Afforestation covering more than a million dunams. Reclamation of land for 1,000 settlements. Environmental projects such as the restoration of over 100 riverbeds, the rehabilitation of the Hula Valley, and extensive drainage in the Jezreel, Beit Shean and Yavne'el Valleys to repair and improve salinated lands. Building dams and reservoirs. Creating some 400 recreation areas, playgrounds and picnic sites in forests. Developing tourism infrastructure.

A liman in the desert

Pundak Sde Boker

In a serene spot in the heart of the desert you'll find **Pundak Sde Boker**, a restaurant near David Ben Gurion's desert home at kibbutz Sde Boker. The restaurant is **kosher** and **airconditioned**. Takeaway meals can be ordered in advance.

Pundak Sde Boker is open for breakfast and lunch everyday. With reservations meals are also served at other hours.

Sunday-Thursday 8:00-16:00
Friday and before holidays 8:00-15:00
Saturday and holidays 8:30-16:00

Phone: 07-560379; fax: 07-560119

Israel Nature Reserves Authority Natureland Pass

When you purchase a **Natureland Pass** you're in for a treat. For an entire month you are entitled to free entry intto Israel's Nature Reserves. From desert oases to fish ponds and swamplands inhabited by migrating birds; from mountain streams to ancient caves and underwater coral gardens. Israel packs more contrast into its borders than any other country.

Your **Natureland Pass** also entitles you to special reductions on:
* Hertz Car Rentals in Israel and Europe.
* Subscriptions to Eretz Magazine.
* Fuji film purchased at the nature reserves.

To purchase your **Natureland Pass**, ask at any nature reserve, or call 02-371257

Index of Tourism Services

"IF ONLY I HAD RESERVATIONS AT A HOTEL IN THE DESERT..." (JEREMIAH 9:1)

Reservation and/or Information Centers

Beer Sheva Tourist Information Office, 6 Ben-Zvi Street. Tel. 07-236001 or 236002.

Arad Tourist Center (Marketing and Reservations). Reservations for flights, hotel rooms, tourist attractions and services in Arad and the vicinity. Tel. 07-958144 or 959333, fax 07-955052.

Negev Highlands Reservations and Marketing. Reservations for lodging, restaurants, tourist attractions, activities, or tours in the Negev Highlands. Tel. 177-022-2646 (toll free), 07-588319 or 07-588290; fax 07-588298.

Eilat Tourist Information Center, for all the information you need for a total holiday experience and/or reservations. At the intersection of Arava and Yotam Roads. Tel. 07-372111.

Lodgings and Restaurants

Mashabei Sadeh Holiday Village, Kibbutz Mashabei Sadeh. Enjoy the tranquil kibbutz atmosphere. On the Beer Sheva-Mitzpe Ramon Highway. Tel. 07- 565134, fax 07-565145.

Ramon Inn (Pundak Ramon). Isrotel's new hotel in Mitzpe Ramon. The inn offers 1½, 2 and 3 room apartments with special amenities to spoil every guest. Reservations desk tel. 177-022-3636 (toll free), 03-5178989, or 07-588822.

Beit Hamburg. A luxurious guest house facing the "land of springs". At the Ben Gurion Campus, just south of kibbutz Sde Boker. For reservations call 177-022-3181 (toll free), 07-565828, or 565902; fax 07-565721.

Zin Restaurant, air-conditioned, offers a wide variety of foods and delicacies. At Sde Boker College. Open 8:00-23:00. Tel. 07-565800 or 07-555998, fax 07-565811.

Special Attractions

Negev Highlands

Mitzpe Revivim. The exciting story of a pioneer settlement; audio-visual presentation. Special activities for groups include programs with professional actors; tour with a "pioneer" or true stories of life experiences; a day in the kibbutz, and/or meals. Tel. 07-562570, tel/fax 562607.

Midreshet Sde Boker's Audio-Visual Program. Unique 45-minute audio-visual presentation on the life and work of David Ben Gurion, at Sde Boker College. Open for groups; entrance fee. For reservations call 07-565717, fax 07-558352.

The National Solar Energy Center. See how solar energy is harnessed to produce electricity, a clean, continuous power source. The tour includes an audio-visual presentation and computer programs. At Sde Boker College. To reserve a tour call 07-555057/9.

Eilat

Dolphin Reef offers snorkeling and diving with dolphins (by reservation) and diving courses at all levels. Tel. 07-375935, fax 07-375921.

ERETZ

THE GEOGRAPHIC MAGAZINE FROM ISRAEL

KNOW IT ALL

You make a point of keeping up with current affairs in Israel. But there is a wealth of exciting information to be learned about the Israel behind the headlines - and new discoveries about its momentous history, diverse peoples, natural treasures, and extraordinary landscapes are constantly being made.

Deepen your understanding and appreciation of Israel by exploring it with ERETZ Magazine.

In 80 pages of vibrant text and spectacular color and black and white photography, ERETZ takes you and your family on a journey through this remarkable land.

ERETZ Magazine, the English-language geographic magazine from Israel
SUBSCRIBE TODAY

A one-year subscription to ERETZ Magazine is only $36, including shipping and handling all over the world.

Write or call:
In Israel:
ERETZ Magazine
P.O. Box 565
53148 Givatayim
TEL. 03-571-4253
FAX. 03-571-4184

All phone numbers are in area code 07 unless otherwise noted.

Highland Highlights
Mitzpe Ramon - Ramat Negev

Negev Highlands Tourism

Yehuda Honeybud, Director

Negev Tourism Development Authority

Ramat Negev Regional Council

Mitzpe Ramon Local Council

RamatNegev Regional Council, 85155 Halutza Mobile Post. Tel. 07-557314, 07-557559, Fax 07-559235

Mitzpe Ramon Local Council, P.O. Box 1, Mitzpe Ramon 80600

RESERVATIONS CENTER. To book hotels, tours, restaurant reservations, etc. 177-022-2646 (toll free number), 588319, or 588290; fax 588298

HOTELS
RAMON INN. 1 En Akev St., Mitzpe Ramon. Tel. 588822, fax 588151
MASHABEI SADEH HOLIDAY VILLAGE. Kibbutz Mashabei Sadeh. Tel. 565134, fax 565145
TELALIM VACATION. Kibbutz Telalim. Tel. 563672. Reservations: 04-9998928
YOUTH HOSTEL, MITZPE RAMON. Tel. 588443, fax 588074
HAR HANEGEV FIELD SCHOOL. Mitzpe Ramon. Tel. 588616, fax 588385

RESTAURANTS
SDE BOKER INN. Near Ben Gurion's Hut. Tel. 560379
ZIN RESTAURANT. At Midreshet Ben-Gurion. Tel.565811
HANNAH'S RESTAURANT. Mitzpe Ramon, next to the gas station. Tel. 588158, fax 587047
GAVISH, catering in the desert. Mitzpe Ramon. Tel. 588054, fax 588883
TZUKIT RESTAURANT. Mitzpe Ramon. Tel. 588079, 586163
HACHAVIT PUB. Mitzpe Ramon. Tel. 588226

TOURS
SEFINAT HAMIDBAR DESERT TOURS CENTER. Mashabim Campsite. Tel. 557315 or 557318
BE'EROTAYIM TOURS. Ezuz. Tel. 555788, fax 554369
CAMEL FARM LTD. Mamshit. Tel. 551054, fax 550965
DESERT SHADE. Mitzpe Ramon. Tel. 03-5756885, fax 03-6130161
SUCCAH IN THE DESERT — A VACATION FOR THE SOUL. Tel. 586280, fax 586464
ACTION TOURS. Mitzpe Ramon. Tel. 588443, fax 588074.
ART IN NATURE, Mitzpe Ramon Colony for the Arts. Tel. 587411, fax 587414
HADDAS JEEP TOURS. 08-436882, fax 08-436898

SITES
MITZPE REVIVIM — MUSEUM OF JEWISH SETTLEMENT IN THE NEGEV. Kibbutz Revivim. Tel. 562570, fax 562607
AVDAT NATIONAL PARK. Ein Avdat. Tel. 550954, fax 586391
BEN GURION'S HUT. Kibbutz Sde Boker. Tel. 558444, tel/fax 560320
SOLAR ENERGY INFORMATION CENTER. Midreshet Ben-Gurion. Tel. 555059, fax 555060
DESERT SCULPTURE MUSEUM. Midreshet Ben-Gurion. Tel. 565720, fax 558352
SDE BOKER FIELD SCHOOL. Live snake collection. Midreshet Ben-Gurion. Tel. 565016, fax 565721
BEN-GURION — DREAM AND FULFILLMENT, audiovisual program. Midreshet Sde Boker. Tel. 565717, fax 558352
VISITORS' CENTER, Be'erot Campsite. Tel. 588620, 588691
BIO RAMON. Mitzpe Ramon. Tel. 588755
ALPACA FARM. Mitzpe Ramon. Tel. 588047, fax 586104
DESERT ARCHERY PARK. Mitzpe Ramon. Tel. 587247